笃行奋进　砥砺远航

——对外经济贸易大学国际经济贸易学院庆祝
建党100周年暨建校70周年师生论文集

主　　编　曹小勇
执行主编　曲佳文
副 主 编　毕　帆

中国商务出版社
CHINA COMMERCE AND TRADE PRESS

图书在版编目（CIP）数据

笃行奋进　砥砺远航：对外经济贸易大学国际经济贸易学院庆祝建党100周年暨建校70周年师生论文集／曹小勇主编. —北京：中国商务出版社，2021.11（2023.3重印）

ISBN 978-7-5103-4050-5

Ⅰ.①笃…　Ⅱ.①曹…　Ⅲ.①中国共产党-高等学校-党的建设-北京-文集　Ⅳ.①D267.6-53

中国版本图书馆CIP数据核字（2021）第208140号

笃行奋进　砥砺远航
——对外经济贸易大学国际经济贸易学院庆祝建党100周年暨建校70周年师生论文集
DUXINGFENJIN　DILIYUANHANG
—DUIWAIJINGJIMAOYIDAXUE GUOJIJINGJIMAOYIXUEYUAN QINGZHU JIANDANG 100 ZHOUNIAN JI JIANXIAO 70 ZHOUNIAN SHISHENG LUNWENJI

主　　编	曹小勇
执行主编	曲佳文
副 主 编	毕　帆

出　　版	中国商务出版社
地　　址	北京市东城区安定门外大街东后巷28号　　邮政编码：100710
网　　址	http://www.cctpress.com
电　　话	010-64212247（总编室）　　010-64218072（事业部）
	010-64208388（发行部）　　010-64515210（零　售）
排　　版	北京宝蕾元科技发展有限责任公司
印　　刷	河北赛文印刷有限公司
开　　本	787毫米×1092毫米　1/16
印　　张	15.5
版　　次	2021年11月第1版　　　　印　次：2023年3月第3次印刷
字　　数	300千字　　　　　　　　 定　价：48.00元

版权所有　盗版必究　盗版侵权举报可发邮件至 cctp@cctpress.com

购买本社图书如有印装质量问题，请与本社印制部（电话：010-64248236）联系

目 录

第一部分 砥砺百年,初心不忘·建党100周年

"三全育人"理论指引下的高校理论社团育人机制创新 ………… 曲佳文 王妍力 003
激发高校学生党支部建设活力的路径探索
　　——以对外经济贸易大学国际经济贸易学院为例 … 闫雪琴 金小娜 王馨怡 010
"四史"教育
　　——高校党支部的必修课 ……………………………… 毕 帆 黄依萌 021

第二部分 经韬纬略,立德树人·建校70周年

军事课教学在推进高校"三全育人"中的作用机制研究 ……… 曲佳文 蔡维明 031
疫情防控常态化下的高校学生管理研究
　　——以对外经济贸易大学国际经济贸易学院为例 ………………… 张晶娟 039
"双一流"建设背景下优化提升研究生生源质量的思考 ………… 王依然 毕晶晶 045
高校应对新冠肺炎疫情的经验与启示 ……………………………………… 陈怡琴 052
财经类高校院级学生管理体制探索
　　——以对外经济贸易大学为例 … 闫雪琴 魏伟斌 金小娜 王 者 陈欣怡 V61
红色经典阅读——高校思政教育的助力者 ………… 毕 帆 王可欣 黄依萌 070
新媒体视域下高校共青团思想引导工作的困境和改进路径 ……………… 杜姝君 078
财经类高校学生劳动教育研究 ………………………… 熊正非 吴比特 王 丹 085

第三部分 合作共赢，接轨世界·入世20周年

The Extrusion Effect of State-owned Enterprises on Private Enterprises' Exports Propensity and Scale ………………………………… 刘舒婷　张国峰　097

The Economic Effect of Hainan Pilot Free Trade Zone Policy based on PSM-DID Model ……………………………………………………… 王心蕙　116

Explore the Influence Factors of International Competitiveness of Intellectual Property Trade
——Based on the Competitive Advantage Theory …………………… 王可欣　137

An Empirical Study on the Impact of the "Belt and Road" Initiative on the Overseas Business Revenue of Chinese Enterprises …………… 何　娟　蒋灵多　158

探讨营商环境对出口增加值的影响
——以"一带一路"沿线国家为例 …………………………………… 蒲海霞　182

The Pilot Policies of Cross-border E-commerce and New Opportunities for China's Import Trade ……………………………………………………… 杨　静　197

转移支付的均等化效果评价 ……………………………………………… 陈　煜　229

第一部分
砥砺百年,初心不忘·建党100周年

1921年，在浙江嘉兴的红船上，国际歌被嘹亮唱响。一个坚定的信仰，一颗炽热的初心，由此被一代代中国共产党党员继承与发扬，筚路蓝缕，披荆斩棘，建立了由人民当家作主的崭新中国，走上中国特色社会主义复兴之路。今日中国的辉煌成就，无不印证着——中国共产党是历史与人民的选择，是带领我们实现中华民族伟大复兴的中国梦的领路人。

"三全育人"理论指引下的高校理论社团育人机制创新

曲佳文[①] 王妍力[②]

摘　要：国家坚持教育的"三全育人"要求，落实立德树人的根本任务，发展素质教育，要求培养全面发展的社会主义建设者和接班人。高校理论社团在当代大学思想教育体系中发挥着重要作用，对于高校的思政建设产生了重大影响。在"三全育人"理论指导下，需要创新高校理论社团的育人机制，提高社团运行效用。本文从当前高校理论社团育人机制现状、创新意义及创新举措三个角度进行论述。重点从发挥高校理论社团思想引导作用、加强实践开辟专业化道路和优化社团管理体系三个角度论述了创新举措。希望通过育人机制的创新，不断激发高校理论社团活力，实现在"三全育人"要求指导下，高校理论社团与思想政治教育的更好融合。

关键词："三全育人"；理论社团；机制创新

高校作为培养中国专业化人才的重要基地，不仅需要加强学生专业方向的理论知识传授，更要加强思想引领建设，做到理论与实践相结合，培养政治水平高、专业素养强的毕业生。中共中央、国务院在《关于加强和改进新形势下高校思想政治工作的意见》中提出坚持全员、全过程、全方位育人的要求（简称"三全育人"）。习近平总书记也在全国教育大会上提出要培养德智体美劳全面发展的社会主义建设者和接班人。"三全育人"理论为高校理论社团的建设与未来发展提供了方向和契机。为了实现"三全育人"的目标，需要利用好高校理论社团，更好发挥其育人机制，实现理论学习和具体实践有机结合，优化高校理论社团管理体系，提高理论社团运行效率，更好发挥高校理论社团的引领作用。

---

① 曲佳文，对外经济贸易大学国际经济贸易学院党委副书记。
② 王妍力，对外经济贸易大学国际经济贸易学院金融学2021级硕士研究生。

在国内高校社团育人机制的理论研究中，谷家川（2020）认为大学社团机制创新需要从社团文化建设、创新运行模式、完善评价机制角度三个角度进行，并且做到理论与实践相融合。薛文辉（2020）从"三全育人"机制角度提出，需要在立德树人理论指引下开展系列实践活动，通过系列文体活动，创新活动内容，加强社团学生负责人培训提升。陈晓宇（2020）在研究中则更加突出高校学生社团组织中党团领导的重要性。针对"三全育人"的发展要求，通过借鉴研究已有的高校理论社团育人机制，并且结合对外经济贸易大学国际经济贸易学院发展实际情况，作出以下创新研究。

一、当前高校理论社团育人机制现状

随着"三全育人"理论在大学校园的发展，高校理论社团数量有了大幅度增加，规模不断扩大，在高校内影响力不断提升。为了满足高校专业课堂与理论实践课堂的互动和融合发展，高校理论社团成为马克思主义理论和实践的重要载体，是专业理论与思想政治沟通的重要枢纽。目前，中国高校理论社团主要呈现以下状况。

1. 学生自主学习能力较强，但缺乏对理论研究的系统性学习

目前，高校内理论社团成员大多来自不同专业背景和不同年级，对理论和研究有着共同的兴趣，同时具有较高的思想政治素养，理论学习研究水平普遍高于高校内其他同学。彼此在志同道合的基础上进行合作学习研究，是学校专业课之余在思想政治学习领域的极好补充，对于高校内马克思主义思想的学习研究具有重要贡献。理论社团内部的学习方式主要集中在社团内部成员间通过查找资料、观看新闻等方式进行自学，部分理论社团会有定期的交流学习活动。这种以自学为主的研究方式，导致目前高校理论社团普遍存在理论研究碎片化、片面化的现象，同学们往往仅凭经验或者兴趣进行理论研究，系统化理论研究能力较弱；多种学科专业成员之间的互补作用没有完全发挥。其主要是因为同学们对于理论社团的系统性认识不足，缺乏专业导师的指导。

2. 对历史理论的研习充分，但缺乏对时政的必要思考与研究

当前高校理论社团研究的内容主要集中于中国共产党党史研究、马克思主义理论研究和中国近现代史研究。开展的活动也侧重于社会主义核心价值观的引领，通过学习借鉴历史经验，发挥好其思想引领的重要作用。但是往往高校理论社团的这种偏重历史研究的活动，对于在校大学生的吸引力较差，同时因为其与时政结合度不足，往往导致研究的实际意义较差，从而不利于培养大学生针对时政的独立思考能力。

3. 开展活动数量充足，但对高校学生的吸引力不足

目前以高校理论社团为核心，依托团委、学生会和志愿团开展的系列活动数量丰富，活动范围广泛，有效配合了高校的思想政治教育工作，活动已经参与进大学生主要的课余活动。但是其目前形式主要依赖于讲座、读书分享会等传统活动，缺少理论和创新性实践的融合，具有时代特色的创新活动数量不足，部分高校理论社团开展的创新性活动也因经验不足导致效果未达预期，从而导致活动吸引力不足或同学们参与热情不高。

4. 社团领导力较强，但内部管理运行机制有待创新

高校理论社团对于其他学生组织的辐射力强，高校普遍将理论社团作为思想引领的重要载体，放在学生活动整体规划的核心位置，以理论指导实践来完善德育体系。但理论社团内部管理运行机制则往往采用传统学生会结构划分具体部门，内部管理松散，管理流程侧重表面；同时也造成机构冗余，效率低下。探索创新属于高校理论社团独特的内部运行机制成为当前需要解决的一项重点工作。

二、高校理论社团育人机制创新意义

高校理论社团是当代大学生学习马克思主义思想，是提高政治文化素养的重要基地，对当代大学生的思想教育工作作出了重要贡献，创新高校理论社团育人机制符合中国教育改革要求。

建设高校理论社团符合2016年共青团中央、教育部联合发布的《高校共青团改革实施方案》中"一心双环"团学组织格局要求，有利于促进学生自主进行理论学习，在高校内形成理论学习的良好风气，将理论内化于心、外化于行，积极践行中国特色社会主义理论。同时高校作为当代人才培养的重要基地，加强思想道德建设，提高高校学生对于马克思主义相关理论的认同感，也成为新时代思想教育的重要目标。高校理论社团通过激发学生自主学习研究的兴趣，极好地促进了高校内思想道德建设工作的顺利推行。同时高校教育要坚持以人才培养为核心，坚持立德树人的教育理念不动摇，培养全面发展的社会主义建设者和接班人。作为"三全育人"的重要载体，高校理论社团创新育人机制具有重要意义。

三、高校理论社团育人机制创新举措

（一）紧抓时代脉搏，加强理论学习，发挥理论社团的思想引领作用

当今中国经济迅速发展，国际形势在新冠肺炎疫情影响下瞬息万变，大学生需要在多变的国际形势下坚定政治理想，树立正确的世界观、价值观和人生观，坚定道路自信与制度自信，发挥自身专业优势。因此，当代高校将培养实用性人才提到了较为

重要的高度，需要学生在日常学习专业课之余，加强对时事热点的学习和研究，培养针对时事独立思考研究的能力；同时更需要加强高校师生的政治理论学习，厚植爱国主义情怀，培养社会责任感。高校理论社团不仅是高校内理论学习的重要阵地，同时也是党团内培养骨干力量的红色摇篮。因此，必须在高校理论社团发展的工作中落实"三全育人"的要求，培养德智体美劳全面发展的社会主义建设者和接班人。

1. 加强社团内政治理论学习，提高学生思想先进性

为了保持高校理论社团的思想先进性，需要提高学生的主动学习意识，日常学习党的先进思想和政策，利用好"学习强国"等党政学习平台，做到随时随地掌握最新政治思想。同时，在提升学生个人自身政治水平的同时，也要加强社团内部研讨及理论成果分享。在指导教师和社团负责人领导下，通过定期开展理论分享会，将理论学习成果以校报或公众号等形式拓展到更大的学习范围，将政治热点及研讨成果固定化，实现宣传效用最大化，从而营造理论学习的良好氛围，提高理论学习效率。

2. 聚焦社会热点，创新开展专业相关系列主题活动

现在高校将培养全面发展人才作为重要目标。理论社团更需要将研究成果在社会问题中进行检验。密切关注国内外新闻及政治动向，紧抓社会热点，就必须将理论学习与社会热点紧密联系，培养学生运用所学理论思考的能力与习惯，培养经世人才。同时，理论社团可以与其他学生组织进行联动，结合社会热点开展专业相关主题活动。开展诸如党史竞赛、征文竞赛等，通过竞赛类活动激发学生的参与热情；在重要历史纪念日，如五四青年节、"一二·九"运动等开展相关活动，为学生提供成果展示平台，丰富学生活动种类，增强思想性和趣味性。

3. 开展理论学习讲座，发挥教师团队和优秀毕业生的帮扶带动作用

由理论社团带头组织，完善高校社团与专业课导师和往届毕业生联动机制，促进形成在导师带领下的理论学习的良性发展闭环。由专业理论研究型导师针对理论研究等不同阶段和不同方向开展系列讲座，对学生在理论研究方法和实践方法上进行指导，引导学生找到正确的理论研究方向，提高社团理论研究效率。在加强导师带头引导的同时，需要完善高校理论社团内部的学习成果传递机制，实现老生帮新生，老一届研究经验新一届共享的良性循环。通过开展毕业生经验讲座、创建理论社团老社员论坛等方法，不断积累往届经验，促进社团的发展和同学理论水平不断地提高。

（二）理论融入实践，开拓理论社团专业化发展道路

在理论研究中，如果空谈理论，会失去研究本身的实用意义，导致研究空洞乏味，缺乏实践借鉴性。但是如果只注重实践，不进行理论的研究学习，又会导致实践无目

的化,缺乏理论指导,也会导致实践效率低下。因此,应在高校理论社团中强调理论和实践的有机结合,加强高校专业知识理论与实践的融合,寻找开辟高校理论社团专业化发展新道路。

1. 组织专业化实践,加强实践的理论成果转化

高校理论社团在加强政治理论培养学习的同时,也要利用好所学的专业知识。以学院为单位,针对本学院专业特点开展相关实践实习,将专业知识、国家政策与实践内容有机结合。在国家扶贫扶智政策指导下,开展相关扶贫支教系列调研,通过实践探究发现痛点,利用专业知识进行帮扶,因地制宜助力当地经济长远发展。完善实习基地建设,给予社团及学生更广阔的实践平台,在合理范围内给予容错空间,鼓励更多学生参与到实践中去。与此同时,创新理论—实践—理论新模式,实践前,针对实践领域内容和专业知识进行自主学习与集体研讨,形成来自书本历史经验的理论研究初期思考;在理论指导下有目的地开展实践,在实践中对所学理论加以印证;最后加强实践后的理论成果转化工作,将实践经验及成果以报告或论文形式进行保存,提高高校学生理论产出能力。同时,为社团后续发展提供理论留存与经验借鉴。

2. 加强个人技能培养,探索青年全面发展新模式

高校理论社团在"三全育人"的教育要求下,不仅要加强学生思想政治水平的提升,更要注重在正确思想引导下的智育体育美育劳育全面育人。协同其他学生组织一起,为高校大学生建立兴趣培养发展平台,完善大学生全面发展教育体系。在具体实践中,可以充分发挥学生自我教育和自我学习的特点,充分利用国家提供的网课资源,以现代多媒体技术为支撑,有效运用多媒体终端,将科技性和时代性融入学生自主课堂。活动围绕国家大政方针开展,从音体美等多个角度开展系列红色展示活动,增强学生的参与积极性,从而落实"立德树人"的根本任务,以社会主义核心价值观为指引,以促进学生全面发展为导向,强化担当,以行践知,推动落实"三全育人"要求,继续探索青年学生全面培养的新模式。

(三) 管理体系优化,发挥理论社团与师生团队的协同促进作用

高校理论社团作为"三全育人"下高校思想道德建设的重要平台,其运行效果与管理体系紧密相连。优化评价竞争机制,完善健全社团内管理体系,充分发挥学生理论社团与在校师生的协调机制作用,可以有效促进理论社团有序发展,增强社团内部的凝聚力和感染力,从而推动高校思政建设。

1. 优化高校理论社团管理体系,提高社团内部运行效率

为了促进高校理论社团活动有序开展,就必须制定符合"三全育人"要求的科学

管理制度，在制度规范下充分发挥组织效能，保证社团的运行有规章制度可循，管理体系明晰，发展方向明确。在社团内部要落实"一心双环"团学组织格局要求，进行部门间整合，扩大理论研究学习部门在组织中人数和效能占比，精简冗余机构，提高团队的理论研究能力。改良在传统学生组织中的三级管理体系，实行项目负责人或者模块负责人直接负责活动的管理模式，精简理论社团内学生领导人数，扩大理论研究队伍。积极寻找与学生会等其他学生组织的合作方式，协同组织活动及后期宣传。

加强高校理论社团骨干培养。严格选拔理论社团负责人，挑选政治理论水平过硬，组织能力优越，具有较高责任心和奉献意识，具有较高综合素质的学生担任理论社团负责人，确保社团管理者具有足够的统筹协调和理论研究能力。同时，选拔具有政治理论研究特长的导师作为社团长期负责人，引领社团按照既定目标长远发展。为了保证理论社团骨干和负责人思想的先进性和引导性，需要通过高校的内部团校培训、党员活动等加强对高校社团内骨干成员的培养，使其深化对立德树人作为教育根本任务的理解，从而才能更好地将"三全育人"融入高校理论社团活动中。

2. 强化高校理论社团服务身份，完善内部奖励机制，激发学生参与活力

作为高校学生组织中思想建设的重要环节，高校理论社团需要明确自身定位，牢固树立服务者意识。严防官僚主义、形式主义等现象的发生。坚持做好政治学习服务工作，带头引领理论研究，为在校大学生提供理论自学方向；组织开展系列思政活动，为在校大学生创建实践学习平台；积极撰写理论成果，为高校大学生提供理论学习范本。切实做好高校学生的理论学习帮扶工作。

同时，在社团内部完善奖励机制，建立健全社团成员评价机制，实行定量化考核标准。通过将社团成员活动出勤率、活动贡献率及成果产出进行量化评分，每学期末进行统计排名，将排名结果与成员综合测评分数挂钩，对表现优异的社员给予额外加分奖励，积分排名与成员留任社团负责人挂钩。同时，鼓励理论产出成果优异的同学参与马克思主义学院专业导师的科研团队，给予其更多理论研究机会，从而激发社团成员积极参与活动的热情，形成良性竞争的社团内部氛围。

3. 健全理论社团、辅导员、专业导师三方协调机制，扩大理论社团辐射范围

目前高校理论社团普遍存在社团自身独立性较强，与学校或学院内的具体学生工作较为脱离的问题，导致理论社团在思政教育领域发挥的辐射作用受到局限。因此，需要创新理论社团、高校辅导员和马克思主义专业导师三方联动机制，整合学校思政教育资源，让理论社团全面融入"三全育人"体系。在理论社团自身层面，积极主动倡导学生和导师建立联系，开辟合作机制；在辅导员层面，需要参与骨干成员的挑选，推荐本年级更适合参与理论研究的同学参与到社团中；此外，从本年级学生实际情况出发，依托理论社团开展人生职业规划、实习方向选择等系列讲座，更好达到第二课堂效能；在专业导师层面，定期邀请专业老师进行马克思主义理论研究方法培训，或邀请专业课老师聚焦中国热点开展系列讲座，提高理论社团的专业性；同时可以邀请专业老师带领理论社团骨干成员进行课题研究，在老师专业指导下，提高理论成果产出质量。三方协调，共同助力高校思政建设，完善"三全育人"体系。

四、结语

目前，高校思想政治工作愈加凸显其重要地位，高校理论社团在宣传与实践马克思主义思想和中国特色社会主义理论工作中发挥着重要作用。因此，需要不断完善高校理论社团育人机制，创新发展模式，引导其正确发挥思想引领作用，配合完善高校"三全育人"体系。

参考文献

[1] 薛文辉，李忻. 构建三全育人工作格局，服务学生成长成才 [J]. 文教资料，2020（6）：120-121.

[2] 谷家川，张永俊. 实践能力：高校专业型学生社团建设研究 [J]. 绥化学院学报，2020，40（5）：108-110.

[3] 陈晓宇. 高校共青团组织加强对学生社团思想引领研究 [J]. 时代人物，2020（5）：0074-0075.

激发高校学生党支部建设活力的路径探索

——以对外经济贸易大学国际经济贸易学院为例

闫雪琴[①]　金小娜[②]　王馨怡[③]

摘　要：党支部是党的基础组织，是党的组织体系的基本单元。党的十八大以来，以习近平同志为核心的党中央高度重视党支部建设，要求把全面从严治党落实到每个支部、每名党员，推动全党形成大抓基层、大抓支部的良好态势，取得明显成效。高校学生党支部作为党支部的特殊组织形式，以其密切联系青年学生的特点和推进学生思想建设提升为前沿阵地的定位，在基层党支部建设中占据重要地位。如何完善高校学生党支部的建设工作并激发其活力，是各高校党建工作开展的重点。本文以对外经济贸易大学国际经济贸易学院学生党支部建设为例，探究目前的建设成果及存在不足，并提出激发党支部活力的建设性方案。

关键词：高校；党支部建设；青年党员；活力

一、高校学生党支部建设工作重要性

（一）服务顶层设计的需要

"扩大基层党组织覆盖面，着力解决一些基层党组织弱化、虚化、边缘化问题"是党的十九大报告提出的核心观点之一。2018年施行的《中国共产党支部工作条例（试行）》同样强调："高校中的党支部保证监督党的教育方针贯彻落实，巩固马克思主义在高校意识形态领域的指导地位，加强思想政治引领，筑牢学生理想信念根基，落实立德树人根本任务，保证教学科研管理各项任务完成。"2018年5月，习近平总书记在

[①] 闫雪琴，对外经济贸易大学国际经济贸易学院本科生辅导员。
[②] 金小娜，对外经济贸易大学国际经济贸易学院财政学专业2018级本科生。
[③] 王馨怡，对外经济贸易大学国际经济贸易学院金融学（国际金融与市场）专业2018级本科生。

北京大学考察时指出,"人才培养体系涉及学科体系、教学体系、教材体系、管理体系等,而贯通其中的是思想政治工作体系"。习近平总书记还这样比喻基层党组织的作用:基层党组织是贯彻落实党中央决策部署的"最后一公里",不能出现"断头路",要坚持大抓基层的鲜明导向,持续整顿软弱涣散基层党组织,有效实现党的组织和党的工作全覆盖,抓紧补齐基层党组织领导基层治理的各种短板,把各领域基层党组织建设成为实现党的领导的坚强战斗堡垒。

通过对重要文件、会议、讲话精神的汇总、学习和研讨,我们可以得出结论:党的基层组织是党落实精神的神经末梢,高校学生党组织是党的基层中极其重要和活跃的组成部分。完善好、发展好高校学生党支部建设工作是服务国家大局和顶层设计的需要。

(二)引领学生群体的需要

青年学生是极具特殊性的群体,做好青年学生的思想政治工作,提升其思想道德素质和专业技能水平是党的工作中不可或缺的一环。一方面,青年学生充满希望且肩负希望,习近平总书记指出:"历史和现实都告诉我们,青年一代有理想、有担当,国家就有前途,民族就有希望,实现中华民族伟大复兴就有源源不断的强大力量。""当代中国青年是与新时代同向同行、共同前进的一代,生逢盛世,肩负重任""广大青年要肩负历史使命,坚定前进信心,立大志、明大德、成大才、担大任,努力成为堪当民族复兴重任的时代新人,让青春在为祖国、为民族、为人民、为人类的不懈奋斗中绽放绚丽之花"。另一方面,青年学生思维活跃、情感充沛且尚未形成完整科学的三观,在目前的环境大背景下,充斥着多样复杂化、需要甄辨选择的信息。因此,在这一特殊人生阶段和复杂外部环境的背景下,正确引领青年学生思想、生活和学习的方向是培养青年学生立德树人、成才报国的决定性因素。

通过对青年群体的针对性分析,我们可以得出结论:高校学生党支部是青年学生群体成长成才道路上的关键指引,完善好、发展好高校学生党支部建设工作是引领学生群体的需要。

(三)激发裂变效应的需要

学生党支部是党的新鲜血液,是未来中流砥柱的中坚力量。高校学生党支部工作是学社连结的纽带,是为社会建设打基础、育人才的关键阵地。做好高校学生党支部建设工作,有利于立足工作本身,依托青年群体积极上进的特点,辐射带动更多的群体,给更多的基层党组织带来振奋人心的精神力量和参考学习的建设模范作用。

通过对高校学生党支部的关联性分析，我们可以得出结论：做好高校学生党支部建设工作的意义不仅在于建设本身，更在于其外部性的集中体现。完善好、发展好高校学生党支部建设工作是激发正面影响向社会全体裂变的需要。

二、高校学生党支部建设实例：对外经济贸易大学国际经济贸易学院党委

（一）情况概述及问卷结果展示

国际经济贸易学院党委作为学校二级党委单位，被评选为全国高校党建标杆院系和北京市先进基层党组织。下属学生（本科及研博）支部13个，支部成员共307人，其中正式党员232人，预备党员75人。从组织结构上看，大体上以学生的教育阶段为标准进行支部组建工作，同时，综合考虑国际经济贸易学院党委自身党员基数较大的客观情况，通过进一步在年级、专业间分组，保证党支部人数适中，能够支持日常支部工作的顺利开展和支部活动的最优参与；在人员分工方面，支委会组建以"1+2+1"为特征，即1位支部书记、2位支部委员分别担任组织委员和宣传委员，再由其中1位委员兼任纪检委员，如支部成员较多，则在原有分工基础上增加委员数量；在支部活动形式方面，以专家主讲的学习讨论及气氛轻松的党建相关文体活动为主，增进党建活动的教育性和趣味性，但两者结合的情况尚未达到预期效果。

为切实了解党支部建设现状，聆听以支部成员为主体的学院同学对党建工作的意见和建议，笔者向本院各学生党支部下发共200份调查问卷，收回192份有效问卷。其中本科学生98人，研博学生94人；从发展阶段来看，有16名预备党员同志和91名正式党员同志参与了问卷调查活动，另85名同学处于入党积极分子阶段。

在党员和预备党员同志被问及所在党支部开展活动的参与频率时，50.63%的同学选择了"一个月1次"，48.10%的同学选择了"一个月2~3次"，另有个别同学选择"一个月4次及以上"。在党支部开展的党建活动中，出现频率最高的是支部大会，其他被提及的形式，以被提到的数量排序，分别有党史党章等学习大会、党建相关的文体活动（如观看电影、重大会议转播、共读活动等）、校外共建活动和民主生活会。在开展的各式各样的活动中，75%的同学能够表现出80%~100%的参与率；在缺席党支部活动的原因一栏中，97.47%的同学选择了"时间冲突"及其他，2.53%的同学因对活动的形式和内容缺乏兴趣而放弃参与活动。

总的来看，支部成员及积极分子给本支部的建设打出了比较高的分数，平均来看达到9.18分（满分10分）。参与者通常选择校外共建活动，如"参观水长城"和"瞻仰烈士陵墓"作为令自己印象最深的党建活动；在校内活动方面，大家一般对自己亲

身参与并进行过观点输出的活动颇为乐道（如读书分享会、电影鉴赏会等）。但也有54.48%的同学认为，目前支部建设活动开展的形式比较单一；37.93%的同学提出，在活动开展的时间、地方上，缺乏对支部成员出席便利性条件的充分调研，导致因时间冲突被迫放弃参与党支部活动的现象出现。另外，还存在活动内容相对陈旧，对作风建设、纪律建设和队伍建设涉猎较少等问题。

（二）优秀党建活动经验：以"共读红色经典，传承红色基因"项目为例

"共读红色经典，传承红色基因"项目是由国际经济贸易学院本科生党支部开展的一项长期党建活动，时间跨度达8个月，参与人员包括师生共123人。本活动通过文献研究、调查研究等手段，深入了解学生党员和积极分子群体的思考维度与学习习惯，探究在该条件下高校学生的生活现状和行为模式变化，从而探讨"共读红色经典"在高校学生党员群体中推进的可行性和有效性，并结合心理学、组织行为学、教育学等学科的相关理论，设计了以"共读红色经典"为载体的高校学生党支部工作创新模式，并最终进行实践检验。

从活动的内容来看，红色经典共读活动注重实践经验与理论知识，坚持将先进思想输入与行动输出相结合，展开了高校党建工作的新途径。从活动的形式来看，设计了云上分享会、线下读书分享会、共读感悟推送制作等多个环节，既适应了后疫情时代集体活动的安全性和可行性的要求，又以多样化的活动方式吸引了支部成员参与的热情。从活动的结果来看，同学们在分组阅读不同红色书籍的前提下形成感悟，以摘抄、共读音频、心得视频等方式展示成果，共形成精品阅读摘抄20余份，共读音频推送4期，读书报告约6000字。通过本次红色经典共读活动，同时利用宣传优势，将支部学习成果向学院内其他同学推广，鼓励积极分子及发展对象、党外群众在支部的带动作用下强化理论修养，积极向党组织靠拢。

值得注意的是，在问卷调查中，相当多比例的本科生党员在被问及"留下印象最深的党建活动"时，都将本次共读活动列在了第一位。

三、高校学生党支部建设现状及成果分析

（一）优点

学生支部的特点主要有对党内活动参与能建立起严肃认识、参与活动热情高、成员综合素质好等。

1. 活动时参与率高

作为支部成员的义务之一，国际经济贸易学院学生支部的活动参与率较高，除个

别同学因时间冲突等原因请假外，参与者到场的情况及到场者对于活动的投入度都较为理想。

2. 活动后评价反馈深刻

支部成员在参与活动后，能从思想高度对活动的性质、意义和成果进行理解与体会，使得支部活动收到反馈良好，成员形成的心得感悟也助力党建活动上升到了新的高度。

3. 宣传资料存留情况好

支部成员重视活动后的资料保存，从以往的新闻稿汇总及党支部手册填写，再到现在的形成新闻推送或制作成果汇报视频，都是学生党员在自身综合素质得到提高的前提下，积极发挥个人特长助力党支部建设的表现。

（二）不足

学生支部党建活动开展的不足主要聚焦在以下方面。

1. 活动前期：理论准备不充分，内部调研不到位

许多同学反映，在活动开展前对于活动内容、相关理论了解不够，有"到了现场才知道活动主题"的现象。这一点会对同学们熟悉相关理论或时政热点并形成自身感悟不利，对活动意义的深化形成阻碍。

此外，成员因时间或地点原因无法出席也逐渐成为高校学生支部面临的重要问题，即每一次活动都会固定出现一部分同学请假的现象。高校作为同时具有教育教学和党政建设的特殊单位，应尽量为学生党员的学习生活及党内生活提供便利，同时，这样做也有助于从源头上解决党建活动参与率的"总有一部分人"请假问题。

2. 活动过程中：内容分配不够平衡，形式创新有待增强

党的建设作为党保持自身性质而从事的一系列自我完善的活动，除日常进行的党务工作外，还包括党的思想建设、组织建设、政治建设、作风建设、纪律建设和制度建设等多个方面。目前，国际经济贸易学院学生党支部在保证日常工作有序开展的前提下所组织的各项活动，对党的各方面建设所涉猎的程度不够平衡，突出表现为政治建设、思想建设、组织建设和制度建设频率较高，但有关作风建设和纪律建设的内容欠缺。

同时，支部成员反映，支部活动开展形式较为单一，多为支部大会、学习大会、座谈会等，双向沟通机会较少且缺乏新颖性，不利于支部活力的激发及可持续性的发展。

3. 活动后期：宣传产出成果不足，活动影响力局限在支部成员内部

与学生党支部良好的宣传资料留存习惯相对应的是，一方面，支部成员面临"有好材料不知道怎么发表"的困境；另一方面，在新媒体方面，学院及党团相关公众号常陷入急需高质量、即时性的内容来充实宣传渠道的窘迫。当支部宣传工作只进行到形成材料环节而没有及时在新媒体渠道发表时，党建目标中对于积极分子及发展对象、党外群众的服务和教育功能就很难得到充分体现。

四、高校学生党支部建设发展方向及优化路径探究

（一）高校学生党支部未来发展方向是建设学习型、服务型和创新型的青春党支部

高校学生党支部以其年龄上的青春性为根本特征，具有以培养人才为主要目标、以党团建设为重要组织形式的特殊身份。在新形势下，学生党支部要立足自身定位，建设学习型、服务型和创新型支部。"学习型"学生党支部的建设作为未来发展的基础和前提，倡导加强理论学习力度；"服务型"学生党支部意在强调支部建设过程中要兼具奉献精神及谦逊态度，着眼于支部服务对象，将活动举办的成果惠及全体同学；"创新型"学生党支部的建设是新形势下对高校基层党组织的必然要求，也是实现"学习型化""服务型化"的关键途径。同时，年龄层次上的年轻化使得学生党支部的思考方式更贴近青年人，死板僵化的传统错误想法在支部内引起的负面反响更加强烈，对于支部活动的态度也呈现出注重活动意义及个人收获的趋势。把握青春的典型特征，才能助力"三型"党支部建设，解决教育意义从活动到内心的"最后一公尺"问题。

（二）高校学生党支部，尤其是本科生支部，要以党建带团建，以团建促党建

高校环境的另一个特殊点在于学生年龄阶层的过渡性，尤其是本科学生，大多经历着作为共青团员、接受团组织的统一管理，到作为预备党员及党员、接受党组织统一领导的过程。同时，出于团员身份的广泛性和便于管理等原因，高校的育人工作一直坚持着"一心双环"的结构，以团委为领导核心进行日常的学生活动。

党组织工作对团组织的日常运行及管理形成理论支撑与客观监督，有利于提高团员对党组织的向心力及在团员队伍中的凝聚力，即"以党建带团建"。同时，在团组织生活已经形成较为成熟的管理架构及组织形式的基础上，学生支部党建存在的活

动开展形式不多样、活动内容落实古板、同学参与积极性不高的问题，可通过团委对于自身工作和发展的保障举措"切实可行、务实有效"的要求得到解决，即"以团建促党建"。

（三）从不同维度完善党建实践路径

1. 精准定位三种服务对象

党支部的工作对象包括党员、积极分子和发展对象、青年群众三类，对应党员管理、党员发展、服务青年群众三项基本职责。定位三种服务对象，要求高校学生党支部扩展视野，深化影响，积极探索服务对象间的带动发展机制，使党支部建设的成果惠及全体同学。

（1）横向扩大视野，拓宽党建活动覆盖面

支部建设活动的组织者和主要参与者是作为支部成员的预备党员和正式党员，但应同时鼓励积极分子和发展对象、党外群众加入党支部建设，如参与支部建设方案策划、以旁观学习者的身份参与支部活动，通过查看活动新闻报道及相关材料的方式自觉向党组织靠拢等。支部建设活动的负责人要积极扩大视野，在更大的党建活动覆盖面下，特别关注支部成员外的同学对于本支部建设情况的评价，不断吸收外部建议，形成以支部成员为输出核心、积极分子和预备党员为吸收中间层、党外群众为更广大的被影响者及客观评价者的"双环多层"思政教育传导结构。

（2）纵向加深影响，增加支部建设活动参与者的主动输出

调研显示，学生对于支部建设活动的评价及在后续活动中表现出的积极性，很大程度取决于自己在活动中的贡献，尤其取决于是否有原创观点的输出机会。作为激发党建活力、深化党建影响的重要手段及有效途径，党建活动的设计应增加观点分享、感想阐述、成果展示等类似环节，鼓励活动参与者主动输出观点、形成个人收获、定期总结新想法新思路，真正打通思政教育到学生内心的传导路径。

（3）树状构建培养体系，以共同发展带动个人成长

结合党员发挥先锋模范作用的义务及党史学习教育动员大会的相关思想，在学院内建立党委—支部成员—预备党员及发展对象—以积极分子为重点的党外群众四级树状党员培养体系。

邀请模范党员和党委相关负责老师，面向支部党员进行党的基础知识、党史学习教育、思政教育方面的演讲或讲座，把牢支部成员的思想关，保证正确三观及准确知识的传播；创新开展"预备党员及发展对象轮回宣讲"模式，在支部党员的引领及把关下，鼓励预备党员及发展对象在班团内开展有关入党流程、时事热点、个人近期思

想汇报的分享，并将宣讲情况及效果纳入对其入党意愿及入党期间表现的考核中，同时形成新闻稿，以多媒体形式汇总系列宣讲成果。为更大程度激发学生参与的积极性，完善双重选择机制，从宣讲的接受者一方出发，可以将聆听宣讲并形成感悟纳入对积极分子及后续有入党意愿的党外群众的考察中，做到既有"推力"，又有"拉力"。

四级树状党员培养体系的建立，使得支部成员的综合素质及能力有机会得到极大的锻炼，为培养一大批素质过硬、可堪大用的青年人才提供平台，并且可以极大地提升广大学生对于中国共产党认识的高度，树立正确的入党动机，充分地了解入党流程，使党的旗帜高高飘扬在同学们日常政治生活中，为后续工作的开展建立坚实的群众基础，源源不断地为党吸引优秀的人才。

2. 统筹着眼六大建设板块

支部建设需要兼顾政治、思想、组织、作风、纪律、制度六大板块。但学生支部由于成员具有年龄层次低、社会阅历少等特点，通常在支部建设中会忽视个别板块，如作风建设和纪律建设，导致其在党建活动中的占比较少，不利于支部的全面发展。

（1）标准化支部建设，普遍关注所有板块

学生支部应平衡分配各个板块建设的机会和时间，通过多样化的活动形式对支部成员的党性进行锤炼。在对学生党员的考核中，也应一以贯之，普遍关注其所有方面的理论学习成果及实践情况。

（2）发挥青年学生支部特点，重点突出个别板块

普遍关注并不等于同等关注，在实际工作中，学生支部应在全面重视各板块的基础上，针对本支部的特点及情况，强调突出对现阶段较薄弱环节的建设。如高校学生可以以党课学习、心得感悟书写的方式进行思想建设，在通过从理论层面了解和理解党组织架构相关知识的方式同时完成政治建设和组织建设。

3. 将不断进取创新的工作精神及关注核心、统筹全局的工作方法贯穿活动始终

当前高校学生党支部建设活动存在的不足中，未对成员出席的情况进行足够的事前调研，从而导致党建活动请假现象成为党建活动难以完全治好的"慢性病"之一。与此相应的是，党建活动形式单一，作为一种"急症"，对于党支部建设的负面影响是致命的。

（1）重视党建工作重心，兼顾成员个人需求

党建活动的活力被完全激发的前提，是参与者的数量及主动参与的意愿得到保证，这也是目前高校学生支部党建活动面临的显著问题之一。对此，支部活动组织者应依据本支部实际情况与不同阶段同学们的学习和工作任务量及紧迫程度，提前进行调研，

确定大多数成员能够出席的时间，并提前通知活动参与者。以通知时间上的提前量，换来出席率可能的提升区间。

（2）从支部实际情况出发，大胆创新具体工作内容

在创新活动形式方面，可以采用向外学习优秀榜样，向内广泛征求意见与延伸现有活动含义相结合的方法，创新活动开展的方式。定期与不同类型支部展开共建或经验分享活动，取长补短，吸收先进建设经验；常态化向全校或全院征集党建新点子、好点子，积极贴近群众，听取群众意见，才能办出真正有趣有样、不脱离群众的好活动；在现有活动基础上，向前或向后延伸一个环节，不仅是对活动本身的创新，更有利于活动意义的深化。如在校外参观活动前增加一场对所参观地点的历史事迹的集中学习活动，或在活动后组织成员制作实践成果汇报视频等，都属于高效且深刻的活动形式创新方法。

4. 把握新形势下特点，形成"互联网+党建"的两线并行新模式

"互联网+"利用信息通信技术及互联网平台，让互联网与传统线下事务进行深度融合，充分发挥互联网在资源配置中的优化和集成作用及新媒体技术的影响力和话语权。新冠肺炎疫情使得高校学生面临着学习、就业、人际交往等多重压力，学生支部的凝聚力容易因支部成员学习生活状态变化，以及无法见面共事而受到负面影响。学生支部达到解决支部成员自身发展问题，促进"支部"整体建设的目标，需要互联网及新媒体作为资源共享的源头活水、形式创新的灵感智库及效果展示的宣传舞台。

（1）资源共享的源头活水：搭建两种互联网平台

现今丰富的网络资源作为几乎零门槛的信息获取方式，一大优势在于无论有怎样的个人成长轨迹，都可能在互联网中找到相似的案例及解决方法。充分利用线上资源搭建党员互助网络平台，对明确支部成员个人发展路径，为其提供个性化指导与帮助具有一定的优势。从线上资源的传递角度来看，当信息从外到内流入支部时，互联网这一"源头活水"同时作为各地党组织建设经验交流与互助的高效平台，可以为创新支部建设活动提供外部建议。

（2）形式创新的灵感智库：统一两类活动形式

在新冠肺炎疫情影响尚未完全消散的情况下，支部建设活动的线上开展起初只是线下形式的替代品，但随着后疫情时代的来临及互联网、新媒体技术的发展，线上开展的党建活动在功能定位和影响意义上，与线下形式是地位平等且优势互补的。将线下活动注重环节流程严肃性的特点与线上活动倡导交流沟通活跃化的特点结合起来，依据实际情况灵活开展党建工作，是新时期最大化提高支部建设效能的重要手段之一。

(3) 效果展示的宣传舞台：惠及三方不同主体

在支部成为资源的发布者并将自身经验发表上传的过程中，通过新媒体手段对支部动态和新思想、新理论进行常态化的整编。第一，做到既把工作干到实处，又把成果摆到明面上，为支部的量化考核提供依据；第二，采用学生喜闻乐见的成果展示形式，激发支部成员参与活动的积极性；第三，对更广大的学生群体来说，以积极正面支部形象的建立，增强网络阵地的吸引力和感召力，将党建工作影响内化于心。

新时代背景下，要将高校学生支部的党建工作提升到新高度，就必然需要依托互联网平台及新媒体手段，将高科技发展的技术优势转化为党支部建设的资源优势、能力优势和传播优势。

五、结语

高校学生党支部因其自身具有的年龄及受教育程度的特征，在支部建设过程中易受活动开展形式和活动策划思路的影响，使得党建工作效果在活动参与度及活动意义内化上打折扣。为激发高校学生党支部建设活力，在定位未来建设方向的基础上，我们要坚持党团共建，着眼三个维度，统筹六大板块，改进工作作风及工作方法，打造线上线下相结合的新时期党建模式。高校学生党组织作为思政教育的主阵地，优化其内部建设，不仅对打造标杆党组织具有重要意义，更有利于将爱党爱国的先锋思想传递给全体学生，助力高校育人工作。

参考文献

［1］中共中央政治局．中国共产党支部工作条例（试行）［N］．人民日报，2018-11-26（001）．

［2］人民日报社．习近平在北京大学考察［J］．人民日报，2018（05）：3．

［3］颜东．六个聚力提升机关党的建设［J］．办公室业务，2021（06）：7-8．

［4］王思琦．高校学生党支部建设的创新与实践研究［J］．党史博采（下），2021（04）：25-26．

［5］庞博，张健．"小切口"提升高校党支部组织力研究：以陕西科技大学为例［J］．陕西教育（高教），2021（03）：4-5．

［6］共青团中央书记处．充分发挥高校共青团在大学生思想政治工作中的生力军作用［N］．人民日报，2017-01-26（009）．

［7］黄文璇．新时代高校基层党组织党员培养教育的实践探索：浙江外国语学院电子商务系学生党支部建设的创新做法［J］．科教导刊，2021（07）：82-84．

[8] 龙志成, 谭珺如. 高校学生党支部建设及作用发挥探索 [J]. 现代企业, 2021 (02): 106-107.

[9] 李德煌. 三级联动提升新时代高校组织建设质量 [J]. 党建研究, 2021 (01): 60-61.

[10] 蔡嘉鑫, 王莹, 段汝和等. 探索高校"互联网+党建"有效模式: 以河北北方学院研究生党支部为例 [J]. 中外企业文化, 2021 (01): 155-156.

"四史"教育

——高校党支部的必修课

毕 帆[①] 黄依萌[②]

摘 要：历史是最好的教科书，学好"四史"可以"看成败、鉴得失、知兴替"。习"四史"，对高校青年党员的世界观和方法论培育有重要意义，"四史"教育应该成为高校青年的必修课，也应该成为高校党支部的必修课。高校青年党员具有的"学生"和"党员"两个属性，对"四史"应进行更广泛而深入的研究，在把握思政课这一主阵地的同时，高校基层党支部应成为青年党员学习"四史"的重要平台。在具体学习实践中，高校党支部一是要把握生活化，贴近实际，让"历史走出教室走进生活"；二是要注重沉浸式，双向互动，提升学生学习参与感与领悟力；三是要年轻态，更新思路，把握当代青年的话语体系。同时，对于学习"四史"的成果，在学习结束后要注意成果固化总结和多次传播。当前，高校党支部在"四史"的学习教育中也遇到广度不够和深度不足的问题。总的来说，"四史"教育作为高校党支部的必修课，应该继续深入推进，把握高校青年特点，力求政治性、学理性和生动性的统一。

关键词："四史"教育；高校党支部；学生党员

一、学习"四史"的理论基础

历史是最好的教科书，中国共产党作为一个善于学习的马克思主义政党，正是通过不断学习才发展壮大的。学习党史、新中国史、改革开放史、社会主义发展史可以"看成败、鉴得失、知兴替"，作为高校师生，学好"四史"有助于在把握历史发展规律的基础上，坚定对中国特色社会主义的"四个自信"，更深刻理解中国共产党的初心和使命，更深刻认识历史和人民选择马克思主义、中国共产党、社会主义道路和改革开放的必然性。高校基层党支部应把"四史"教育当作支部建设的"必修课"，既与

[①] 毕帆，对外经济贸易大学国际经济贸易学院本科生辅导员。
[②] 黄依萌，上海交通大学文创学院2021级硕士研究生。

高校思政教育保持一致性,也要把握基层支部的先进性。

"四史"教育不仅是党政干部的必修课,也应该成为高校青年的必修课。党的十八大以来,习近平总书记高度重视对"四史"的学习。2020年1月在"不忘初心、牢记使命"主题教育总结大会上的讲话中,习近平总书记强调:"把学习贯彻党的创新理论作为思想武装的重中之重,同学习马克思主义基本原理贯通起来,同学习党史、新中国史、改革开放史、社会主义发展史结合起来,同新时代我们进行伟大斗争、建设伟大工程、推进伟大事业、实现伟大梦想的丰富实践联系起来。"回看100年来中国共产党的历史经验,我们可以发现,如果这个世界上最大的政党想要保持先进性和纯洁性、永葆青春活力,需要广大青年,特别是青年党员的努力。从时间的历史、现实、未来三个维度看,加强"四史"教育有助于继承和发扬宝贵的思想传统,从现实来看会为改革与发展提供思想助力;而着眼未来,加强"四史"教育意在指向更加灿烂辉煌的未来。高校青年学习"四史"建立起正确的历史观、国家观和民族观,进而通过思想指导实践,成为合格的社会主义建设者和接班人。

学习"四史",对高校青年党员的世界观和方法论培育有重要意义。2020年6月习近平总书记给复旦大学《共产党宣言》展示馆党员志愿服务队全体队员回信中写道:"希望广大党员特别是青年党员认真学习马克思主义理论,结合学习党史、新中国史、改革开放史、社会主义发展史,在学思践悟中坚定理想信念,在奋发有为中践行初心使命。"学习"四史"能使青年党员进一步理解唯物主义历史观的基本理论和方法论,做到实事求是研究"四史"。习近平总书记基于客观性、辩证性、人民性三重视野,提出了实事求是的历史观,这是对历史的科学认识:历史是一脉相承的历史,历史是曲折发展的历史,历史是人民创造的历史。

青年党员在学习"四史"的过程中要坚持唯物主义历史观的方法论,要认识到实事求是原则与坚持党性和科学性原则不是对立的,而是统一的。坚持实事求是,要以正确的思想路线、科学的理论方法为指导学习"四史",也要注意把握整体性和辩证思维。整体性原则意味着"四史"学习要把握历史、理论与实践的密切关系,既要求青年党员抓住每部历史的重点来学,更要把握共性,从整体上学习主流和本质、理论和历史、经验和教训。青年党员在学习时应该注意到,不应该将历史割裂或者对立,要把历史性论断、历史性成就、历史性变革、历史性结论作为整体来把握。"四史"就其主体而言可以说是一部近代以来中华民族的伟大复兴史,是围绕中国共产党创建和发展的历史这个"骨骼"展开的。坚持辩证思维,一方面,就是要在"四史"学习中正确认识历史上的失误与错误,"使失误和错误连同党的成功经验一起成为宝贵的历史教材";另一方面,分清主流和支流也十分关键,要避免历史虚无主义。这既是学习"四史"的要求，也是学习"四史"的目的之一，为我们在新时代有效抵御历史虚无主义提供了根本遵循。

二、高校党支部的"四史"学习实践

高校青年党员具有的"学生"和"党员"两个属性，对"四史"应进行更广泛而深入的研究，在把握思政课这一主阵地的同时，高校基层党支部应成为青年党员学习"四史"的重要平台。习近平总书记曾语重心长地说："做好基层基础工作十分重要，只要每个基层党组织和每个共产党员都有强烈的宗旨意识和责任意识，都能发挥战斗堡垒作用、先锋模范作用，我们党就会很有力量，我们国家就会很有力量，我们人民就会很有力量，党的执政基础就能坚如磐石。"提升高校基层党建要在质量水平上下功夫，具体到"四史"教育中，那就是要坚持抓基层支部的"四史"学习工作，强基础，开展各种形式的"四史"主题教育活动，充分发挥基层党支部的战斗堡垒作用，更好地教育管理党员，加深对中国共产党发展历史的认识理解，有效引领带动群众，形成高校内学习"四史"的良好氛围，不断激发师生的积极性和创造性，全面增强高校基层党组织的生机与活力。具体来看，应把握"生活化、沉浸式、年轻态"三个特征开展高校党支部的"四史"实践。

（一）生活化：贴近实际，让历史走出教室走进生活

高校党支部的成员多为青年学生党员，未走出"象牙塔"，社会阅历浅，对知识理论的认知未完全形成体系，严肃的"四史"教育反而适得其反，不利于青年党员学习领会，因而，"四史"学习应贴近生活。更具体来说，要创新学习方式，摆脱在课堂学理论的刻板印象，以更丰富的方式讲解"四史"。

其一，让历史走出教室走进生活，就是要在教室外的实践中学习"四史"。高校党支部可以充分利用当地红色资源，红色遗迹、伟人故里、博物馆和档案馆等，处处有鲜活的"四史"学习素材。同时，各高校党委可以充分统筹各基层党组织资源，开展离退休党支部与青年学生支部的户外共建活动，在户外实践的过程中，离退休老党员们以亲身经历讲述的一手史料或转述得知的相关"四史"史实，都是极佳的"四史"学习资源，这些会收获比思政课堂更好的传授效果。

其二，让历史走出教室走进生活，就是要在课堂外润物无声中学习"四史"。信息互联网时代，"四史"学习，特别是青年群体的"四史"学习应创新方式，更多地与互联网接轨。如网友逆光飞行（真实姓名林超）创作的《那年那兔那些事儿》（以下简称为《那兔》）就是一部收获极高关注与热度的爱国主义科普漫画。动画版以近现代

历史事件为题材，每集时长不到十分钟，以兔子等小动物为主要角色，于2015年3月开始在各大网络视频播放平台播出。每集故事基于史实，如1950年的长津湖战役，《那兔》以生动幽默的动画语言表达，如"雪地里的兔子们纷纷起身战斗，口中高喊：'我们的口号是，专打鹰酱，不疼不要小钱钱！'"，在剧中体现了兔子们保护种花家的责任感与使命感，让人自然带入抗美援朝战争期间无数"跨过鸭绿江"的戍边战士，在寓教于乐中学习"四史"。至今《那兔》在哔哩哔哩网站共有超3亿的播放量（截至2021年5月），并于2021年出版动画周边手账本《兔子的征程是星辰大海》。其选用在青年群体中占比高的平台投放"四史"教育资料，并以贴近当代青年人生活的方式使他们潜移默化学习"四史"，这是让教育走进生活的最佳例证。

（二）沉浸式：双向互动，提升学生学习参与感与领悟力

近年来，思政课课堂不断改革创新课程模式，但不变的是要把握思政课教学政治性与学科性的统一。从总体上看，"四史"的内容都能直接或间接地融入思政课的教学中。传统的课堂式教学是"老师讲，学生听"，属于老师对学生的单向传播，没有形成交流互动，传播效果差；近年不断改革的思政课课堂强调丰富的实践，让学生成为课程的主体，极大提升了学生的课程参与感。高校基层党支部的"四史"学习，一方面可以作为思政课的补充，强调沉浸式学习"四史"；另一方面也作为思政课课堂理论学习的纵深，通过各类双向互动体验更好领悟"四史"中蕴含的理论。

"四史"学习的双向互动，即强调不是只有老师讲，而是要老师和学生一同评议，一同发表观点，"有来有往"。2017年，习近平总书记在中国政法大学考察，《习近平与大学生朋友们》一书中曾记载，参加民商经济法学院"主题团日"时，几位同学从不同角度畅谈观看电影《焦裕禄》的体会，习总书记认真倾听，并参与讨论。习总书记说："消除贫困就是不忘初心，不忘焦裕禄精神的初心，不忘老革命和老红军的初心。"从当下联系过去，从影片联系实际，"四史"教育在无形之中展开，这种平等的对话令人获益匪浅，非常值得各高校基层支部在党日活动中学习借鉴。

书中还写道："总书记在与我们互动交流时，跟我们一起分享了他父亲的故事，感觉就像是一个长辈在给孩子们讲故事，充满关怀与期许。"讲故事也是学习"四史"的好方法。习近平总书记曾强调，"要讲好中国特色社会主义的故事，讲好中国梦的故事，讲好中国人的故事，讲好中华优秀文化的故事，讲好中国和平发展的故事"，中国共产党的发展并不缺乏好故事，但欠缺传播的合理路径，这是针对国际传播讲的，但同样适用于"四史"的研究和学习。在"四史"的教育过程中也要遵循当前社会的传播习惯，适度减少宏大叙事，多关注微观个体，如开展听亲人讲"四史"等活动，

由点到面，坚持家校同行、师生同行，引导青年学生坚定不移与党中央同心同路、同向同行。

（三）年轻态：更新思路，把握当代青年的话语体系

高校基层党支部作为高校思想政治教育的重要组成部分，应不断创新发展适应当代青年话语体系的思政教育话语体系，增强思想政治教育话语体系的学理性、亲和力和针对性。关键就是要通过"四史"学习研究强化形成历史自觉，以历史自觉推动高校思想政治教育话语体系发展。

要通过学习"四史"形成历史自觉，重要的一环就是要阅读经典书籍。但面对时空差距甚远的红色经典，如何让青年学生想读、读通、读懂？这需要党支部等基层组织的负责人在书籍选择和阅读引导方面下功夫。一方面，"领学人"要选择适合高校青年阅读的读物，具体到基层党支部，应选择在理论思想上更深入、有难度的"四史"作品进行学习研究；另一方面，面对高深的文献，"领学人"要选择更符合当代青年理解的方式领读。如对外经贸大学国际经济贸易学院本科生党支部在学习《毛泽东选集》时，"领学人"从当前高校青年的热点、痛点话题"内卷"引入，结合《毛泽东选集》中的经典章节语段，与当下现实紧密结合，青年面对前途的迷茫，要相信"星星之火，可以燎原"。"内卷"并不是唯一的出路，如果能掌握正确的方向、适当的方法，青年人虽初出茅庐但也能有一番自己的事业，将青春华彩写在祖国大地上。经典之所以愈久弥新，正因其理跨越百年而毫不褪色。

在夯实高校基层党建方面，习近平总书记指出："高校党的基层组织建设要适应高校发展趋势，遵循高校特点和规律，创新体制机制，改进工作方式，提高党的基层组织做思想政治的工作能力。"适应不同学科特点的青年群体进行"四史"学习研究，这也是各高校党支部工作应注重的一环。《习近平与大学生朋友们》书中就记载了时任厦门市委常委、副市长的习近平指导厦门大学经济系的一名同学学习《资本论》的故事。作为经济类专业的高校学生，研究"四史"更要研究马克思政治经济学原理，细读前人智慧，更好服务中国特色社会主义经济建设。

三、学习"四史"的成果与难点

高校党支部的"四史"学习应特别强调成果固化，以期使"四史"研究获得更好效果，青年党员在学习中更有收获。具体而言包括以下两个方面。

要固化成果，一是要在每个"四史"主题活动结束后做好总结工作，学生党支部内部做好高年级与低年级党员的"传、帮、带"。每次活动的总结回顾，也是再一次梳

理学习"四史"的过程,同时,在这个过程中党支部能认识到活动的不足与欠缺之处,在下一次活动中加以改进。由于高校学生党支部具有人员流动性大的特性,开展学习活动时也应该把握自身特性,特别是高校学生党支部开展"四史"教育时应该要对经典理论、书籍、影音作品等进行反复多次的学习,这就要求组织内部成员有极强的责任意识,每个支部青年党员从加入组织到离开组织都应该经历从"学习"到"助学"的过程,这个过程是助人的过程,也是深化"四史"学习研究的有效途径。

要固化成果,二是要将"四史"学习成果做形式多样的信息化呈现,以丰富的多媒体形式留存学习材料和心得体会,达到多次传播的目的。如在进行"四史"经典书籍阅读活动时,可以将青年党员的读书笔记等材料以微信推送、H5等新媒体形式留存。青年学生可充分发挥主观能动性,针对书中的情节、观点,组织阅读分享会,或制作短视频、播客等便于社交媒体传播的阅读体会,将支部"四史"学习成果扩大化,由基层党支部带动辐射更多的高校青年群体学习"四史"。

当前,在高校党支部的"四史"学习教育中也遇到一些问题,可以总结为"广度"和"深度"两方面的问题。广度不足是指高校党支部在开展活动时没有积极创新活动形式,支部的"四史"学习教育无法与高校思政教育主阵地——思政课堂形成相互补充、促进的作用,支部的部分活动内容和形式与思政课的重叠部分较大,恐难以调动青年学生积极性,也降低了学生的学习效率。深度不够是指高校党支部没有在"四史"学习中发挥青年党员的先进带头作用,学习的内容无法沿着思政课的脉络继续推进深入,青年党员没有借主题教育活动深入学习"四史"相关理论知识,强化"四史"教育成果。总的来说,"四史"教育作为高校党支部的必修课,应该继续深入推进,把握高校青年特点,力求政治性、学理性和生动性的统一。

参考文献

[1] 程美东,刘辰硕. 从三个维度理解加强"四史"教育的重大意义 [J]. 思想教育研究,2020 (12):14-17.

[2] 顾钰民. "四史"学习与加强思想政治理论课建设 [J]. 理论与改革,2021 (01):26-29.

[3] 胡静波. 中国特色社会主义整体性特征的三个维度 [J]. 科学社会主义,2020 (04):67-72.

[4] 王炳林,刘奎. 关于学习党史、新中国史、改革开放史、社会主义发展史的思考 [J]. 思想理论教育导刊,2020 (08):64-71.

[5] 魏晓文,秦雪. 历史虚无主义批判的三重逻辑:学习习近平关于"四史"的

重要论述[J].思想教育研究,2020(09):25-30.

[6]许月.习近平科学认识历史的三维视野[J].思想理论教育导刊,2020(08):154-159.

[7]朱喆,王芳.历史自觉与思想政治教育话语体系创新发展[J].思想教育研究,2020(12):43-47.

第二部分
经韬纬略,立德树人·建校70周年

1951年,党和国家部署建立中央人民政府贸易部高级商业干部学校,1984年,学校正式更名为对外经济贸易大学。对外经济贸易大学始终坚守为党育人、为国育才的初心使命,历经70年发展壮大,在学科建设、人才培养、科学研究和国际交流等方面保持着国内领先水平,培育出众多活跃在经济、贸易、法律、国际事务等领域的杰出人才,为我国乃至世界经济社会发展贡献贸大智慧。

军事课教学在推进高校 "三全育人" 中的作用机制研究

曲佳文① 蔡维明②

摘 要：军事课教学是提升高校大学生军事理论知识水平，夯实大学生军事实践技能基础，强化大学生国防教育和爱国主义教育的重要形式，对提升大学生综合素质，助力大学生全面发展具有重要作用。"三全育人"的全新时代背景对高校军事课教学提出了更高的要求。通过研究，笔者发现对标"三全育人"要求，军事课教学存在着专业教师配置不齐，全员育人作用发挥不到位；教学环节不连续，全过程育人作用发挥不到位；教学协调联动不充分，全方位育人作用发挥不到位三个方面的主要问题。为此，军事课教学可以通过强化军事课教学人才队伍建设，补足军事课教学全员育人短板；延长军事课教学时间"战线"，提升军事课教学全过程育人实效；提升军事课教学质量，筑牢军事课教学全方位育人防线等举措进一步提升军事课教学"三全育人"实效，从而助力高校"三全育人"工作，落实立德树人根本任务，培养堪当大任的时代新人。

关键词："三全育人"；军事课教学；军事理论；军事训练

2016年12月，习近平总书记在全国高校思想政治工作会议上提出"三全育人"的要求。2018年教育部在《教育部办公厅关于开展"三全育人"综合改革试点工作的通知》（教思政厅函〔2018〕15号）文件中提出了"三全育人"的概念。"三全育人"的内涵是指全员育人、全过程育人、全方位育人。全员育人是指从育人的主体出发，强调在高校的各类育人工作中注意主体的多样性，注重发挥全部主体的育人作用，而不是仅发挥某个或某些主体的作用；全过程育人是指从育人的时间发展角度出发，对

---

① 曲佳文，对外经济贸易大学国际经济贸易学院党委副书记。
② 蔡维明，对外经济贸易大学国际经济贸易学院本科生辅导员。

育人工作进行纵向界定，强调重视高校育人的过程管理，注重教育的连续性、持续性，因为人才的培育是一个循序渐进的过程，需要更多的时间和更丰富的内容，而不是通过短时间的灌输式教育可以一蹴而就的；全方位育人是指从育人工作的各个角度出发，对育人工作进行横向分析，强调对育人活动的效果和不足进行全方位、多角度和系统化的综合分析，从而补足育人工作的横向短板，提升育人工作实效。自2003年军事理论课以必修课的形式在全国高校普及以来，军事课教学在我国的发展已有近20年的历史。军事课教学内涵丰富，既涉及学生军事理论知识的讲授、军事实践技能的训练、国家安全观念的培养，又肩负着集体荣誉感养成、爱国主义教育、纪律意识提升和集体主义精神培养等重要责任，是培养优质大学生士官和德智体美劳全面发展的新时代人才的重要环节。在中国特色社会主义新时期，在"三全育人"的全新要求背景下，高校在推进"三全育人"工作中对军事课教学提出了全新要求，军事课教学自身要对标"三全育人"要求，找出缺点和不足，实施改进而提升效果，实现"三全育人"目标，而后才能反作用于学校的"三全育人"工作，推进高校"三全育人"工作深入发展。

一、军事课教学的发展历史

我国军事课教学的开始，要追溯到1985年教育部等六部委联合发文决定在部分院校开展军事技能训练试点。2003年，教育部和相关部门要求普通高等学校以必修课的形式开设"军事理论"课。1985年，军事课教学有了统一的教学大纲。2019年1月，教育部、中央军委国防动员部联合制订了《普通高等学校军事课教学大纲》（简称《大纲》），《大纲》中具体指出："军事课是普通高等学校学生的必修课程。军事课由'军事理论''军事技能'两部分组成。"其中"军事理论"教学时数36学时，记2学分。该部分课程可由各普通学校自行制订教学计划、考核方式等统一管理方式，通常运用网络化教学手段在多媒体教室进行大班上课。"军事技能"训练时间2-3周，实际训练时间不得少于14天112学时，计2学分。其教学形式一般为普通高校针对入学新生开展的军事训练，各高校根据实际情况自行确定军事训练的时间和地点，制订军事训练方案，确定军事训练内容，通过实践训练提高学生对军事技能的了解与掌握，帮助学生养成良好的生活习惯，增强学生的组织纪律性、集体荣誉感和爱国主义精神。

二、军事课教学在高校推进"三全育人"工作中的重要性

军事课教学是有效提升大学生军事理论知识和军事实践技能，开展大学生国防安全教育和爱国主义教育的主阵地。普通高等学校是我国人才培养的基地，大学生爱国主义精神培养和国防意识的提升对国家安全战略发展有着重要意义。青年学生是我国

未来发展的中流砥柱，也是我国国防安全建设的人才基础，因此，针对大学生开展的国防教育是全民国防教育的重中之重，而军事课教学是高校开展大学生国防安全教育最基础、最普遍、最有效的方式。从 2003 年普通高等学校的"军事理论"课正式被确立为全国高校统一开设的必修课开始，我国高校军事课教学工作已经开展了 20 多年，取得了较好的育人成绩，如形成了较为完整的课程体系、探索出了军事训练的方式与方法，在增强学生爱国主义精神、大局意识和国防意识，培养学生责任感、使命感，提升学生综合素质方面切实发挥了重要作用。

军事理论课教学是国家相关法律法规的要求。2001 年通过的《中华人民共和国国防教育法》第十五条、第十六条规定体现了国家对高校推进国防教育的要求，其中既有对课程设置的要求，也有对课程模式的要求，充分体现了军事理论课程和国防教育对大学生的重要性。而 2004 年教育部发出的《教育部办公厅关于加强普通高等学校军事课教学工作的意见》也表明了教育部的观点：军事课程教学应当在高校课程中占有一席之地，高等学校必须重视起来这一点，军事课程教学应当成为大学生的必修课程。这些规定和要求在一定程度上体现了世界大环境的现状，面对中美贸易摩擦、国际地区冲突和新冠肺炎疫情蔓延等问题，我们要做的是在这些浪潮下武装好自己。由此观之，国家教育法规和教育部相关文件对普通高等学校开展军事课教学都做出了明确、具体的规定，国家高度重视，教育部高度重视，军事理论课教学的重要性不言而喻。

军事理论课教学是普通高等学校贯彻"三全育人"要求，构建德智体美劳全面培养教育体系的重要一环。在当下教育的大环境中，党和国家对大学生普遍的要求是全面发展的高素质人才，而军事课教学的内容丰富，形式多样，既有军事理论的讲授，又有军事技能的实践提升，有利于提升大学生的军事理论水平和军事技能。在理论教学层面，涉及政治、经济、军事、国防等多个方面的知识，可以说基本涵盖了古今中外的各类知识。同时，军事、军队、军人、国防等相关知识又将爱国主义、集体主义、使命感与责任感等重要精神内涵包含其中，使大学生学习军事理论课程不只是能了解一方面的知识，而是获得全面的知识，受到各种正能量精神的鼓舞与感召，实现身心的全面健康发展。在实践教学层面，军事技能课教学通过为期 14 天左右的军事技能训练，引导学生实地了解军营生活，感受军队文化，提升自身军事实践技能，这对大学生集体荣誉感的培养和团结协作能力的提升具有重要意义，同时，可以通过军事技能训练实践引导大学生树立热爱祖国、崇尚荣誉、拥军爱民和无私奉献的高尚情操。

三、军事课教学在高校推进"三全育人"工作中存在的问题

"三全育人"的理念要求军事课教学实现全员育人、全过程育人、全方位育人，将

军事课的育人效果最大限度地发挥。从军事理论课被确定为高校大学生必修课以来，经过多年的发展，军事理论教学和军事实践训练体系日臻完善，开设了完整的有关军事理论教育和国防教育的必修课程与选修课程，教学方法和手段也在不断改进，时至今日，军事理论课程已经在大多数高校课程中占有一席之地。对标全员育人、全过程育人和全方位育人的"三全育人"要求，军事课教学在三个方面还都存在着一些缺点和不足，这些缺点和不足在一定程度上影响和限制了军事课教学的育人实效。对标"三全育人"的要求，找出军事课教学存在的问题并加以解决，是提高军事课教学育人实效质量的前提。具体来说，当前军事课教学在以下三个方面存在问题和不足。

1. **军事课教学专业教师配置不齐，全员育人作用发挥不到位**

一方面军事课教学专业教师人员配备不齐。目前，绝大部分高校军事课教师除很少一部分外聘军事人员外，大多数是高校自己配备教师，其中军事课专业教师较少，大部分高校选择由思想政治课教师、辅导员兼任军事理论课教师。同时，大部分高校的军事课教师待遇难以落实，教师水平参差不齐，存在较大差距。另一方面，军事课教学缺乏独立的教学部门，大部分高校的军事课没有独立的教学部门，大多数高校是在其他教学部门（如教务处、体育部）或行政部门（如学生处、武装部）下设教研室。由于军事课学科不同于其他专业学科，学科界定不独立，专职教师处境较为尴尬，待遇难以按照其他专业课教师标准落实，教师发展通道也较为狭窄，导致从事军事课教学的教师难以全身心投入，教学的创新动力不足。高校军事课教学专职教师队伍人员不足，课程专业建设滞后，缺乏专门的负责部门，导致对高校军事课教学课程内容研究不足、课程内容专业性不强、科研成果少、评价考核松懈、教学质量不高。除此之外，对军事课教学其他相关校内人员资源利用不充分，如各高校都有参加大学生士兵计划，但退役归来学生的朋辈激励作用未完全发挥，大学生退役士兵是学生的同龄人，却是在军队学习、生活、训练和执行过任务的人，他们的2年军旅经历和所学、所思、所悟都可以经过引导和培训后转化为军事课教学宝贵资源。目前，各高校对这部分学生的作用还有待进一步挖掘。

2. **军事课教学环节不连续，全过程育人作用发挥不到位**

一方面，大多数高校军事实践技能训练时间不充足，训练效果无法保证。在军事实践技能训练安排实际操作过程中，各高校为确保学生的身体健康和生命安全，会适当降低军事实践技能训练难度，适当降低相关要求，致使大学生军事技能训练效果远远达不到教学大纲的要求。目前，全国高校军训一般安排在新生入学前后，主要内容包括队列训练、内务整理、军体拳、匕首操学习、会操评比等。同时，受教学时间安排的影响，最低14天集中训练的时间要求没有根本保证，训练效果往往不尽如人意，不能完全达到军事技能训练的目标。除此之外,部分高校选择在校内军训,由在校的大学生退役士兵担任教官,教官的专业程度不够在一定程度上也使军事技能训练效果大打折扣。另一方面,军事理论课教学一次性开展,从时间维度上看学生军事理论学习"一劳永逸"。目前,大部分高校的军事理论课教学以专题讲座或基础必修课程的形式安排在大一学年或大一上学期,作为新生入学后的基础课,一般学习时长为36学时,学生考核通过后获得相应学分即完成军事理论课学习,在以后的大学生活中将不再有军事理论课的相关学习任务,这在学习时间维度上形成了军事理论课学习"一劳永逸"的局面。而事实上,军事理论知识的学习应该是一个长期的、反复多次的学习过程,因而军事课教学全过程育人功能的发挥还远远不够。

3. 军事课教学协调联动不充分,全方位育人作用发挥不到位

一方面,学生不够重视,导致教育难度增加。对对外经济贸易大学国际经济贸易学院2019级本科生进行线上问卷调查,共收到有效问卷286份。问卷统计结果显示,针对"你对军事理论课教学重要性的认识程度"这一问题,选择"是培养方案要求的基础必修课"的学生占59%,选择"是大学生全面发展必须提升的素养"的学生占24%,选择"学校安排的课程或讲座,按要求参加"的学生占17%。针对"你在军事理论课教学课程或讲座的听课状态"这一问题,选择"全程认真听讲座"的学生占15%,选择"大部分时间是在认真听讲座或听课"的学生占27%,选择"选择性听课,只听自己感兴趣的内容"的学生占52%,选择"基本未在听课"的学生占6%。调查结果大体上反映了军事理论课学习情况的现状:学生对军事课的学习不够重视,缺乏学习军事理论知识的热情和兴趣,学习效果较差。另一方面,高等学校对军事课教学缺乏足够重视。普通高等学校在面临繁重的专业课教学任务和巨大的科研、就业压力的情况下,对与学校优势专业不太相关联的军事理论课程未给予足够重视,实施过程中大多数以能完成基本任务为目的,要求自然不会很高,教学质量也就难以保证。除以上两个方面外,相比于思想引领的各类"第二课堂"相关活动长期、定期举办,军事理论学习和国防安全教育的"第二课堂"相关学生活动的举办数量也是远远不足的,在一定程度上限制了军事课教学全方位育人功能的发挥。

四、军事课教学在高校推进"三全育人"工作中的改进措施

1. 强化军事课教学人才队伍建设,补足军事课教学全员育人短板

课堂教学是军事课教学的主阵地,军事课教师是军事理论课程的直接讲授者,是传授军事理论知识和普及国防教育的一线力量,各高校应重视军事课教学和军事课教师队伍建设。具体来说,学校应当就军事课教师进行专门选拔,选聘具备专业知识和

教学经验丰富的教师组建专职军事课教师队伍。另外，学校也应当重视军事理论这门课程，将它与学校其他课程一视同仁对待，充分重视对学生的军事理论教育，成立专门的军事课教学教研组，确保教学经费、教师待遇、教学时间三方面政策落实到位。充分发挥在读退役大学生士兵在军事课教学中的作用，发挥其朋辈激励作用，可以将相关学生组织起来，根据教学内容和课程体系组织他们进行集体备课，选拔优秀学生担任小讲师，结合其自身经历向同学们讲述军事课专业知识。同时，发挥退役大学生士兵和各类学生骨干在"第二课堂"活动组织中的作用，结合军事课教学内容和重要时间节点，针对各个年级的学生开展丰富多彩的军事理论知识和军事技能学习活动，形成"第二课堂"与第一课堂相互联动、相互促进的良好局面，全面提升军事课教学的育人效果。

2. 延长军事课教学时间"战线"，提升军事课教学全过程育人实效

一是要努力保证军事技能训练的时间和训练效果。军事技能训练不同于课堂教学，有其特殊性和专业性，需要有专门的军事训练营地和专业的军事教官才能确保军事训练的育人效果，各高校应提高对军事训练的重视程度，根据本校的课程教学安排，协调同一区域内其他高校，错峰安排军事训练，确保军事训练能够达到设定的育人目标。二是要提升军事理论课教学的全过程育人实效，可以参照"形势与政策"课程将总共2学分的课程平均分配到每个学期都有课程学习的方式，延长军事理论课教学的时间跨度，从一个学期集中授课变为6个或8个学期分散授课，消除学生军事理论课学习"一劳永逸"的刻板印象，引导学生树立军事理论知识和国防教育知识需要长期学习、自觉学习和常学常新的学习理念，以课堂教学为阵地，以"第二课堂"活动为补充，构筑军事课教学全过程育人新"战线"。三是丰富军事理论和国防教育相关"第二课堂"活动，可以参照高校日常思想引领相关"第二课堂"活动，针对各个年级、各个层次的学生设计开展丰富多彩的军事课教学相关"第二课堂"活动，与军事课课堂教学互相联动、互相补充，形成课上课下协调联动，各个年级学生全面参与，筑牢军事课教学全过程育人基石。

3. 提升军事课教学质量，筑牢军事课教学全方位育人防线

一方面要强化学生认识，提高学生对军事理论知识和国防安全的重视程度。目前，普通高校学生全部为"90后""00后"，他们出生在和平年代，成长在物质生活丰富的安逸环境中，缺少国防使命感和责任感，大多数人将军事课视为无关紧要的副课，不愿去花费更多的时间和精力进行军事课学习。所以，要提升军事课教学全方位育人实效，首要措施必然是提升军事课教学的主体——学生对军事课和国防教育的重视程度。各高校应该加大对军事课教学重要意义的宣传，加强对学生的引导，强化学生的认识。

同时，可以通过适当提升课程难度、改变课程考核方式等措施，增加学生实际学习的机会，以引导学生更加认真地进行军事理论学习和军事训练。另一方面，要对军事课教学方式进行创新，着力激发学生学习的热情和兴趣，提升学生学习军事课知识的积极性和主动性。针对军事课教学中的军事技能训练和军事理论课程教学，结合互联网和新媒体技术，创新授课方式，以学生喜闻乐见的形式进行军事课教学。军事训练作为大学生开始了解国防教育的第一途径，既要在大学生可以承受的范围内适当进行实践训练，也要借助各种现场举例讲解，更可以组织大学生参观军营，观看军人演武等来进行实地教学，通过多元化的教学方式提升教学效果。军事理论课程讲解作为大学生深入了解军事理论知识和国防教育知识的途径应当在内容上下苦功，通过丰富的教学内容激发学生的学习兴趣。这就要求授课教师应具备一定的专业性及对课件的筹备能力，比如，教学内容可以结合时事，由当下的某个时事热点入题，由浅入深地引出要讲的主题。另外，授课教师可在课堂上多放一些有关的视频资料或者多开展一些讨论活动，让授课气氛更加活跃。

五、结论

军事课教学是提升高校大学生军事理论知识水平，夯实大学生军事实践技能基础，强化大学生国防教育和爱国主义教育的重要形式，对培养新时代人才具有重要意义。"三全育人"的全新背景对军事课教学提出了更高的要求，要想助推高校"三全育人"工作，军事课教学需要对标"三全育人"要求，针对自身不足，通过强化军事课教学人才队伍建设，补足军事课教学全员育人短板；延长军事课教学时间"战线"，提升军事课教学全过程育人实效；提升军事课教学质量，筑牢军事课教学全方位育人防线等举措进一步提升军事课教学"三全育人"实效，从而助力高校"三全育人"工作，落实立德树人根本任务，培养德智体美劳全面发展的社会主义合格建设者和可靠接班人。

参考文献

[1] 刘志坚."三全育人"视阈下高校校友协同育人的系统探究[J].南京理工大学学报（社会科学版），2021，34（04）：88-92.

[2] 刘杰，吴倩倩，王东红."三全育人"视域下学生党建推动学生管理工作路径探析[J].湖北经济学院学报（人文社会科学版），2021，18（08）：108-111.

[3] 刘静，万明，赵小惠."三全育人"理念下高校课程思政建设路径的探索[J].大学，2021（50）：110-112.

[4] 袁二凯，龙洋.新大纲背景下高职院校开展军事理论课的路径探究[J].北

京财贸职业学院学报, 2021, 37 (02): 60-64.

[5] 谢菲菲, 李雷. 课程思政视角下高校军事理论课教学效果提升路径的思考 [J]. 科教文汇（下旬刊）, 2021 (05): 40-42.

[6] 蒋百平. 高职院校军事理论课教学改革问题与对策研究 [J]. 广西教育, 2020 (47): 49-50, 64.

[7] 邹小雨. 高职军事理论课教学存在的问题及对策 [J]. 现代职业教育, 2020 (43): 100-101.

[8] 邹小雨. 高职院校军事理论课教学实效性实现路径探讨 [J]. 现代职业教育, 2020 (39): 160-161.

[9] 时慧. 大思政视野下高校军事理论课教学探索 [J]. 卫生职业教育, 2020, 38 (05): 41-43.

疫情防控常态化下的高校学生管理研究

——以对外经济贸易大学国际经济贸易学院为例

张晶娟[①]

摘　要：疫情防控常态化下，学生的发展环境悄然变化，学生管理工作压力较大，学生的疫情防控对应急管理和部门协作提出了更高要求。面对挑战，需要以思想政治工作为引领，推进理想信念教育常态化制度化建设；坚持全员全过程全方位育人，推进"三全育人"工作常态化制度化建设；加强学生事务规范化和精细化管理，完善学生干部培养和学生组织管理，推进学生科学管理常态化制度化建设；完善学生管理工作模式，推进信息管理常态化制度化建设。

关键词：疫情防控；常态化；高校；学生；管理

2020年初暴发的新冠肺炎疫情深刻影响着高校的教育教学和日常管理工作。目前，疫情防控已经进入常态化阶段。疫情防控无小事。疫情防控常态化对高校学生的管理工作提出了新的挑战，高校需要采取切实有效的应对举措。

一、疫情防控常态化对高校学生管理工作提出的新挑战

（一）学生的发展环境悄然变化

在疫情常态化下，由于疫情防控的要求，很多线下活动转成线上活动，面对面解决问题的方式经常被腾讯会议和微信沟通所替代，学生学习、生活、实习和就业的发展环境发生了显著的变化。

在学习方面，部分线上课程的教育教学方式对学生个体提出了较高的要求，特别是学生的自觉自律意识。在线上教学过程中，教师很难关注到每个学生的学习状态，

---

① 张晶娟，对外经济贸易大学国际经济贸易学院研究生辅导员。

反馈和互动也受到一定程度的限制。如果学生上课不能集中精力，学习效果必然会受到影响。

在生活方面，学生出入学校的频次和社团活动的规模都受到不同程度的约束，限制了学生人际交往的可能性，朋辈互助的力量存在一定程度的弱化趋势。在高校阶段，朋辈互助是学生重要的社会性支持力量，在朋辈互助中可以发现和化解很多问题。如果朋辈互助的支持力量出现弱化，部分问题就会搁置甚至隐匿。

在实习和就业方面，由于疫情影响，优质的实习和就业机会更加稀缺，学生参与实习和就业也受到疫情管控措施的限制。学生的选择和行动都受到了一定程度的约束和影响，甚至导致某些学生产生了焦虑情绪。

（二）基层学生管理工作压力较大

国际经济贸易学院辅导员负责学生人数较多，本、研辅导员所带学生数量远远超过1∶200的要求比例；在学生类别上，既有统招统分学生，也有委培学生、双培学生，不同类别的学生对应不同的管理要求；在是否住校上，有的同学在校住宿，有的同学校外走读，为疫情常态化期间的管理增加了难度。

在疫情防控常态化下，学校出台了多种管理学生行动轨迹的方法，如青春求真打卡记录、校园系统申请离校返校、一人一案的位置变动等。上述多种方法虽然有利于学校掌握学生的行动轨迹，但由于多种统计方法并行，许多数据暂时无法兼容和批量导入或删除，多重数据的交叉统计使辅导员的压力陡然增加。

少数同学不遵守管理要求，不按照要求办理系统离校返校并申报一人一案的位置变动，对整体学生数据统计的及时性和准确性造成不利影响。疫情防控期间，要求离京后返京返校的同学提供核酸检测证明。个别同学不能够积极主动配合学校完成规定要求，给基层学生工作部门和辅导员的审核管理带来较大的压力。

（三）对应急管理和部门协作提出了更高要求

高校疫情防控常态化下，应急管理成为重要的工作内容。国际经济贸易学院学生数量较多，在校学生处于集体住宿状态，一旦出现和新冠肺炎疫情直接或间接关联的个体，基层学生管理部门和辅导员必须第一时间积极应对，严密排查，避免疫情发展。

高校疫情防控是一项长期和系统的工作，需要校医院的专业认定、保卫处的进出入管理、信息处的大数据支持、学生工作管理部门的计划部署和学院的具体落实等。部门协作的效能将直接影响高校疫情防控工作的效果。同时，在疫情防控常态化下，高校是社会治理链条中重要的环节。高校疫情管理不再是高校本身的工作，还需要和教育部门、卫生防疫部门、社区管理等部门协同作战，才能压实四方责任，确保疫情防控无死角。

二、疫情防控常态化下高校学生管理工作的应对举措

面对疫情防控常态化下高校学生管理工作的挑战，基层学生管理部门要发挥主导作用，整合资源，以思想政治工作为引领，推进理想信念教育常态化制度化建设；坚持全员全过程全方位育人，凝心聚力，推进"三全育人"工作常态化制度化建设；加强学生重大事务规范化管理，重视学生个体事务精细化管理，完善学生干部培养和学生组织管理，推进学生科学管理常态化制度化建设；完善学生管理工作模式，提高学生管理工作信息化水平，推进信息管理常态化制度化建设。

（一）推进思想政治教育常态化制度化建设

2017年2月27日，中共中央、国务院《关于加强和改进新形势下高校思想政治工作的意见》（以下简称《意见》）指出，要提升基层思想政治工作质量和水平。加强学校思想政治工作，加快构建学校思想政治工作体系，实施时代新人培育工程，完善青少年理想信念教育齐抓共管机制，培养德智体美劳全面发展的社会主义建设者和接班人。

基层学生工作管理部门要将思想政治工作融入学生的学习和成长过程中，重视在理论和实践方面的教育与引导，为学生发展提供保障。

（1）国际经济贸易学院（以下简称学院）的学生党团组织机构完善，多年来形成了良好的工作机制，在党员和入党积极分子培训方面形成了良好的传统。学院二级党校和学习社为理论方面的教育引导提供了优质的平台。

（2）在实践方面，学院组织丰富多彩的党日团日活动，如参观北大红楼等教育基地、读书讨论会、党日团日知识竞赛等，将理论和实践相结合，在实践中升华学生的共产主义信仰，坚定学生的共产主义信念。

（3）在保障方面，学院支持德智体美劳全面发展，在传统团学工作基础上，增设大学生兴趣发展中心，拓展学生的兴趣，增进学生的交往，提升学生的综合竞争能力。

学院以思想政治工作为引领，教育人、锤炼人、培养人，提升学生学习发展的内生性动力，提高学生严格要求自己的自觉自律意识，培养学生人际交往的沟通能力和全面发展的综合素质。

（二）推进"三全育人"常态化制度化建设

《意见》提出，"坚持全员全过程全方位育人。把思想价值引领贯穿教育教学全过

程和各环节,形成教书育人、科研育人、实践育人、管理育人、服务育人、文化育人、组织育人长效机制"。

学院是承担人才培养、教学管理、科学研究和社会服务的基层组织。学院只有坚持全员全过程全方位育人,才能够应对新阶段的挑战,凝心聚力,完成教育使命。

全员育人,要求无论是专业教师、辅导员,还是行政管理干部,都要以育人为中心,转变传统观念,调整工作方式,重视优秀校友和优秀家长等校外教育力量,调动一切积极因素为育人工作提供助力;全过程育人,要求学院教职员工尊重教育教学规律和学生成长成才规律,在课程设计、党团社团等实践活动策划、学生重大事务管理工作中秉承可持续发展的科学理念,使学生们在学习中获得真知、在实践中沉淀素养、在管理中感受教育温度;全方位育人,要求学院教职员工能够突破传统的教育场域限制,重视网络教育阵地建设,提供大学生喜闻乐见或参与度较高的教育资源,积极拓展第二、第三课堂,使学生的课堂学习与社团活动、社会实践有机结合。

(三)推进学生科学管理常态化制度化建设

高校的人才培养具有重要的战略意义和社会意义。人才培养,不仅是专业知识和技能的培养,更是德智体美劳综合素质的培养。高校学生管理工作在促进学生德智体美劳全面发展方面发挥着重要的作用。在疫情防控常态化下,人才培养对学生的科学管理工作提出了更高的要求。

1. 学生重大事务规范化管理

教育学生、培养学生要从尊重学生开始。目前,高校大学生主体是"90后""00后",他们有着强烈的自主意识和维权意识,敢于正面表达自己的意见和态度。无论从教育主体的工作理念,还是从教育客体的利益诉求,规范学生重大事务管理工作都是非常必要和重要的。

从范围来说,涉及大多数学生利益或者影响较大的学生事务都属于重大事务;从性质来说,关乎学生根本利益和重要利益的事务都属于重大事务;从紧急程度来说,学生出现突发和紧急状况都属于重大事务。

重大事务的科学化管理,需要贯彻以人为本的理念,需要重视学生的根本利益和合理诉求,需要制定配套的管理规范和制度。学院在学校的章程和总则基础上,根据学院的学科特点和学生具体情况,制定一系列综合测评规定、奖学金评定办法、优秀学生干部评选办法、优秀毕业生评选办法、推优和入党积极分子推选办法,让制度发挥教育导向的积极作用,引导学生全面发展,提升学生学习和发展的内生性动力;制定相应的约束和监察制度,对于违反校纪校规和公序良俗的言论行为予以相应的批评和处分，发挥制度的强制约束作用。

2. 学生个体事务精细化管理

如果说学生重大事务关注到学生群体的整体利益和学生个体的重要利益，那么精细化管理就是尽可能覆盖全体学生的利益和诉求，尽可能保障每名学生都不被忽视。

学院学生人数较多，本、硕、博学生数量约占学校学生总数的1/4。辅导员负责的学生人数已远超过规定的师生比1∶200。在这种现实条件下，除了一对一的深度辅导外，辅导员需要采用更加科学有效的方式方法提升精细化管理水平。

（1）辅导员需要重视分析系统大数据

通过大学生心理测评数据分析，对于有明显和潜在心理问题的学生，进行一对一的深度辅导并追踪了解其发展动态；通过大学生家庭贫困情况调查数据分析，对家庭经济状况困难的学生给予更多关注和了解，做好学生基本情况台账，合理分配学生资助专项资源；通过学生成绩分析，对出现较多不及格科目或成绩下滑严重的学生，逐一了解具体情况；通过打卡记录晚归数据分析，了解晚归学生的具体原因，加强引导教育。通过系统数据的筛查，可以有效帮助辅导员锁定需要精细化管理的重点群体。

（2）辅导员需要重视开展分类指导

通过学生的人口统计属性和特点进行分类指导，根据具体工作要求，将民族、性别、层次、专业、年级、兴趣等变量进行组合，开展小范围的精细化辅导工作。通过调查问卷了解学生的偏好和诉求，再进行精细化辅导。例如，毕业阶段，可以对考研、出国和就业进行分类指导，也可以在考研、出国和就业栏目下进一步细化分类。

3. 完善学生干部培养和学生组织管理

学生的科学管理需要规范化制度化，更需要贯彻落实。学生干部和学生社团是贯彻落实的重要力量和组织保障。学生工作部门和辅导员要按照德才兼备的用人原则，组织学生民主推选有责任心和管理能力的学生干部；需要悉心培养学生干部，设计奖励约束机制，鼓励学生干部发挥才干、多做实事，避免学生干部独断专行，促进学生干部个人和团队协同发展的良性循环。

学生组织是学生干部发挥作用的平台，学生组织的设置和管理直接影响学生干部的作用发挥。学生工作部门和辅导员需要整合功能相同或相近的学生组织，使得各类学生组织分工明确，各司其职，减少内耗和推诿，不断完善学生组织的管理流程。

（四）推进学生信息管理常态化制度化建设

在疫情防控常态化下，学生信息管理不仅是技术手段上的一种辅助，更是深刻地改变着学生管理的工作模式。搜集和分析整理信息，成为学生管理决策的基本前提。

1. 充分利用学校的学生信息管理系统

学校的学生信息管理系统主要集中于学生学籍管理、成绩管理、科研管理和第二、第三课堂的管理。通过学生学习、科研和第二、三课堂社团活动的信息，基层学生工作部门和辅导员可以了解学生的整体态势与个别学生的具体情况。

2. 充分利用信息平台和统计工具

疫情期间，腾讯会议和网络教学平台等已经普及使用，成为学习、工作的重要保障。在疫情常态化下，腾讯会议和网络教学平台等也将持续发挥作用。在高校学生管理事务中，在线即时统计工具、问卷统计工具等可以高效完成信息的共享、输入和输出问题，提高了工作效率。

3. 充分利用主流平台的学生管理信息

学生管理信息的主要渠道就是教育部、北京市教委与学校的官方网站和官方微信推送。同时，学生管理部门和辅导员需要密切关注高校学生聚焦度高的哔哩哔哩、知乎等网络平台，把握基本舆情，了解学生思想动态，对于突发舆情给予及时引导。

疫情防控常态化下，高校学生管理工作需要"因事而化，因时而进，因势而新"，坚持育人为本，德育为先，构建"三全育人"工作格局，创新工作理念和方法，助力大学生德智体美劳全面发展。

参考文献

[1] 中共中央、国务院印发《关于新时代加强和改进思想政治工作的意见》[EB/OL]. 2021-07-12. https://t.ynet.cn/baijia/31096688.html.

[2] 中共中央国务院印发《关于加强和改进新形势下高校思想政治工作的意见》[N]. 人民日报，2017-02-28（1）.

"双一流" 建设背景下优化提升研究生生源质量的思考

王依然[①] 毕晶晶[②]

摘 要:"双一流"建设和新媒体技术的发展为高校的研究生招生工作带来了机遇与挑战,如何抓住机遇,应对挑战,趁势而为,优化提升研究生生源质量成为各大高校必须直面的重要议题。本文针对当前研究生招生(以下简称研招)工作面临的主要问题与挑战,探索优化提升研究生生源质量的路径,提出高校应首先从管理理念上提高对研招宣传与咨询工作的重视,建立健全研招宣传工作机制;以"双一流"建设带动人才培养质量的提升,从根本上增强对优质生源的吸引力;推进研究生招生考核方式的改革,为拔尖创新人才的遴选提供保障;积极利用新媒体技术实现精准高效的研招宣传;在宣传对象上精准定位,锁定聚焦目标生源群体,构建系统性、长效型、全方位的宣传内容体系。在立足传统渠道的同时,不断开拓新的宣传渠道,并定期进行研招宣传效果评估反馈,调整完善研招宣传方案,力争不断优化提升研究生生源结构。

关键词:"双一流"建设;研究生招生;生源质量;研招宣传

建设世界一流大学和一流学科(以下简称"双一流"建设),是党中央、国务院为提升中国高等教育综合实力和国际竞争力作出的重大战略决策,是实施科教兴国、人才强国、创新驱动发展战略的重要组成部分。《统筹推进世界一流大学和一流学科建设总体方案》中明确提出,以培养拔尖创新人才为核心任务,而研究生教育作为国民教育体系的顶端,是培养高层次人才的主要途径。优质的生源无疑为提高人才培养质量提供了良好的前提与基础,这一点已成为各大高校的共识,因而,研究生招生工作中围绕优质生源的竞争愈加激烈,当前形势下高校研招工作机遇与挑战并存,如何保

---

① 王依然,对外经济贸易大学国际经济贸易学院讲师、研究生教务员。
② 毕晶晶,江苏经贸职业技术学院助理研究员。

障和优化提升研究生生源质量已成为高等院校需要认真思考和努力探索的问题。

一、当前高校研究生招生面临的机遇

（一）"双一流"建设助力高校和学科发展，增强对优质生源的吸引力

新的时代背景下，党和国家对于研究生教育高度重视。2020年7月召开的全国研究生教育大会开启了研究生教育发展的新篇章，也必然会推动研究生教育迈上新的台阶。一方面，"双一流"建设在助推高校和学科发展的同时，也必然吸引更多优质生源的关注和报考，为当前研究生招生质量的提升带来了新的发展契机；另一方面，生源质量的提升又会进一步促进高校"双一流"建设，在保障和提升生源培养质量的基础上，相互促进，良性循环，相得益彰。

（二）信息化时代为研究生招生提供多样化的宣传手段和平台

信息化时代伴随着5G等移动通信技术的发展，各种新媒体层出不穷，方兴未艾。社交平台和自媒体高度发达，集各种宣传优势于一体的融媒体宣传理念也为高校研究生招生工作带来了前所未有的便利、快捷与高效。其不仅提供了多样化的宣传手段和平台，也可以用年轻人喜闻乐见的方式增强与目标生源群体的交流与互动，改进研招咨询和宣传的实效。同时，人工智能、云计算、大数据等技术的运用又可以及时分析挖掘和精准定位潜在目标生源，便于进行研招宣传效果的跟踪反馈，以及研招宣传方案的调整改进。因此，善用新媒体技术可以使高校的研招工作如虎添翼，达到事半功倍的效果。

二、当前高校研究生招生面临的挑战

（一）考生选择自主多元化，高校研究生招生竞争日趋激烈

当前我国研究生招生方式中推荐优秀应届本科毕业生免试攻读研究生（以下简称"推免"）被公认为是提升优化研究生生源质量最重要的途径和来源。获得本科推免资格并符合"双一流"建设高校接收推免生条件的学生，通常都是本科期间学业表现优秀的学生，因而，各大高校围绕推免生的招生大战可谓竞争激烈。教育部办公厅2014年发布了《关于进一步完善推荐优秀应届本科毕业生免试攻读研究生工作办法的通知》，强调所有推免生均享有依据招生政策自主选择报考招生单位和专业的权利，推荐高校要充分尊重并维护考生自主选择志愿的权利，不得将报考本校作为遴选推免生的

条件，也不得以任何其他形式限制推免生自主报考。这样既保障了考生自主选择推免院校和志愿的权利，同时也加剧了高校之间的推免优质生源的竞争。近年来，各大高校通过提前举办夏令营、预推免等方式加大宣传力度，提前招生日程，力争广纳优质生源。但由于学生自主多元化的选择，每个学生在预推免阶段，在时间不冲突的情况下，可以选报多所院校，因而，往往会导致优秀的学生获得多个学校的拟录取资格，但最终只能选择其一放弃其他，而高校却因为招生政策和时间节点的限制，无法有效递补而导致推免名额浪费、推免招生指标未能充分利用的尴尬。外校优质生源不足加上本校优秀生源的流失，共同造成了研招工作的痛点与难点。

（二）各高校对研招宣传的重视程度不同，研招宣传工作机制有待完善

由于目前各高校对于研究生招生宣传工作的重视程度有所不同，投入力度也有差距。有的学校相当重视，不断建立健全招生宣传工作机制，设立招生专员，组建研招咨询宣传队伍，经常性地开展或参与各种形式的招生宣传和咨询活动；而有的学校研招宣传工作刚刚起步，从事研招宣传与咨询的人员匮乏，只有研究生教务管理人员，且往往身兼教学培养、学位管理等多重工作，在各类别层次的硕博研究生招生季工作任务繁重，难以抽身开拓招生渠道，也难以取得理想的招生宣传效果。

（三）研究生招生考核方式对于拔尖创新人才的选拔效果仍有待改进

2015年，国务院印发的《统筹推进世界一流大学和一流学科建设总体方案》中对培养拔尖创新人才的建设任务做了如下要求："着力培养具有历史使命感和社会责任心，富有创新精神和实践能力的各类创新型、应用型、复合型优秀人才。"目前国内高校硕士研究生入学统一考试（以下简称"统招"）初试主要包括统考科目和各高校业务课自命题科目。总体而言，在统招初试阶段，大多还是以识记性的专业基础知识的考查为主，且目前初试成绩还是占据主要权重，对于具有创新思维、研究能力和培养潜质的拔尖创新人才的选拔效果还有待改进。

（四）研招宣传大都局限于传统方式，未能充分利用新媒体信息技术增强宣传实效性

新媒体技术的蓬勃发展虽然为高校研招工作带来了利好与机遇，但反观目前，大部分高校的研招宣传模式还局限于传统方式，未能与时俱进地回应社会发展和考生需求。从日常的招生咨询实践中不难发现，考生咨询内容实际上大多是招生单位已公布

的信息，但考生却往往不知从何查询。究其原因，不外乎学校的招生简章、招生专业目录与院系介绍、导师信息等相关资讯分散在各个不同的网站页面，缺乏有效整合或一体化的信息链接及打包推送服务，且大多数学校的研招信息只能登录PC端网页版查看，尚未开发移动客户端、小程序或浏览体验较好的WAP版，致使考生需要花费较多的时间和精力去搜集各方面相关信息进行比较选择和决策。除了少数一直关注、报考意向坚定明确的学生外，不容易获取潜在目标生源的注意力，不利于招生宣传效果的落实。

三、优化提升研究生生源质量的路径

（一）高校管理理念上，需要提高研招宣传与咨询的重视程度

抓住机遇应对挑战，实现研究生生源质量的优化提升，高校必须首先从管理理念上切实加强对研究生招生宣传与招生咨询工作的重视程度，加大工作力度和经费投入，配备专业的研招咨询与宣传工作队伍，并不断完善研招宣传工作机制。毕竟研招工作具有很强的政策性、政治性与纪律性要求，必须进行必要的培训，由既熟悉研招政策又了解学校、学院及专业情况的人员担任。在人员组成上，应注重发挥导师的宣传带动效应，调动知名专家、学者教授等硕博研究生导师参与研招宣传与咨询的积极性；配合研招管理人员、院系研究生教务员、辅导员从各个层面的介绍，以及校友的宣传推介，同时注意吸纳已录取在校生或拟录取新生，聘任他们作为本科生源学校的"校园大使"，发挥朋辈的示范和带动效应，多管齐下以利于打开市场，增强外校学生的关注和了解。当前，高校普遍十分重视本科招生，对于研究生的招生宣传起步相对较晚，然而"酒香也怕巷子深"，在这个信息冗杂的时代，谁能有效抓住受众的注意力，谁就能占据制高点掌握主动权。

（二）以"双一流"建设和人才培养质量的提升，切实吸引优质生源

能否有效提升生源质量，归根结底还取决于人才培养质量作为支撑。以"双一流"建设带动学校师资力量、科研水平、国际交流等综合实力的发展，提升学校和学科专业排名，才是最有力的招生宣传。持续不断地改进优化培养方案和课程设置，切实提高人才培养质量，并以培养质量和就业水平为依据，结合国家社会发展需要，科学合理地测算分配招生计划，并进行动态调整，实现研究生招生、培养与就业的良性互动，才能切实从根本上提升和优化研究生生源结构。

（三）推进研究生招生考核方式的改革，为拔尖创新人才的选拔提供保障

教育部、国务院学位委员会2017年印发的《学位与研究生教育发展"十三五"规

划》中明确指出，要深化研究生考试招生改革，完善多元化招生选拔机制。进一步深化硕士研究生考试招生改革，推进分类考试，优化初试科目和内容，强化复试考核，加强能力考查，注重综合评价，建立健全更加科学有效、公平公正的考核选拔体系。各高校需要以此为指导，抓紧探索和推进适宜于拔尖创新人才选拔的研究生招生考核方式的变革，并制定明确细致的考核评价标准。

（四）积极利用新媒体技术，推进精准高效的研招宣传

研招宣传工作要达到理想的宣传效果，有效吸引和不断拓展优质目标生源，离不开科学合理的顶层设计和研招宣传方案的制订完善，首先需要明确向谁宣传、宣传什么、如何宣传及宣传得怎样几个问题。

1. 宣传对象：锁定目标生源群体，进行精准宣传

研招宣传工作需要精准定位，瞄准锁定目标生源群体，聚焦发力，好钢用在刀刃上，才能达到事半功倍的效果。精准宣传的理念源于企业的精准营销，就是恰当的产品能够在恰当的时间、以恰当的方式送达恰当的客户，从而提升客户体验和满意度，增强用户粘性。研招宣传的内容便是高校为满足学生考研选择需求所提供的产品。

（1）积极开拓校外优质生源市场，不断扩大关注范围

如何精准锁定目标生源群体，发掘潜在生源对象，就需要综合利用大数据、云计算、AI技术等进行用户画像。同时，重视人际传播和自媒体的扩散传播效应，如通过朋友圈、微信群、社交媒体平台等的裂变式传播，快速拓展和锁定潜在生源群体的广泛关注，从而进行研招宣传相关信息的定向长效推送，打造贴心的信息服务切中考生实际需求。例如，国防科技大学、广西大学等高校在2020年的研招录取工作时，创新性地采用中国教育在线开发的"招生喜报"的新型宣传方式，通过考生在查询录取结果或收到录取通知书时，扫码生成个人专属考研喜报，分享转发至朋友圈、微信群等。考生在分享被录取喜悦的同时，也很好地带动了学弟学妹和亲朋好友等对其考取院校的关注了解，从而获取更多潜在生源，提高了学校的品牌影响力。

（2）重视留住本校优质生源，改变本校研招宣传"灯下黑"的局面

"双一流"建设高校拥有优质的本科生源。但近年来，由于考生报考选择日益自主多元化，以及高校研招竞争的白热化等因素，很多高校对于本校本科生的研招宣传的力度和重视程度往往不够，理所应当地认为本校学生已经对本校的研招政策和优势有所了解，致使研招宣传存在"灯下黑"的现象，导致本校优质生源的流失。其实针对广大本科生普遍的考研需求，研招宣传理应想得靠前、做得长远，管理服务贴心细致、全面周到，通过组织多种多样的活动，尽早将本校的研究生招生、培养、奖助、就业

等方面的资讯有效传达给本校学生，实现本科新生入校后的无缝衔接，增强本校学生的归属感和认同感。

2. 宣传内容：构建系统性、长效型、全方位的宣传体系

全媒体时代，虽然媒体格局、传播方式、舆论生态等都发生了较大变化，但"内容为王"始终是内在要求。向目标受众持续提供更权威、专业、多元、深度的传播内容，以及便捷的资讯获取方式，在很大程度上决定和影响着目标受众群体的长效关注和选择。研招宣传要拓宽思路和视野，设身处地地站在广大考生的角度，想考生之所想，全方位地展示学校和学院的建设发展成果，包括师资力量、科研实力、社会服务、国际交流、社会声誉、评估排名，以及教学培养、就业情况、校友风采和奖助政策等激励机制。

不断完善、设计整合学校和学院官网（包含电脑版和移动端）、官方微信公众号等宣传平台的资讯推送，必要时可以开发研招掌上 App 或研招咨询系统及小程序等，使得考生能够"一站式"便利获取相关信息。运用 AI 技术，对常见的共性问题，可采取关键词匹配等算法第一时间给出标准化的统一解答；对一些个性问题，则根据问题性质和责任归属，转接人工咨询解答，可以提供贴心高效的研招咨询，也能减轻大量的重复性咨询工作，使招生工作管理人员能够腾出时间和精力更好地思考和改进研招宣传工作。

3. 宣传途径：立足传统渠道，开拓新的宣传平台

总体而言，各大高校研招宣传方式可以概括为"引进来"和"走出去"两种途径，又分别涵盖线下线上不同方式的宣传推介活动。

（1）引进来

"引进来"，顾名思义就是把外校优质生源或目标生源群体引领请进校园，向其近距离直观展示学校和学院各方面的办学情况及特色优势。近年来，国内主要高校纷纷通过开展夏令营等推免提前选拔活动，预先锁定目标优质生源，通过邀请校内外知名专家、学者、教授和业界导师、杰出校友等进行学术报告和讲座交流，让考生真切了解和感受学校氛围，获得与学术大咖面对面接触交流的机会，通过选拔考核获得拟录取资格的学生在获得本科学校推免资格后，可以免试直接报考心仪院校，这个方式受到很多考生的青睐。此外，高校还通过举办校园开放日、各种学科竞赛、学术创新论坛和研讨会等活动，为外校优秀学子搭建校际交流的机会和平台。虽然自 2020 年以来，由于新冠肺炎疫情的影响，很多线下活动不得不转为线上举办，但由于参与活动成本的减少，以及新兴技术手段的发展成熟，宣传活动效果并未受到太大影响，未来可以搭乘信息化时代新媒体技术的顺风车，探索更加高效便捷的宣介方式和窗口平台。

(2) 走出去

"走出去",是指本校研招宣传咨询工作组积极主动走出校园,联系目标院校生源群体,扩大研招宣传范围,提升高校的知名度和影响力。传统的"走出去"方式主要包括高校参与中国教育在校等权威教育机构组织的官方专场研招咨询与宣讲会,但缺点是往往因为时间地点的局限而无法真正对焦高校自身的目标生源群体,缺乏宣传的针对性和有效性。为弥补此种方式的不足,目前不少高校的研招工作组尝试主动联系目标生源高校或相关院系专业的老师,面向特定目标群体进行重点推介。当前,随着新媒体技术的广泛运用,不少高校采用线上直播方式,邀请专业领域拥有较高学术声望的知名导师、院系领导及专家学者,以访谈、介绍等多样化的形式,通过研招网,以及抖音、快手等社交软件直播平台同步直播,并在线及时与全国各地广大考生积极互动、交流、答疑,取得良好的宣传效果。同时,因其可以在一定时间范围内无限次回放的特点,突破了参与时间和空间的限制,更好地满足了考生的观看需求。

4. 宣传效果:定期进行研招宣传效果评估反馈,以数据指导调整研招宣传方案

研招宣传工作要形成完整的闭环,每年招生季结束后,要注重及时分析总结并反馈研招宣传实效。通过各项数据和调研结果分析,梳理并总结招生宣传实际做法对于招生结果的影响因素和相关性,汲取经验不断调整改进研招的宣传方式、内容,进一步精准聚焦目标生源群体,从而持续优化和提升研究生生源质量。

参考文献

[1] 吴瑞华. 研究生招生精准宣传研究 [J]. 高教论坛, 2020 (9): 82-85.

[2] 教育部办公厅. 教育部办公厅关于进一步完善推荐优秀应届本科毕业生免试攻读研究生工作办法的通知 [EB/OL]. 2014-08-04.

[3] 国务院. 统筹推进世界一流大学和一流学科建设总体方案 [EB/OL]. 2015-10-24.

[4] 中华人民共和国教育部,国务院学位委员会. 学位与研究生教育发展"十三五"规划 [EB/OL]. 2017-01-20.

[5] 靳慧,刘佳,曹兵. 提高研究生招生宣传效力的思考:以北京化工大学为例 [J]. 北京化工大学学报(社会科学版), 2017 (1): 79-82.

[6] 常江,田浩. 新媒体时代"内容为王"的新标准 [J]. 青年记者, 2018 (4): 14-16.

高校应对新冠肺炎疫情的经验与启示

陈怡琴①

摘　要：新冠肺炎疫情暴发以来，高校坚决执行党中央有关工作部署，严格落实教育部等有关部门工作要求，守好"责任田"，护好"一校人"，积极承担了疫情防控的责任与使命。高校不断健全各项机制，在疫情防控工作中始终坚持党的领导，压实防控责任，筑牢校园安全防线。同时，积极开展社会服务、在线教育教学、心理援助等创新工作形式和方法，做出了很多积极有益的尝试，切实维护了师生生命安全和身心健康，取得了良好的防控效果，积累了丰富的疫情防控经验。当前，新冠肺炎疫情防控趋于常态化，高校应增强忧患意识，及时总结疫情防控的有益经验，做好系统性、前瞻性谋划。

关键词：新冠肺炎疫情；高校经验；常态化启示

新冠肺炎疫情暴发以来，党中央高度重视，把疫情防控作为头等大事来抓，始终把人民群众的生命安全和身体健康放在第一位。习近平总书记时刻关注疫情形势，亲自指挥、亲自部署，提出坚定信心、同舟共济、科学防治、精准施策的总要求。高校作为疫情防控中的重要力量，坚决落实中央有关部署，深入学习贯彻习近平总书记重要讲话和指示精神，始终坚定并积极有效地应对疫情。在疫情暴发时压实防控责任，努力确保师生生命安全和身体健康，同时，积极开展社会服务。疫情稳定时，适时有序推进学生返校复课工作，积极探索疫情防控方法和措施。当前，我国疫情防控取得重要阶段性成果，但全球疫情暴发大流行态势依然严峻，全国疫情反弹点状发生潜在隐患并未解除，疫情处于常态化防控阶段。高校必须保持高度警惕，坚持疫情防控常态化思维、落实常态化举措，主动谋划，健全机制，着力建立并完善常态化疫情防控体系。

---

① 陈怡琴，对外经济贸易大学国际经济贸易学院副研究员。

一、高校参与疫情防控的责任与使命

在党中央的坚强领导下,全国上下团结一心共抗疫情,各行各业积极主动参与,共同努力应对新冠肺炎疫情带来的种种挑战。疫情就是命令,防控就是责任,责任重于泰山。高校立足自身,充分发挥相关学科优势,义不容辞地投入疫情防控斗争中。高校具有师生人数众多、来源省份广泛、开学返校跨地区乃至跨国流动加大传播风险等特点。因此,高校疫情防控成效具有重要风向标意义。

(一)加强健康教育,成为完善高校治理体系重要内容

高校应落实教育部2017年印发的《普通高等学校健康教育指导纲要》有关要求,积极开展"师生健康、中国健康"主题健康教育活动,把健康生活方式、疾病预防、心理健康、安全应急与避险都纳入高校健康教育体系。增强防病意识,掌握常见疾病的预防原则和常规措施,提高防控传染病和慢性非传染性疾病的能力。新冠肺炎疫情暴发以来,高校对于抓好健康教育有了更深刻认识,做好防控工作对高校健康教育工作有着直接的推动作用。高校应积极拓展健康教育思路、开辟健康教育新途径、完善健康教育举措,通过讲座、开设通识课程等方式强化公共卫生知识的传播。利用抗击新冠肺炎疫情、推进疫情防控工作提供的有利契机,加大健康科普知识宣传教育力度,着力改变部分学生不良的卫生习惯、促进学生养成健康文明的生活方式,进一步提高学生的健康意识,维护和促进他们的健康安全。

(二)高校发挥人才和资源优势,服务公众彰显社会服务功能

在新冠疫情大暴发时,这场突发的灾难式疫情使人们普遍受到了较大的心理冲击乃至产生心理危机,维护人们的心理健康此时显得尤为重要,这就需要相关心理疏导及咨询工作及时跟进。有关高校应利用自身心理学及医学等学科优势,主动开展各类心理咨询和援助工作,通过开设心理热线、网络咨询、选派专业人员赴一线等方式,有针对性地开展心理咨询和干预,帮助医护人员、民众等克服消极心理,减少疫情带来的心理伤害。拥有附属医院的高校应积极组织动员一大批医学专业学生投入重点地区开展疫情防控和定点诊疗救治服务。这些都是打赢疫情防控阻击战最后胜利不可或缺的重要组成部分。在疫情逐步缓解和结束后,学生心理疏导援助的需求并不会随之中断,后疫情时期的心理恢复和重建是一场"持久战"。

（三）高校用好科研优势推进科研攻关，直接为打赢疫情防控阻击战作贡献

科学研究是高校的一项重要职能，高校有义务也有能力为抗击新冠肺炎疫情提供智力支撑。高校的科学研究职能，决定着高校在疫苗开发、药物筛选、医疗救治、智能机器人研发等方面能够发挥重要作用。战胜疫情离不开科技支撑。高校依托多学科特点及人才优势，加大专项科研攻关和科技创新投入，加快成果转化及在疫情防控中的实际应用。高校可以充分发挥有关智库的作用，针对经济金融、公共卫生、信息技术、管理决策等领域为党和国家提供政策咨询建议。高校还可以深化校企合作、校地合作，加强属地联动，为打赢疫情防控阻击战积极贡献智慧和力量。

（四）高校维护学校稳定，促进社会稳定要求必须加强疫情防控

高校具有自身特殊性，不仅在校生人数较多、学生规模大，而且学生来源地域较广，其中来自国外的留学生也占有较高比例。一旦发生任何不良事件，都有可能产生较大的负面影响。学生公寓、学生食堂、教学楼、图书馆、体育馆、学生活动中心、校园超市等学生日常学习和生活的主要场所多为室内封闭环境，人群聚集密度大、流动性较高，疫情传播风险大。由于高校的特殊性，社会对其关注度普遍较高，高校能否有效防控疫情，维护师生生命安全和身体健康，适时恢复正常教育教学秩序等，对于社会安全和稳定都至关重要。高校一旦出现疫情防控疏漏或发生聚集性疫情，不仅影响学校的安全和稳定，而且极有可能成为影响社会稳定的重要因素。

二、高校疫情防控的主要做法与经验概述

在一年多的疫情防控工作中，高校坚决并贯彻落实党中央的有关决策部署，充分发挥自身优势和社会职能，不断完善疫情防控体系，积极改进疫情防控管理方法和有关措施，取得了很好的成效，探索并积累了丰富、宝贵的抗疫经验。

（一）发挥政治优势，加强党的领导

党组织的坚强、有力领导至关重要。新冠肺炎疫情暴发后，高校党委积极响应党中央、国务院和教育部的重要部署与有关要求，第一时间严密组织、健全机制，成立新冠肺炎疫情防控工作领导小组和院（系）基层防控工作组，将相关防控工作前移，制订防控工作方案和突发应急预案，发挥基层组织的战斗堡垒作用，确保防疫责任层层有效落实。切实把党的政治、思想、组织、作风、纪律等各方面优势转化为疫情防控各项工作中的无私奉献和全身心投入，发挥党员的战斗力，让党旗不仅飘扬在疫情

防控的各个区域，更飘扬在每个党员的心中。疫情初期，武汉防控形势十分严峻，所有在武汉的高校都充分发挥党员干部抗疫先锋作用，分批分组进入社区和街道值守，完成感染人员、密接人员等的排查工作及部分校内临时封闭区域管理等任务，主动扛起许多急、难、险、重工作，始终站在抗疫一线。许多高校纷纷向党员师生发出倡议书，要求大家始终站在一线，在各项抗疫工作中冲锋在前。各高校始终精准摸排师生员工情况并及时有效梳理上报，召开专题会议，研究、落实抗疫工作方案及分工和推进，及时有效解决抗疫过程中遇到的各类实际问题，加强实地督查指导，严格落实相关防控措施、严密校园管理，确保疫情防控工作扎实有效有序推进。此外，各高校依托学校新闻网、官方公众号等渠道，及时发布疫情有关政策、抗疫进展，普及相关防控知识，提高师生防控能力。大力宣传报道基层先进典型，不断凝聚和传递疫情防控正能量。

（二）压实防控责任，严密校园防控

建立健全上下联动、快速沟通机制，日报告、日研判机制及疫情防控属地上报等机制。根据部门特点和疫情防控需要，成立各类疫情防控专项工作组，由学校综合协调部门牵头，教务、组织、人事、后勤、保卫、校医院、学工、宣传、财务、离退休、工会、纪检监察等部门负责人和相关人员组成。武汉理工大学成立由党委书记和校长任指挥长的"疫情防控指挥部"，坚持"四早原则"，完善"早发现"机制，畅通"早报告"渠道，采取"早隔离"措施，落实"早治疗"要求，提前组织部署到位。很多高校通过多部门联防联控，建立信息报送、学生工作、教学科研、隔离观察、安全稳定、教职员工与离退休人员等专项工作组，健全工作机制，协同高效，确保在疫情防控工作中学校安全正常运转。高校党委实行全天候人员线上值班值守，院（系）等二级单位也分别成立工作小组，扎实有力推进防控举措落实。高校纷纷利用大数据和先进技术手段提升疫情相关数据的上报效率和精准度，进一步完善微信打卡，依托校园信息一体化优势，有效运用二维码简化在校师生进出校园的相关审批机制，提高疫情防控的管理效能。加强人员排查和校园防疫，严守校门第一道防线，内防扩散、外防输入，筑牢校园安全防线。此外，高校根据疫情防控进展不断完善疫情防控工作方案，动态调整有关疫情防控措施，严格落实有关部门的各项防控要求。

（三）利用自身优势，主动服务社会

在疫情暴发初期，许多有附属医院的高校发挥医疗专业人才资源和医学科研优势，积极驰援湖北省尤其是武汉市抗击疫情，为疫情防控特别是保护人民生命安全作出了积极的贡献。例如，华中科技大学 10 家附属医院均为定点诊疗救治医院，投入了大量的一线医护人员，保障了众多医疗床位。附属协和医院在湖北省率先成立新型冠状病毒核酸检测实验室，发布治疗策略，首次提及阿比多尔抗病毒策略并被写入《新型冠状病毒肺炎诊疗方案（试行第六版）》规范，90% 住院患者为重症患者。附属同济医院将各院区均改为定点医院，重症患者数、可用床位数、发热门诊接诊量均为武汉市最多；支援火神山医院、雷神山医院建设，建设 2 家方舱医院，首创诊疗快速指南，联合专家团队发布重症诊疗与管理共识。高校主动发挥科技创新主体地位，高质量执行基础研究和原始创新任务，找准科研攻关突破口，靶向发力，主动启动疫情的应急攻关科研项目，主动承接国家重大科技攻关项目，在溯源、检测、传播途径、动物模型和疫苗等前沿问题、关键问题上投入研发力量。许多高校积极参与并加紧针对新型冠状病毒的相关科研攻关及有关疫苗研发。清华大学、北京大学、复旦大学等高校关于单克隆抗体研发取得新进展。厦门大学、四川大学、清华大学等高校从多条技术路线推进疫苗研发。疫情暴发初期，很多高校利用自身优势加强心理援助，通过网络宣传、开通咨询热线、QQ 平台网络咨询、组建防疫抗疫专业心理援助队等方式，对感染人员及家属、医护人员、社区工作者、志愿者、广大人民群众等提供多项心理咨询、疏导、治疗等专业服务，凸显人文关怀。此外，许多外语类高校利用自身的语言优势，为外籍医疗专家等提供专业的多语种翻译和服务工作。

（四）推进在线教学，保障学习需求

教学工作是高校最基本的职能，新冠肺炎疫情给高校教学工作带来很大挑战。高校主动工作前移，预先做好网络在线教学各项筹备工作，摸排网络教学可能性、师生认可度、学生端网络普及度及开展必要的信息采集工作，对教师在线教学能力进行调研，征求教师对于教学平台使用的建议，并对线上教学及学生线上答疑等进行相关示范和培训，使高校线上教学整体平稳有序。高校依托腾讯会议、学校 TAS 平台、中国大学 MOOC 等，开展以录播、慕课课程观看和在线直播课程及在线辅导等多种方式的网上教学活动。高校大规模开展网络教学，将疫情危机转化为教育信息化改革机遇。各高校充分运用多年来在线课程建设与应用成果，创新教学模式，提高学生对在线教学的满意度。例如，清华大学建立分层教学管理体系，通过院（系）院长（主任）工作群、教学主管群、任课教师群、课程研讨群等，逐层落实学校对教育教学工作各项要求，逐一检查任课教师对教学技术掌握情况、教学内容修订情况、授课设备准备情况，保持与每位学生联络通畅，确保课堂"一个都不能少"。许多高校利用在线教学工作群、研讨群、技术保障群等，实时解答教师在网络教学备课和授课过程中的各类实际问题。高校根据自身学科及课程特点，设置"录播＋线上辅导""直播＋线上辅导""录播＋直播答疑"等模式，切实保障了各类课程的实际教学效果。在加强和提升在线教育质量与教学效果的同时，高校还重视并完善线上督导，加强学生评价，确保线上教学内容和质量。我国的教育尤其是高等学校利用互联网技术，迅速实现了线上与线下的对接和转换，教学活动依然正常运转，部分教师和学生实现了从"一无所知"到逐步适应，从仓促"应战"到"平稳"过渡，从"痛苦的磨合"到逐渐喜欢，每一所高校都实实在在地感受到了互联网和科学技术的力量，显示出了我国高校强大的教育应急能力和较高的专业水平。

三、对高校常态化疫情防控的启示

在新冠肺炎疫情防控趋于常态化的形势下，高校应及时总结前一阶段新冠肺炎疫情防控的有效做法和有益经验，继续健全各项机制，压实管理责任，探索常态化疫情防控的各项有效措施，对于疫情防控乃至应对突发公共卫生事件都具有一定的启示。

（一）强化常态防控，必须加强党的领导

在疫情防控过程中，高校各级党组织充分发挥主动性、积极性，有效调动党员干部带头投入疫情防控工作，发挥全体党员应有的模范作用。事实证明，党委总揽全局、全面领导，基层组织作用突出，党员先锋模范作用发挥显著，党的政治建设、组织建设、思想建设、作风建设、纪律建设和制度建设等基础工作好的高校，就能在疫情防控中担负起责任、经受得住考验。高校党委在新冠肺炎疫情常态化防控工作中应进一步担起政治责任，继续统筹协调疫情防控和教育教学各项工作，全校防控工作一盘棋，统一领导、统一指挥、统一行动，加强统筹协调，细化防控任务，压实防控责任。根据防控工作中存在的问题，及时调整或完善思路与对策。高校领导要加强危机应对，并将危机长效管理纳入学校治理体系，提高常态化防控意识，做好常态化防控心理准备和工作准备，提高警惕性和敏锐度。高校要继续加大经费投入，用于新冠肺炎疫情防控物资购置，确保常态化疫情防控工作物资需求。高校要建立和完善分级响应机制，根据疫情级别采取相应的应急措施。根据新冠肺炎疫情期间工作预案，结合当前及今后一段时间疫情防控常态化的新形势和新任务，未雨绸缪，早筹划、早部署。制订学生复学、返校后疫情防控工作方案，制订港、澳、台地区学生及留学生分类防控工作方案及具体措施，外防输入、内防扩散。制订疫情期间违规行为处理工作方案，制定并细化疫情防控期间校园管控制度、网络教学质量保障制度和管理制度等，加大对相关工作的巡查和督查力度。

（二）优化在线教育，注重质量提升

新冠肺炎疫情的暴发直接推动和促进了高校网络在线教学的发展。网络教学具有方便快捷、选择性大、自由度高等许多优势，为疫情期间高校正常教学提供了强有力的支持。常态化新冠肺炎疫情防控的新形势下，对高校改革传统教学方式、推动在线课程建设发展、虚拟仿真技术运用于网络教学来说，都是良好契机，高校要利用好这个契机、转化好这个契机。但网络教学也存在一些短板，如线上交流互动性不足或不深入、教师的平台使用技术待提高、学生硬件参差不齐、线上教学督导困难等，这些都影响着教学质量和教学效果，应引起高度重视。高校要完善软硬件环境和相关设施，调研师生教学需求，加强与相关网络平台的合作，有针对性地提升教师在线教学平台的技术水平和服务能力。同时，要积极引导和帮助学生提高网络自主学习能力，转变原有传统课堂学习观念，使学生快速适应并实现将线上线下教学内容有机结合，将线上线下学习优势完美融合。重新组织教学设计，做到线上授课前导读，线上授课中研学，线上授课后促学，从而真正达到深度学习的目的。严密防范网络教学风险，加强授课内容的审批和监管，对录播课程做到监管前移，对直播课程加强在线听课督导等，防止出现不当、敏感言论，必要时暂停相关课程。

（三）发挥科研优势，着力服务社会

要继续依托高校学科优势，有效助推科研发力和专家智库发声，充分发挥高校社会服务功能。要加大疫情防控科研项目支持力度，引导专家学者深入探讨新冠肺炎疫情给经济金融、国防科技、医疗卫生、社会工作、国际合作等领域带来的新的研究课题，如疫情及防控对国内经济的影响及应对策略、如何利用云技术提升新冠肺炎疫情防控效果、疫情防控对高校党建工作的新启示等，力争取得丰富的研究成果并有效转化，为疫情防控建言献策、贡献力量。

（四）采取有效措施，着力保障就业

高校学生毕业就业是关乎学生切身利益的大事。高校要积极应对可能产生的风险和突发情况，做好舆情工作，有效维护学校稳定。常态化疫情防控形势下，高校学生学位论文将有可能采取网络答辩的形式，要精密设计网络答辩流程，确保程序规范、标准统一，做好指导和帮扶。充分利用新媒体、针对网络便捷的优势，开拓就业渠道，寻求就业服务工作的新途径和新方法；出台相关举措，组织网络招聘会、云面试，完善签约及就业手续办理流程，减少减轻疫情对学生就业的影响。要依托"高校毕业生全国网络联合招聘——24365校园招聘服务",为毕业生提供每天24小时全年365天的网上校园招聘服务,促进毕业生就业。

(五)持续心理援助,助力疫后应对

疫情发生后,恐慌、孤独、苦闷、焦虑、挫败、悲伤等负面情绪不断滋生。疫情防控大环境下,高校学生由于普遍居家时间较长,由此引发的学业就业焦虑情绪带来了较大的心理压力,这类心理问题短时间内可能有所缓解,但需要持续关注并提供心理援助。学生长时间停课居家到返校复学,可能产生由学习、生活的不适应而引发的心理不适应。高校要将心理干预纳入常态化疫情防控工作方案,持续完善心理健康服务,做好疫后心理普查工作,积极有效开展心理疏导,避免复学后心理压力叠加。要加强对学生的关爱,有效避免因心理、负面情绪等问题诱发的极端行为。设计并举办疫情后心理体验交流会、开展艺术治疗等,引导学生通过合理方式和途径宣泄情绪,进行积极的心理调适。

(六)深刻总结思考,加强"抗疫精神"教育

全国上下抗击新冠肺炎疫情过程中,党中央的坚强领导,各地各部门的积极落实,都积累了丰富的工作经验,为今后应对公共卫生领域突发重大事件提供了宝贵的经验和范本。高校要汇集整理抗疫中的优秀工作方法、抗疫工作笔记、个体抗疫日记等,为常态化疫情防控提供可参考及借鉴的范本。民族强盛、国家强大都需要精神支撑。在这场没有硝烟的新冠肺炎疫情防疫阻击战中,涌现出了众多"最美逆行者"——白衣天使、解放军战士、科技工作者、社区工作人员、大学生等,他们舍生忘死、逆行而上,他们忠于使命、无私奉献,全民参与、友爱互助,全国上下众志成城、万众一心,凝结成为伟大的"抗疫精神"。"抗疫精神"是一笔宝贵的精神财富,高校要用这种伟大的"抗疫精神"教育、引导、激励当代大学生不断培育和践行社会主义核心价值观,勇于担当、甘于奉献、乐观向上,与国家同呼吸共命运,承担应有的社会责任,在应对疫情中淬炼成长。

参考文献

[1] 中华人民共和国教育部. 教育部关于印发《普通高等学校健康教育指导纲要》的通知. 教体艺〔2017〕5号,2017-06-14.

[2] 晋竹筠,张冰彭,文彬. 新冠肺炎疫情防控期间高校学生心理状态调研与辅导员心理援助工作初探[J]. 云南农业大学学报(社会科学),2021(15):127-133.

［3］陈翔，胡志斌. 高等学校新型冠状病毒肺炎防控指南［M］. 北京：人民卫生出版社，2020：22.

［4］王慧敏，许敏. 抗击疫情：高校科研协同攻关机制探析［J］. 中国高校科技，2020（5）：5-8.

［5］邬大光，李文. 我国高校大规模线上教学的阶段性特征：基于对学生、教师、教务人员问卷调查的实证研究［J］. 华东师范大学学报（教育科学版），2020（7）：1-30.

［6］刘向兵. 关于高校党委担当有为打好疫情防控阻击战的系统思考［J］. 中国高等教育，2020（5）：8-10.

［7］周翔. 疫情下高校"停课不停学"线上教学可持续发展的探讨［J］. 福建教育学院学报，2020（4）：75-77.

财经类高校院级学生管理体制探索

——以对外经济贸易大学为例

闫雪琴[①]　魏伟斌[②]　金小娜[③]　王　者[④]　陈欣怡[⑤]

摘　要：本文旨在通过对对外经济贸易大学及其他财经类院校的学生管理体制现状的调研，发掘当下财经类院校学生管理体制存在的问题及原因，并进一步提出针对性优化措施，为提高财经类院校学生管理体制运行效率、创建及完善财经高校特色育人体系提供方向。

关键词：财经类院校；学生管理体制；优化措施

一、当代财经类院校学生管理体制现状

根据对中南财经政法大学、中央财经大学、上海财经大学、江西财经大学等财经类院校的调查了解，我们发现当下财经类院校学生管理体制大体上为辅导员—班主任—班委三级式分级管理，但各个院校又存在其自己的独创之处。现以对外经济贸易大学为例，详细介绍财经类院校学生分级式管理体制及各级管理负责内容。

（一）对外经济贸易大学学生管理体制

对外经济贸易大学学生管理体制大体上也为三级式分级管理，不同的是这三级分别为辅导员—年级大班（团）委—行政班班（团）委。辅导员每院每年级设置1位，主要负责总揽该年级学生事务，其职责范围包括但不限于学生的学习、生活、情感、就业等问题，对每位学生的大学生活负责；年级大班委作为链接辅导员、学生干部和

---

① 闫雪琴，对外经济贸易大学国际经济贸易学院本科生辅导员。
② 魏伟斌，对外经济贸易大学国际经济贸易学院经济学专业2018级本科生。
③ 金小娜，对外经济贸易大学国际经济贸易学院财政学专业2018级本科生。
④ 王　者，对外经济贸易大学国际经济贸易学院国际经济与贸易专业2018级本科生。
⑤ 陈欣怡，对外经济贸易大学国际经济贸易学院国际经济与贸易专业2018级本科生。

全体学生三个主体的桥梁，其主要职责是协助辅导员配合学校、学院处理年级事务，并为学生多方位服务提供制度保障；行政班班委主要负责管理各自所在行政班的班级内部班、团事宜，协助辅导员及年级大班委开展年级工作。除三级式管理体制外，国际经济贸易学院同时还有班主任—班主任助理两个职位立于三级之外：班主任每院人数依行政班的数量而定，每个行政班配置 1 名班主任，主要负责指导行政班班委开展班级工作和班级团队建设；班主任助理一般为同学院同专业大二学生，在大一学生入学时成为其行政班班主任助理，协助辅导员和班主任对大一学生进行相应的心理辅导及学业辅导，直接接受辅导员的管理。

（二）其他财经类院校学生管理体制

中南财经政法大学在该校学生进入大二后，学校会为每个学生分配导师进行学业上的辅助；上海财经大学有些院设置了优秀学长学姐一对一辅导同学。江西财经大学相比较其他财经类院校在学生管理体制上设置存在较大不同，该校不设置辅导员及行政班班委，但设置班主任、助理班主任和下班党员。每班一位班主任，班主任作为主要负责人；助理班主任由大三学生担任，每年更换一次；下班党员仅在学生大一时存在，之后不再跟随设置。

二、财经类高校院校学生特点与现行管理体制优势

（一）财经类院校学生特点

1. 学生与业界接触多，"功利心"较强

由于财经类院校具有就业导向性强、应用需求大的专业特色，其学生在理论学习与实践过程中都相对其他专业而言与社会中的企业、机构、部门等有更深地接触。一方面，学习时在课程教授过程中必然需要借鉴企业的实例来讲解，实习时更是深入企业直接感受其运作模式和内部文化，心理上也清楚自己未来会走向业界。因此，学生会更早、更深地以业界标准为衡量自我发展的标尺，更加专向化地朝着企业需求的方向发展自我。另一方面，多年来的"经管热"使得经管行业日趋饱和，导致行业内部人才的竞争态势愈发残酷和激烈。故而，在日常活动和比赛中更具有目的性。

以对外经济贸易大学为例，各个专业都与经管有着千丝万缕的关系。在学习上，实例是最好的论证，老师在课堂上无论是为了清晰地解释晦涩难懂的理论，还是回答同学关于知识的疑问，都会高频率地用到企业或经济体的实例；在日常生活中，学生组织和社团活动的外联赞助、学校或学生组织的大咖讲座及各类考证培训机构都在不

断地向学生灌输业界的"人才需要"和"生存法则";在纳入必修学分的实习过程里,大家都在想方设法找寻适合自己的岗位。此时,找到一份称心如意的实习工作并成为其"青睐"的对象已然是一种刚需。在此种环境下,面对着激烈的竞争环境,学生在参加活动或各类比赛之前都会更多考虑"有用"与否。因此,经管专业学生更具有功利性。

2. 注重综合能力的培养,社团组织多

同样是受到业界影响,财经类院校学生会更加注重综合能力的培养。不同于理工科专业,财经类专业作为应用性极强的社会科学专业,学生不仅要求有足够的专业知识,还必须具备更强的软实力来领导、组织和表达,即综合能力。因此在都有锻炼自我能力需求的情况下,财经类院校一大明显现象便是学生组织和社团多。

(二)现行管理体制的优势

1. 班主任助理制

无论是步入校园之初,还是在大学前行的漫漫长路,优秀的学长学姐往往能给予我们意想不到的引导和帮助。但由于时间和精力有限,大部分学长学姐只能在开学之初带给"萌新"较多帮助,因此,班主任助理(以下简称班助)对学生意义重大。每一所学校都有自己的"生存法则",对于财经类院校新生而言,如何思考与选择适合自己的发展方向和道路、如何锻炼通往目标必备的技能、如何在各具特色的学生组织和社团中抉择、如何与企业打交道等,都是无法避免的必修课,班助所扮演的角色便是引路人。与此同时,由于大学里班主任角色的淡化,班助也承担着指导班级干部开展学生工作的责任。

以对外经济贸易大学为例,开学之初,班助引导班干部开展班会和团务活动;学期中,班助有一对一谈话,无论是学习中、生活中还是心理方面的困惑都可以与之交流,平时班助更是作为班级的一员在班群里随时可以和同学交流。

班主任助理有以下优势:

(1)同辈交流更顺畅无障碍

同样作为学生的他们更能与同学放松地敞开心扉互相交流,对于学生而言,再平易近人的老师也难免有师生之别,但是学长学姐却是自己的同龄人,更能畅所欲言,说出心中的困惑。

(2)相比于老师有更多精力帮助学生

班主任老师还有学术上和教学上的工作,辅导员老师更是需要兼顾整个年级的学生,而班助相比之下有更多的时间和精力来帮助学生,需要时一条微信便能很快得到回复。

(3)时间和空间上更便于处理紧急情况

在发生紧急或特殊情况时，班助往往比老师能先得到消息，并且便于及时采取行动处理相应情况。

2. 年级大班长制

在高校学生管理工作中，辅导员需要独自对接本院一个年级所有学生，工作量过于繁重，哪怕每个班都有班干部协助管理，面对重要的任务时也难免效率不足，尤其是人数多的大院。因此，辅导员需要有协助处理年级工作的助手——年级班长，上可对接学校职能部门，下可引导班级干部完成工作任务。设立年级大班长在学生管理体制中的优势：

（1）进一步完善学生管理架构

从只有辅导员老师—班干部—学生的管理模式变为辅导员老师—大班长—班干部—学生。一方面，减轻了辅导员在直接对接过程中的压力；另一方面，也增强了管理架构的层次性，有助于年级工作更加流畅地开展。

（2）便于帮助辅导员了解同学情况

同为同级学生的年级大班长不仅能迅速了解同学的情况，相比于班干部，与辅导员老师更加联系紧密的他们还能及时地将信息反馈给老师，成为学生与辅导员老师之间高效沟通的桥梁。

三、现行学生管理体制中存在的主要问题

在高校学生管理工作范围进一步扩展延伸、管理体制进一步创新改革的今天，财经类院校在学生管理体制上体现出了其独特的优势。与此同时，延续传统管理体制和发展创新过程中暴露出来的问题依旧很多，对学生管理体制的革新优化刻不容缓。以对外经济贸易大学（以下简称贸大）现行学生管理体制为例，存在的主要问题有如下几个方面。

（一）班主任管理工作"名存实亡"

贸大现行的学生管理体制，能够通过辅导员制、大班长制、班级助理制三项制度的齐头并举，充分调动资源、发挥各方作用。与此同时，班主任的学生管理工作却已经名存实亡。除了其他几项制度在很大程度上分担了班主任工作这一主要原因，班主任制本身的不完善、学生管理工作制度的顶层设计不合理也是重要因素。为各行政班配置专属班主任的初衷无可置疑，但缺乏配套完善的班主任考核制度、班主任教学任务和科研任务繁重、辅导员和班主任之间长期缺乏有效沟通、顶层设计没有强调班主任作用等，却都会推动班主任这一"优质资源"变成"闲置资源"。如何充分发挥班

主任乃至各种校园"闲置资源"在学生管理工作中的作用，减少人才资源浪费，形成高效有序的学生工作体制，是贸大也是各大高校需要面对并解决的难题。

（二）基层学生干部被动完成工作

贸大的基层学生干部群体，包括按行政班配置的团支书、班长。基层学生干部队伍在学生管理工作中的作用是不可小视的。一个合格的基层学生干部能够将自己负责的集体管理得井井有条，能够将本级工作及时且高质量地与上级对接。而一个优秀的基层学生干部则应当在完成份内工作的基础上，积极主动承担能使集体管理工作得到改善的其他各项工作。学生干部大多数能在刚上任时做到尽心尽力，但是却有相当一部分学生干部工作积极性和主动性随着在任时间的增长大打折扣，只会等着完成辅导员或大班长布置的份内工作，完成工作被动化。一方面，与基层学生干部群体思想素质不过硬、工作态度不够端正有关；另一方面，也有（财经类院校学生）过于功利化的因素。这里的过于功利化包括过分追求在学生工作上的功绩、过分追求个人利益从而忽视学生管理工作两方面含义。此外，对于基层学生干部的考核评比制度不够完善，长效激励机制的缺乏也是重要原因。

（三）学生自我管理能力有待提升

注重锻炼学生的自我管理能力，是贸大现行学生管理体制的一大特点。贸大实行的大班长制和班级助理制都是学生自我管理的典型。大班长需要协助辅导员完成全年级学生工作的策划，独当一面完成一整个流程的学生工作；高年级优秀学生作为班级助理，需要了解并解决班级学生心理、学业、就业等问题，一定程度上也分担了辅导员的工作。这两项制度都对学生自我管理能力提出了更高的要求，对切实落实自我管理体制形成了更大的挑战。就自我管理体系中的学生干部而言，因为缺乏管理经验和社会经验，其在自我管理方面的专业化能力亟待提升。例如，应对突发事件的处理能力、与学生会谈的能力、团队合作的能力和组织策划的能力。此外，贸大仍不够重视引导学生干部将自我管理工作中的经验性总结转化为系统性成果，这一点，在强调和重视学生综合素质的今天是极大缺憾。

四、优化措施

（一）行使班主任职能方面

1. 建立科学全面考核机制

将班主任职责履行情况纳入教师的综合考评要求中，有利于提高教师对于班主任角色的重视程度。在提高教学水平与科研水平的同时，用自己的专业知识和教学经验为学生答疑解惑，辅助辅导员在学生的学业发展方面提出建设性和个性化指导意见。

同时，考核标准应当从学校自身特点出发制定，综合考虑教师队伍负担，避免使班主任任务的完成影响正常的教学科研进程，给教师造成心理负担，从而不利于班主任队伍基础的进一步扩大。

2. 构建师生间直接高效沟通渠道

一些班级的班主任与学生联系得不够紧密，学生即使有了学业和生活上的问题也不能或者不敢于找班主任老师咨询。在这种情况下，学校可以通过构建官方通道，如公众号或网站等方式，将班主任与学生串联起来，以制度化或惯例化的形式定期督促师生进行直接而高效的一对一沟通。此举一方面增加了班主任老师对于班级事务的了解与参与，一方面也将成熟的求助答疑渠道呈现给学生，真正发挥班主任老师的指导作用。

3. 提高辅导员——班主任对接频率

辅导员的工作具有广泛性和复杂性。对于学生的多方面情况有较为深入的掌握，但在专业发展方面与学业指导方面有时存在着短板；而班主任老师作为专业教师团队中的一员，在学术引领与学业辅导方面有着独特的见解，却有时因为对学生个体的不熟悉不了解而错过沟通机会。基于这样的互补性，辅导员老师与班主任老师应建立长效持续制度化对接机制，提高对接频率，增强学生管理信息的及时传达与互换，通过多方面观察，为学生建立起立体的个人档案，从而在学生管理与个人发展指导等方面达到新高度。

（二）发挥学生干部作用方面

1. 建立以工作表现为核心，工作态度为综合考察指标的大数据导向考察机制

在学生管理体制中，对管理效果产生着最大影响的就是学生干部的工作能力与态度。在进行干部团队管理的过程中，一种科学全面的长效考察机制是必需的。以工作事项为划分依据，记录学生干部在一学期或一学年中的工作表现，如资料提交是否准时、资料内容是否正规、信息传达有无晚传达或错误传达现象等。在考核期限到期时，将工作表现数据化，作为评价干部工作表现的核心数据。

在重点考察学生干部工作表现的同时，还应当将学生的评价和反馈纳入评判体系。通过分发不记名问卷等方式，收集有关学生干部平日工作态度的信息，要求他们为干部打分。在班内学生真实数据的支持下，对干部的工作态度作出准确的评判，并与工作表现一同综合考虑，最终作出有理有据和科学全面的干部评价。

2. 多方式和多途径增强学生干部团队自身责任感与信念感

通过开办讲座和座谈会，邀请优秀学生管理工作者进行经验分享等多种方式与途径，增强干部为同学服务的谦卑感与信念感，在提高自身工作水平的同时，杜绝打官腔、搞小动作等不良风气的产生。通过典型榜样与自身工作过程中的反思总结，从内心深处树立起对于学生管理工作的正确认识，才能在日常工作中表现卓越，为学校整体的学生管理工作体系添砖加瓦。

3. 利用科学有效团建活动提升干部团队内部默契度

在学生干部团队内部，利用团建活动等方式，在工作之中与之外培养默契和队友的感情，才能在复杂的工作执行过程及特殊情况中，保证干部团队内部的凝聚力和工作热情度，从而助力工作开展的统一协调和团队合作的顺畅有效。

（三）提升广大学生群体配合度与幸福感方面

1. 学生管理工作过程透明化规范化

在进行学生管理工作的过程中，将信息传达通路与工作开展思路进行及时、准确、全面的发布，不仅可以避免学生对干部队伍产生质疑与不配合，更有利于自身工作的梳理。透明化的工作，不等于完全的信息发布，但及时有效的信息传递是必要的。

在规范化方面，应综合利用传统及现代信息保存制度，做到事事有处可查。为传统工作设计规范化上报表格及反应机制，并定期向同学汇报日常工作进展及创新之处。

2. 搭建高效优质的建议反馈系统

建议建立个性化建议反馈系统，使有关于学生管理工作的意见和建议得到重视与及时反馈。此举不仅有利于学生管理制度自身的推陈出新，更有利于学生与学院管理老师进行有效沟通，及时了解学生的声音，避免因工作开展情况不佳而导致的学生与学院间矛盾。

3. 提升针对性素质教育水平

从财经类院校学生功利性强的特点出发，设计具有针对性的素质教育活动，如加大对典型人物的宣传力度，在大型活动的举办上调动其积极性，以成就感带动参与感，以仪式感造就参与集体活动的幸福感。此举使学生自我发展道路上的功利化不会成为集体生活中的绊脚石或学生管理工作中的拦路虎，同时也有益于学生的长远发展与人生境界的提升。

4. 开辟集体精神文明建设的新途径

以宿舍文明建设等为正面例子，开辟集体精神文明建设的新途径。以宿舍风气、班级风气的建设，带动面向全体学生的正能量建设。

（四）学生管理系统整体协作方面

1. 建立分工明确，问责直接的学生管理系统

在校内事务传达办理的过程中，分工的模糊会导致负责人相互推诿，学生怨声载道。明确工作职责的边界，各司其职，专业化的分工有利于减少类似现象的发生。同样，明确的分工体系，也意味着各方责任明确，可以通过直接问责来定位问题所在并监督改正，这有助于学生管理机制的自我进步。

2. 提高管理系统内部沟通频率

在分工明确的基础上，不能将一件事务的管理过度拆分，各相关系统及部门需要定期进行有效沟通，及时进行信息同步及互相监督，共同分享创新成果，以提高工作效率为最终目标。

五、结语

从以上分析和调查中可知，当下财经类院校学生管理体制受财经类院校功利性较强这一本质影响，存在着某些环节名存实亡、被架空、没有什么实际作用效果，以及基层学生干部工作较为被动等现象，从而导致整个管理体制效率较低，学生受益程度倾向于分化，并造成部分学生自我管理意识差的结果。

针对此类问题，我们认为一是多极化管理各级之间缺乏相互监督与沟通交流，机械式地开展工作，在学生管理上缺乏生机与活力；二是管理体制整体缺乏相应激励机制，在功利性较强的财经类院校中缺少这一点无疑是各级学生干部尸位素餐的原因；三是考核机制的缺失也在一定程度上导致了学生干部管理体制效率低下。

对此，根据对外经济贸易大学国际经济贸易学院的实际情况来看，我们建议从分级式管理体制整体出发，加强整体各级之间的协调性与沟通交流，完善层层监督考核机制；再到每一级明确各级分工，加强学生干部能力培养、学生干部团队精神培养等，每级学生干部、老师加强关注学生身心健康，及时层层上报。与此同时，向学生实行公开、透明化的管理，采用公示考核结果、嘉奖情况等方法定期进行公示干部评分，及时听取广大学生群众意见，从而适时调整管理方案，最终在长期探索出最适应财经类院校的学生管理体制。

参考文献

[1] 杨韶春，张辉，施继生. 高校校院两级管理体制下的学生工作研究 [J]. 大理大学学报，2019，4（03）：116-120.

[2] 杨晓君. 高校学生干部团队管理中项目制的新尝试: 以黎明职业大学工商管理系团队建设为例[J]. 长春教育学院学报, 2011, 27 (03): 86-90.

[3] 尚龙女. 关于提高学生骨干管理能力的思考[J]. 湖北农机化, 2019 (24): 37.

[4] 许瑜. 基于立德树人背景下的高校学生管理研究[J]. 读与写（教育教学刊）, 2019, 16 (09): 46-47.

[5] 白丽君, 刘伟, 唐亮. 基于立德树人理念的高校学生管理工作分析[J]. 智库时代, 2019 (15): 92+94.

[6] 石旭. 基于学生主体的高校学生管理工作的优化措施[J]. 才智, 2018 (34): 250.

[7] 王楠. 我国高校学生管理模式的若干思考[J]. 课程教育研究, 2018 (12): 177-178.

[8] 王碧昱, 于广杰. 学生自主管理团队建设中的学生干部培养[J]. 今日科苑, 2010 (16): 200.

红色经典阅读——高校思政教育的助力者

毕 帆[①] 王可欣[②] 黄依萌[③]

摘 要：红色经典著作反映着中华民族发展的重要时代，诠释着永不磨灭的时代精神，在阐述特殊时代印记和政治因素上具有不可忽视的作用。因此，高校红色经典阅读是培养学生、发展党建的需要。这既是新时代青年对经典的诉求，也是党支部教育的刚需和高校思政课堂教育的重要补充。红色经典阅读作为高校进行思政教育的一种重要方式，在推进的过程中存在较为明显的难点，包括：阅读方式刻板，多元化不足；缺乏理论基础，深入性有限；知行相互分离，生动性欠缺。党支部作为红色经典阅读活动的推动者，应该创新阅读方式并积极开展主题活动，采取"线上＋线下"等新型开展方式，充分发挥党员的带头作用，让实践活动深入结合思政课堂，对提高学生道德素质修养、助力学生塑造正确三观、丰富思政教育内容、推动高校"三全育人"建设等具有深远意义。

关键词：红色经典阅读；高校党支部；思政教育

一、高校红色经典阅读是培养学生、发展党建的需要

近年来，有关传统文化、红色经典、革命历史旧址等方面的学习教育升温，红色经典阅读越来越受到人们的重视。各高校、高校党支部也以此类主题开展多项活动，丰富青年学生视野，溯源历史，领会中国共产党发展历程的艰辛，放眼未来，树立远大志向。各高校开展红色经典共读，主要是对红色经典文学作品阅读进行论述分析，学习领悟其中内涵。

---

① 毕帆，对外经济贸易大学国际经济贸易学院本科生辅导员。
② 王可欣，对外经济贸易大学国际经济贸易学院西方经济学2021级硕士研究生。
③ 黄依萌，上海交通大学文创学院2021级硕士研究生。

（一）形势判断：新时代青年对经典的诉求

在红色经典阅读活动开展过程中，要注意进行形势判断。新时代高校青年生长于21世纪，他们的视野、观念，感知世界的方法与结论与20世纪出生的青年有很大差别，要观察到新时代青年对红色经典的诉求在近年来大幅提升。某些活动参与者，包括组织者都会有一些困惑，甚至带着"刻板印象"觉得红色经典著作拥有其特定的时代含义，与当前的生活产生较大距离，参与者在进行阅读的时候底气不够充足，将愉悦心灵、充实学习教育的活动认为是"例行公事"。这是不正确的观念。近年来较为突出的一点就是越来越多的年轻人开始读起了《毛泽东选集》，并成为悄然兴起的一种"新风潮"。

电商平台上，《毛泽东选集》（以下简称《毛选》）销量不断增加，一跃成为平台热销产品之一。当代年轻人尽管带有"追新"的标签，但仍然对《毛选》等书兴致勃勃，1977年版的《毛选》第5卷甚至出现了供不应求的局面。除电商平台外，在以"年轻人潮流文化娱乐社区"著称的网络视频平台上也不乏朗读《毛选》的视频，且视频的点击量相当可观。

近年来，特别是新冠肺炎疫情暴发以来，面对纷繁的社会变化，面对百年未有之大变局，青年人容易陷入迷茫，这种迷茫进而带来无力感。而《毛选》《青春之歌》等红色经典著作，逐渐被青年一代发现并视为宝藏，成为青年人重新审视世界的标尺和思想武器。

（二）两面共振：作为高校思政课堂教育的补充

高校对学生进行思想政治教育的方式从总体上可以分为"显性思想政治教育"和"隐性思想政治教育"两种。高校思政课堂属于非常具有代表性的"显性思想政治教育"途径之一；"隐性思想政治教育"顾名思义，是指在对高校学生进行思政教育时并非采用课堂、报告、讲座等方式，而是将教育逐步融入日常生活中，让大学生在耳濡目染，潜移默化中达到了思政教育的目的。红色经典阅读就是"隐性思想政治教育"的典型途径。

高校思政教育任重道远。传统的"显性教育"很可能因为执行的不规范、老旧化，从而起不到效果甚至适得其反，运用经典阅读方式的"隐性教育"，作为思政课堂的补充，能坚定高校学生思想意志，引领学生践行社会主义核心价值观，为中国梦的实现而不断奋斗。

开展阅读红色经典活动要加强红色经典文献的深度挖掘与利用，充分考虑经典阅读方式的亲和性、考核的科学性、引导的针对性、组织的协同性等，并加以创新，结合大学思想政治教育需求和当代大学生的心理特点选择红色经典书籍，使阅读经典真正成为马克思主义理论学习的绿色通道。

（三）支部建设：反复阅读红色经典是支部教育刚需

通过对高校学生党员调查显示，当前大学生党员阅读红色经典所面临的最大障碍是阅读时间匮乏。在当今时代，大学生面临着课业学习压力大、课余学生活动多的局面，尽管学生在阅读方面的兴趣浓厚，但也会受到其他课业活动压力的制约，从而搁置阅读。因此，将阅读红色经典作为大学生党支部的日常化活动，不仅保证了党员的阅读时间，也能够调动党员阅读红色经典的积极性。

高校党支部的红色经典阅读特别要强调成果固化，以期获得更好效果，青年党员在学习中才会有收获。由于高校学生党支部具有人员流动性大的特性，开展学习活动时也应该把握自身特性，特别是高校学生党支部开展红色经典阅读时应该要对经典理论、书籍进行反复多次的学习，每个支部青年党员从加入组织到离开组织都应该经历从"学习"到"助学"的过程，这个过程是助人的过程，也是深化经典学习研究的有效途径。

二、高校红色经典阅读发展之路任重道远

习近平总书记曾强调要"把红色基因传承好"。红色经典作为中国深厚的文化软实力，作为中华民族重要的宝贵思想和文化财富，蕴含着丰富的民族记忆和民族文化。红色经典书籍作为红色内涵的载体，完美展示了爱国主义、集体主义和民族精神的有机结合，彰显着前辈的优秀品质和英雄气概会深刻鼓舞着后辈。

（一）推进高校经典阅读的难点

1. 阅读方式刻板，多元化不足

当下，网络阅读的潮流席卷了整个社会，人们日常生活中纸质书阅读的时间不断被网络阅读占据，国民纸质书的阅读率连年走低。现在高校学生逐渐成为移动互联网"原住民"。在日常生活中，高校学生的学习与阅读主要针对提升自身的专业课素养，对于文史哲方向的经典著作涉猎甚少，奔走在教室和图书馆之间成为高校学生的主要行动轨迹。他们由此留下的时间是碎片化的，在碎片化的阅读时间里理解内容较为艰涩难懂和思想具有特殊时代背景的红色经典，是一件较为勉强的事情。同时，高校在开展"红色经典阅读"的相关活动时在创新活动形式上非常有限，单一的阅读方式在

面对新媒体时代的信息爆炸时显得格外单薄且枯燥，多元化不足，难以与渗透方式多样的娱乐文化相抗衡。

2. 缺乏理论基础，深入性有限

在当今快节奏时代，大学生阅读量严重不足的问题愈发突出。精细研读逐渐转变成泛泛浅读，阅读时间越来越被压缩，很多书籍只是匆匆掠过，并不做深入探究。尽管随着互联网的迅速发展，学生接触到的书籍琳琅满目，但其中却鱼龙混杂。尤其是在红色经典著作方面，很多学生缺乏该方面的理论基础，得到的教育仅限于有限的思政课堂，学习内容有限，深入性有限。同时，高校党支部的红色经典学习教育没有与高校思政教育主阵地——思政课堂形成有效的相互补充、促进的作用，而且支部的部分活动内容和形式与思政课的重叠部分较大，学生学习的内容无法沿着思政课的脉络继续推进深入，教育成果难以得到强化。此外，在学习过程中，青年党员的先进带头作用并没有充分发挥，难以调动青年学生积极性，学生学习效率较低。

3. 知行相互分离，生动性欠缺

通过对高校学生进行调研，数据表明，认为红色经典具有传承的必要性的学生占97%，认为红色经典有助于大学生建立核心价值观的学生占82%。然而，阅读过10部红色经典书籍的学生仅有12%。由此可见，高校大部分学生在认知上对于红色经典的阅读价值保持认同态度，说明红色经典在大学生的思想中有很强的重要性。但是对红色经典的阅读主动性不强，阅读现状堪忧。尽管学生在思想上对红色经典著作表示肯定，但行动落后于思想，没有积极去学习阅读红色经典著作，没有将"认识"与实际生活相联系，付诸行动。在红色经典学习方面存在的"知行分离"的现象，以及高校学生生动性欠缺的问题，将对红色文化的传播与发展产生不良影响。因此，在推进"红色经典"教育时，应把握高校青年特点，力求政治性、学理性和生动性的统一。

（二）开展高校经典阅读的途径

1. 创新阅读方式，积极开展主题活动

如何充分利用高校学生的碎片化阅读时间，将红色经典阅读渗入生活的方方面面，是值得高校党支部思考并付出努力的地方。制作浅显易懂的小视频和校园广播，对红色经典的精华进行萃取和展开，通过生动的讲述和视频资料的辅助，充分发挥现有新媒体手段的独特优势，让高校学生在闲暇之时有兴趣、有意愿地了解红色经典，认识到红色经典的文学性；积极开展"红色经典"主题活动与读书会，选出表现优异的讲述人，配合纪录片与优秀的影视资料，让红色经典与高校学生的生活经历结合，贴近校园、贴近学生、贴近生活；充分发挥红色经典扎根群众的优势，抓住学生最关心的

问题，与学生心贴心、面对面地交流，唤起学生心中的民族情感与爱国情怀，激发学生的讨论热情；以红色经典为核心内容，突出思想导向功能，推动阅读红色经典的双向互动，鼓励学生在"输入"后积极"输出"自身体悟，从红色经典的内容本身扩展到本人或祖辈生活中的所悟所感，使学生爱上红色经典，领悟红色经典背后蕴含的深刻思想价值与广博的生活经验。

2. **打通线上线下，发挥党员带头作用**

随着信息技术的日新月异，传播平台与媒介多样化发展，人们不再局限于传统的纸质阅读方式，新兴的网络阅读方式凭借快速、便捷的特点备受人们青睐。因此，党支部在开展"红色经典"阅读活动时，应充分考虑大学生的阅读习惯，有效地利用新媒体方式，同时积极开展"线上+线下"的共同活动，发挥两种手段的不同优势，提升高校学生与党员的参与感。

鼓励党员发挥带头作用，消除一线教师在展开阅读时出现的不自信情况。坚定红色经典永不过时的信念，铺开共和国和华夏民族近代史中的百年风云画卷，积极地引领着高校学生正确且深入地解读红色经典，充分钻研其中蕴含的深刻思想，让高校学生能够真正深切地从现实和情感的双重方向理解革命的不易和先辈的无畏。同时，从中学习革命精神，激励学生在生活中发扬革命精神，传承民族精神，弘扬爱国主义情怀，完善学生的人格特征，提高红色经典文本阅读教学的成效。让红色经典能够坚持"常态化"的推广，于潜移默化中熏陶大学生心灵，让"红色基因"能够真正地扎根于大学生内心。

3. **推进实践活动，深入结合思政课堂**

高校党支部应深入了解学生党员和积极分子群体的思考维度和学习习惯，探究现下高校学生的生活现状和行为模式变化，有针对性地推进实践活动。通过大范围系统问卷调查的方式，了解当下高校大学生的所思所想，目前高校学生党员的阅读现状，分析高校学生对当下红色经典著作的认识和评价；与高校学生党员骨干、学生积极分子进行访谈，深入了解高校学生经典阅读的现状及推进"红色经典"中可能遇到的问题。对外经济贸易大学国际经济贸易学院本科生党支部即通过文献研究、调查研究和实验研究等手段，结合心理学、组织行为学、教育学等学科的相关理论，设计以"共读红色经典"为载体的高校学生党支部工作的创新模式。在早期调研的基础上，设计有针对性的"共读红色经典"模式；结合新时代下学生党员的阅读习惯和学习特点，改进原有的交流方式和工作语言，创新高校学生党员教育方式；关注当代高校学生的个性特点和活动偏好，从学生需求和未来发展出发，改进原有的内容设计和运行模式，开展以"共读红色经典"为载体的高校学生党员教育新形式。通过重温红色经典的活动实践，高校学生对中国革命成果取得的艰难性有了更深刻的认识，同时也对党的路线、方针和政策有了更深入的了解。

让红色经典阅读融入思政课堂，将红色经典中具有时代意义的理念与思想提取出来，与马克思列宁主义、毛泽东思想、邓小平理论、"三个代表"重要思想、科学发展观和习近平新时代中国特色社会主义思想有机结合，在前人不断探索和积累，乃至饱含血泪思考的基础上，充分利用红色经典中丰富的政治知识和政治智慧资源，在完成知识性目的的同时提升智慧增量，提高洞察力与感悟力，自我反省；与中华民族危急关头的伟大思想家和文学家进行对话，倾听他们对重大政治问题和社会问题的观点，站在他们的高度上继续前行，了解政治思想中的超越性与可控性、可行性的分歧，使高校学生学习观察政治问题的基本理论立场与方法，认清思考、观察政治问题的方法论与知识论预设，建立对政治世界的本质、起源与一般规律的基本看法；促进学生关于政治理想、政治规范的思考，为政治评价和认识政治现实打好理论基础。

促进"神入"的移情式理解，使高校学生将自己摆在红色经典中主人公"同样"的位置上，模拟并"神入"主人公所在的场景、情境、环境等"语境"，探究其思想世界，体会作者的语言表达、修辞策略中的言下之意与弦外之音。

完成外部审视与"概念化"处理，即立足马克思列宁主义、毛泽东思想、邓小平理论、"三个代表"重要思想、科学发展观和习近平新时代中国特色社会主义思想，站在今天的政治平台上，去把握红色经典中理论或思潮在中国共产党百年历史和共和国发展史中的影响，评估其所提出或者解决的问题在现代中国社会中的地位，并分析其对现代生活的意义。

积极运用比较的视野与方法，探讨红色经典中存在哪些认知上的局限与偏差，其中的人物或者说作者在思考、认识社会问题与政治问题时走过哪些弯路，留下了哪些教训。坚持科学严谨的态度，既要反对与防止对红色经典的任意曲解和牵强解释，也要遵守学风规范，进行批判式继承与发扬。

三、开展高校红色经典阅读意义非凡

（一）提高道德素质修养，助力学生塑造正确三观

红色经典阅读具有非常强的道德教育功能。道德教育贯穿于学生受教育阶段的始终，其作用的重要性不言而喻。红色经典主要描述革命、战争等特殊年代，其中蕴藏着更为高尚的道德情操和更加严格的道德规范。因此，在通过阅读红色经典对高校学生进行思想政治教育时，也间接地对其进行着道德教育，而且指导作用更为显著。

红色经典教育不仅对大学生的思想道德修养有重要的影响,而且对高校学生三观的形成作用也非常明显。红色经典中鲜活的人物不仅可以激起学生的阅读兴趣,更会让学生得到心灵的洗礼、精神的升华,潜移默化中使学生能够以经典著作中的人物为榜样,学习英雄身上的爱国主义精神和崇高道德品质,提升思想素养,拔高精神境界,有利于高校学生树立正确三观。例如,《青春之歌》作为红色经典著作的代表之一,其中蕴藏的先进文化会助力高校学生建立起爱党爱国的信念意志,其思想教育作用是很强大的。

(二) 丰富思政教育内容,推动高校"三全育人"建设

红色经典阅读是高校进行思政教育的一种重要方式。教科书作为一种通论性的著作,包容的学术观点和理论应当尽量全面,但在信息爆炸的时代,一本书企图容纳所有的观点是既不可靠也不必要的,而编者的选择性原则会让我们失去一部分对历史过程的认知。红色经典阅读作为对思政课程的补充和对历史教育的深化,代表着中华民族发展的重要时代,诠释着永不磨灭的时代精神,在阐述特殊时代印记和政治因素上具有不可忽视的作用。基层党支部通过开展高校学生党员"共读红色经典"的实践活动,不仅给基层党支部注入新的活力,而且从很大程度上丰富了高校思政教育的内容,推动着高校"三全育人"建设。高校作为教育的载体,作为意识形态的前沿阵地,其思想政治教育一直是我国高等教育常抓不懈的一项重要任务。将红色经典逐渐渗透到高校思想教育之中,于潜移默化间不断加深学生对于红色历史的认识,有利于高校学生了解自身文化的文化谱系,理解政治社会化的过程,形成正确的政治立场和爱国主义情怀,并与社会主义核心价值观相贯通,最终形成坚定正确的政治观;有助于高校全员形成系统合力对高校学生进行全方位教育,全面提升人才的培养质量,贯彻推进"三全育人"工作。

参考文献

[1] 吴凌. 红色经典阅读及对其的思考 [J]. 语文建设, 2016 (07): 39 - 41.

[2] 马乙玉. 大学生党员红色经典阅读现状调查分析 [J]. 学校党建与思想教育, 2016 (18): 27 - 28.

[3] 任鹏, 田鹏颖. 马克思主义经典品读在思想政治理论课教学中的改进与加强: 以"毛泽东思想和中国特色社会主义理论体系概论课"为例 [J]. 思想教育研究, 2017 (07): 79 - 83.

[4] 王荣. 当代大学生传统经典著作阅读现状探析 [J]. 思想教育研究, 2015

（02）：95-98.

［5］杨婷婷.高校图书馆红色经典阅读推广实践与启示：以新疆师范大学图书馆为例［J］.文化产业，2020（18）：125-126.

［6］习近平.用好红色资源，传承好红色基因，把红色江山世世代代传下去［J］.新长征（党建版），2021（06）：4-11.

［7］钱雅玲.高校图书馆红色经典阅读推广研究：以龙岩学院为例［J］.龙岩学院学报，2019，37（01）：118-122.

［8］邱建玲.大学阅读推广的实践路径：注意力视角［J］.大学图书馆学报，2016，34（01）：83-87.

［9］杨晓慧.高等教育"三全育人"：理论意蕴、现实难题与实践路径［J］.中国高等教育，2018（18）：4-8.

新媒体视域下高校共青团思想引导工作的困境和改进路径

杜姝君[①]

摘　要：随着互联网时代的兴起，新媒体运行在契合互联网时代的轨道上与传统媒体比较而言，更具先进性。各大高校是共青团思想传播与引领的主要阵地，新媒体视域下共青团开展思想引导工作的优劣势必会对大学生的思想和行为产生各种影响。然而，当各大高校共青团在新媒体视域下开展思想引导工作时，也面临一些问题，遇上险阻，陷入困境，这警醒着我们需要透过现象抓住问题本质，产生新思路，探索价值度高的改进路径，为新时代高校学生的高质量思想引导提供优越的环境。本文通过阐述新媒体视域下高校共青团思想引导工作的现状，分析在新媒体思想引导工作中遇到的困难，将理论与实践相结合，探究出在新媒体视域下高校共青团应该采取哪些有效的路径克服困难。

关键词：新媒体；引导工作；困境；改进路径

一、新媒体视域下高校共青团思想引导工作现状

随着互联网时代的发展，新媒体进入大家的视野。新媒体是继报纸期刊、电视广播等传统媒介之后发展的新型业态，具有渠道多样、覆盖率极高且推广形式丰富的典型特征。新媒体的迅速发展改变了人们认识世界、了解世界的方式，给人们的生活、工作和学习带来了新的景象，具有鲜明的时代特性。其将便捷性、交互性、时效性等优势充分融入传播交互过程，已成为人们思想传播、情感表达的重要工具。

高校共青团组织具有凝聚青年、引领青年、服务青年的工作特点，作为直接联系青年学生的基层组织，面对新媒体带来的巨大变革，应充分发挥其在青年中的吸

---

① 杜姝君，对外经济贸易大学国际经济贸易学院研究生辅导员。

引力和影响力，积极探索思想传播新模式，主动占据思想引导的主阵地。新媒体视域下高校思政教育工作的开展，需要全面搭建线上宣传平台，营造丰富的线上、线下相融合的育人场景，深入开发"智慧团建"系统功能，充分发挥新媒体对高校共青团思想引导工作的促进作用，提高高校共青团工作的有效性，全面服务大学生成长成才。

因为新媒体技术的出现，信息的传达、反馈及互动机制产生变革，共青团工作的开展也受到多维的影响：一是交流媒介的多样性，微博、微信公众号、各类短视频 App 等新媒体平台作为青年人的线上聚集地，均成为青年人接收信息及发出声音的重要平台；二是反馈机制的互动性，各类平台的涌现及移动端的使用使得信息的互动更加迅捷，青年人可以通过弹幕、评论等方式表达情感，传达观点，每个人都能成为信息的发布者；三是传递内容的丰富性，作为内容蓝海，新媒体媒介提供了体量庞大、内容丰富、形式新颖的海量信息，涉及各种领域，广泛的资源可用于思政教育，因此，新媒体成为青年学子丰富的教育资源。立德树人，德育为先。伴随着新技术的发展，新媒体视域下共青团思想引导工作面临着诸多机遇与挑战，共青团工作的开展应深入挖掘更契合当代青年的学习需求和生活方式的思想引领方式，全面革新工作理念，利用新媒体工具探索出价值更高的工作思路和路径，进一步加强共青团思政引领工作。

二、新媒体视域下高校共青团思想引导工作困境

虽然新媒体技术给高校共青团思想引导工作的开展带来了很大的便捷性，但当前仍面临许多巨大的挑战，其中既有当前团组织自身工作方式的相对落后，也有外来环境带来的消极影响。

（一）思想引导方式单调

当前，新媒体视域中高校对共青团思想引领的媒体引导渠道过于单调。在思想传播及宣传的过程中，除了微博、微信公众号等常规选择，一些短视频网站和直播平台，如抖音、快手等符合青年人日常交流需求，流量较大的平台仍较少出现共青团思想教育的宣传。同时部分线上学习平台，内容更新速度较慢，内容建设仍待进一步更新。此外，在利用新媒体宣传的过程中，仍存在形式大于内容，理论知识不透彻、学习领悟不深入、"走过场"开展学习的问题。对于一系列思想引导活动，学生未能从实践中真正得到教育与熏陶，并将理论"入脑、入心"。同时，网络上蔓延的一些不良舆论对高校共青团工作也会产生无形的压力。

（二）引导重点难以突出

高校学生通过新媒体在互联网上看到许多复杂多元的信息，尚无经验的青年学生对互联网的信息难辨真假。当前大学生个性特点突出，实际上需要分类、分批乃至个体化的精细引导。但当前的情况是，共青团在开展思想引导工作的过程中，在以团支部为主体开展教育活动时，对所有青年团员依旧采用一以贯之的集体引导，未充分考虑学生个体差异，导致引导的重点难以突出，部分学生不能切实领悟理论价值和思想内涵。因而，引导在思想上的凝聚力就容易削弱。

（三）新媒体监管难度较大

互联网的信息是广阔性的，它携带的各种信息无论是有益或者有害的都是难以避免的，高校共青团在新媒体视域下开展思想引导工作，也避免不了互联网带来的弊害。处于大数据时代的今天，高校学生的日常学习与工作更是与互联网密不可分，学生新媒体用户日渐增多。与此同时，网络安全的监管机制尚在建设中，对于共青团思想引导的合理监管难度也不断提高。新媒体视域下，各大媒体为高校提供有用信息内容的同时，夹杂了许多垃圾信息和虚假信息，这对高校学生在吸收学习有用信息的过程中较容易产生不良影响。

（四）"信息茧房"易产生异化

由于新媒体先进的技术算法，会导致各种信息会依据受众者的兴趣来推荐，使受众者容易偏向某一个模糊的方向，久之则陷入一种追求自身自由的圈子，形成"信息茧房"。而受众者中不乏反主流的群体存在。因此，倘若不提高对网络舆论的正确引导能力，学生的价值观容易产生歧化。

三、新媒体视域下高校共青团思想引导工作改进路径

互联网存在海量的信息，新媒体平台的多样性可以提供内容丰富的学习活动平台给青年学生。新媒体应与传统的思政教育方式相结合，结合主题团日活动，以团课的方法开展思政教育。因为传统的思想引导方式在整个思政教育工作进程中始终发挥着重要作用，饱含其独特的优势性，而将新媒体作为载体穿插其中，可保证及时有效地传递信息。共青团组织应有效运用各类新媒体媒介，以短视频、公众号文章等多种形式，利用声音、影像及图文并茂的方式将需要传播的思想和文化内容传递给学生，同时利用新媒体媒介中人人都是发言人的特点，鼓励青年学生发挥主体作用，激励主动

参与、带动引领。特别是发挥学生党员的带动作用，加强学生党支部与团支部的融合，以党建带团建，使思想引导的过程更具趣味性，让传统和新媒体各取所长，优势互补，实现融合的最佳效果。

（一）基本原则

新媒体平台融入高校思想政治工作的方式与内容都要"因时而进、因势而新"。具体而言，新媒体视域下高校共青团思想引导工作创新发展，必须重点坚持以下几个原则。

1. 坚持"以人为本"尊重个体化差异

在互联网迅速发展的时代背景下，高校团组织在思想政治教育的开展中，必须尊重学生的主体地位，更加体现出对学生个体的人文关怀。例如，灵活使用学校现有的大数据平台，充分掌握学生的个体情况、兴趣偏好、思想动态等信息，根据相关数据整理出精细的引导方案。结合新时代青年人的情绪发展和个体性格特点，多注重日常关怀、互动沟通，少采取概念灌输、刻板说教，充分尊重个体的差异性和独特性，多利用场景教育，为学生提供结合自身体验的自我学习、自我教育的平台。

2. 全面把握新媒体传播规律和特点

利用新媒体平台建立健全线上思政和线下育人双向融合的联动机制。具体来讲，一方面要利用好新媒体平台，充分利用其承载的丰富多彩的信息资源，创新高校共青团组织思政引领的内容和形式，增强团组织的亲和力和感召力。高校共青团干部要重视并深入研究新媒体的传播规律和特点，通过"网络＋思想教育"的深度融合，打造出既有学理性又有感染力的"智慧课堂"，将思想理念与认识深度融入学生的日常生活和工作之中。另一方面，需要强调的是，新媒体平台还承载着宣传弘扬正能量的重要责任和榜样育人的重要使命。高校共青团组织应充分挖掘校园内的榜样事迹和典型案例，利用新媒体平台的传播速度快、覆盖面广等传播规律和特点，引导学生从小事做起、从身边的事做起，形成"比学赶帮"的良好校园风气。

3. 坚持运用系统化思政育人原则

高校共青团组织要始终坚持体系化、系统化的思政育人原则，积极搭建好思政育人平台，加强团支部基层建设，找好工作抓手。统筹高校"大思政"格局下各方思政力量，协调推进教育、管理、服务联合育人机制，全面促进高校治理能力和治理体系的现代化发展。

（二）核心理念

新媒体视域下高校共青团工作开展应重点做好以下三点。

一是要将统一思想、凝聚力量作为思想宣传、思政引导工作的核心环节，更加主动地去把握党中央及上级党委的要求，自觉承担起举旗帜、聚民心、育新人、兴文化、展形象的使命。

二是团属媒体平台主要面向青年，因此，相比于其他官方媒体，更要围绕青年的兴趣，关注青年的需求，追随青年的脚步，将思想引领工作融入融媒体建设中。

三是要加大校园媒体人才培养力度，培养出一批新媒体技能运用熟练的宣传思想工作队伍，更高质量地推进共青团媒体融合向纵深发展，助力学生思想教育发展。

（三）改进路径

1. 加强新媒体产品创新设计

高校共青团要围绕立德树人的根本目标，结合上级团组织要求开展团日活动，要注重内容的设计更加迎合青年人的话语体系，促进第一二课堂融合。需要以创新意识广泛开展服务青年、引领青年的相关工作，采取多种灵活的思想引导方式，让广大青年充分感受到思政教育主体内容本身的魅力与情感。

以"青年大学习"网上团课为例，作为一个"周更"的网络课程，这门课程凝聚了共青团组织及制作团队的创意巧思。它灵活地将政治理论课创新融合为青年人喜闻乐见的"网红短视频"，把"治国理政的大道理"转化为"入脑入心的小道理"，成功展现了新媒体视域下共青团思想引导工作的全新开展模式。目前，"青年大学习"每期学习人数约 4500 万，已成为全团出力、全团动员、全社会有感的"最强"政治理论课。作为一项成功的实践，"青年大学习"团课值得进一步挖掘并广泛推广其制作方式及运行模式。

同时，通过新媒体媒介讲好大思政课也是发挥高校共青团思想引导的重要途径之一。共青团应结合青年特点，加强思政教育的时代性和感染力，深入挖掘思政教育好模式、好案例、好经验，将传统"灌输式"的说教转化为"启发式"的引导，将被动接受转化为主动求知，因地、因人、因事、因时制宜讲好大思政课，使新时代思政教育焕发勃勃生机。正如陈培永所说："最鲜活的思政课，不是干巴巴的书本，而是亿万中国人写在祖国大地上的青春华章。"高校共青团组织要努力发挥宣传引导作用，推出更多符合青年接受习惯的新媒体产品，围绕习近平总书记在 2021 年两会期间提出的善用"大思政课"的工作要求，广泛开展线上线下交流与实践活动，大力培养青年的历史视野和实践精神，引领青年成长成才。

2. 线上线下融合育人

在新媒体产品设计创新的基础上，高校共青团组织可依托新媒体平台发布内容丰富、形式多样的"二三课堂"活动，把思政教育与校园文体活动、志愿服务、实践实习等活动结合，实现线上线下融合育人。具体来讲，可充分整合校内育人资源，利用各类校园文化活动平台，举办网络征文、微电影、网上红色经典诵读、线上歌曲传唱等内容丰富、形式多样的红色教育活动，让学生在积极向上的网络文化活动中受到教育和启迪。同时，可将团学活动纳入学生"二三课堂"体系，严格学分获得与考评制度，有效记录团员参与情况，以评促学，提高团员对学习活动的参与度，以开拓创新的精神有效推进线下活动育人与线上思政育人的有机融合，提升育人能效。

3. 定期开展团干部培训

新媒体视域下高校共青团思想引导工作面临新的挑战和发展契机，应第一时间建立融媒体平台，广泛动员高校教师参与团的工作，形成强大的育人合力。同时，高校团委需要加强对二级学院团委的指导并积极组织基层团干部的培养工作，拓宽青年团干部发展路径。例如，可结合新媒体渠道创办"团干部提升计划"，定期开展培训工作，鼓励基层团干部线上线下交流与合作，开拓工作视野，形成人才保障。特别需要提升青年团干部的信息化能力素养及风险应对能力，使其不仅能够利用新媒体平台开展宣传引导工作，而且能及时预防和应对随时可能产生的网络舆情与不良影响。

4. 打造新时代"智慧团建"

高校共青团应积极利用新媒体平台打造新时代"智慧团建"，形成富有时代感和吸引力、思政特色鲜明的"共青团网络工作体系"。第一，依托新媒体平台充分发挥共青团的"引领"工作职能。引导广大青年树立远大理想抱负，坚定理想信念，培养广大青年成为具有正确政治立场，坚定马克思主义信仰的时代新人。例如，可以通过采访优秀团员，分享优秀经验，传播正能量，深度挖掘和讲述他们的优秀品质与奋斗经历，充分发挥优秀团员、团支部等的榜样作用，通过线上展播方式展现他们良好的精神风貌，在全校范围内宣传优秀典型，以优秀者的榜样力量和丰富经验来激励青年大学生向朋辈看齐，奋进逐梦。第二，依托新媒体平台充分发挥共青团的"凝聚"工作职能。各级团组织可以开创具备吸引力内容的公众号或者视频号，向广大青年大学生推送党的理论和政策、社会新闻热点、心理健康、就业指导等内容，专栏内容要及时更新，及时反映社会动态，保持发布信息的新鲜度，以此来吸引大学生的主动关注和积极交流，形成核心凝聚力。第三，依托新媒体平台充分发挥"服务"职能。共青团组织可以通过线上服务公众号或小程序，打破服务潘篱，积极做好学生的权益服务工作，一方面增强其服务的便利性，另一方面提升青年学子对共青团新媒体平台的使用率与信任度。同时，共青团还可利用后台程序搭建平台用户"大数据分析"专栏，可以通过浏览数据如阅读量、下载量等分析青年学子的关注点和偏好，对平台内容进行适时调整，使其越来越受到更多大学生群体的关注和喜爱。

历史浩浩荡荡，时代向前的脚步从未停歇。将新媒体融入高校思想政治教育工作体系之中，要让互联网这个最大变量变成事业发展的最大增量，是新时代高校思想政治教育工作实现创新发展的重要举措，对促进大学生成长成才意义重大。新时代的高校共青团思想引导工作既要激发出传统育人平台的最大效能，又要积极开拓和发展新媒体阵地，为培育担当民族复兴大任的时代新人贡献力量。

参考文献

[1] 张策，张耀元. 新时代背景下新媒体融入高校思想政治教育的价值、原则及路径［J］. 国家教育行政学院学报，2020.

[2] 王春华. 新媒介环境下高校共青团工作的思考［J］. 现代教育，2011.

[3] 黑龙江共青团. 青年大学习·一起学党史：在新形势下坚持和发展中国特色社会主义［EB/OL］．［2021-06-21］澎湃新闻.

财经类高校学生劳动教育研究

熊正非[①] 吴比特[②] 王 丹[③]

摘 要：劳动教育是新时代党对教育的新要求。高校在推进劳动教育高质量发展的过程中发挥着支撑引领作用，高校劳动教育水平从劳动精神面貌、劳动价值取向、劳动技能水平等方面对新时代社会主义建设者和接班人的素养产生决定性影响。财经类高校以财经类专业为主要学科，是高等教育战线的重要组成部分，但因自身特质在开展劳动教育过程中面临着学生劳动价值观冲击、财经类专业限制、师资力量不足等挑战。财经类高校应当深刻领会劳动教育的目标要求，准确把握劳动教育鲜明的思想性、突出的社会性和显著的实践性，探索一条结合学校实际、适合学校特色、发挥学校优势的劳动教育实施路径，使学生树立正确的劳动观念，具有必备的劳动能力，培育积极的劳动精神，养成良好的劳动习惯和品质。

关键词：财经类高校；劳动；劳动教育

劳动教育是新时代党对教育的新要求，是中国特色社会主义教育制度的重要内容，是全面发展教育体系的重要组成部分，是大、中、小学必须开展的教育活动。高校每年为社会输出数以万计有素质的普通劳动者和越来越多的创新人才与高素质人才，在推进劳动教育高质量发展的过程中发挥着引领和支撑作用。高校劳动教育水平从劳动精神面貌、劳动价值取向、劳动技能水平等方面对新时代社会主义建设者和接班人的素养产生决定性影响。财经类高校以财经类专业为主要学科，是高等教育战线的重要组成部分，但因自身特质在开展劳动教育过程中面临着一定挑战。探索一条结合学校实际、适合学校特色、发挥学校优势的劳动教育实施路径，是财经类高校落实立德树人的根本任务，是构建五育并举人才培养体系的重要任务和必然要求。

[①] 熊正非，对外经济贸易大学国际经济贸易学院本科生辅导员。
[②] 吴比特，对外经济贸易大学国际经济贸易学院金融学2020级本科生。
[③] 王丹，对外经济贸易大学国际经济贸易学院物流管理专业2020级本科生。

一、财经类高校开展劳动教育的现状

（一）学生的劳动观念与劳动能力"错位"

1. 劳动观念较强，但存在知行不一的倾向

本文以 290 名财经类高校学生为样本展开问卷调查。调查结果显示，88.96% 的学生同意"劳动是人类发展和社会进步的根本力量"，86.20% 的学生同意"劳动是人生一切成功的必经之路"，78.97% 的学生同意"奋斗本身就是一种幸福"，由此可见多数学生具备正确的劳动观念和较强的劳动意识。但是涉及学生自身的劳动意愿和选择时，74.83% 的学生"能够积极参加公益活动和志愿服务活动"，68.97% 的学生"能够自觉参与校园爱国卫生运动"，58.96% 的学生表示"能够对自己从事的事业不求回报地热爱和付出"。部分学生尚未实现观念认知与实际行动的统一。

2. 掌握基本劳动技能，但与学段要求不符

根据问卷调查结果，绝大多数学生具备基本的劳动技能，能够完成小学和初中学段的劳动教育目标，但相比于更高学段的要求仍存在一定差距。90.68% 的学生"能够独立完成个人物品整理清洁"，89.65% 的学生"能够进行简单的家庭卫生打扫和垃圾分类"，72.76% 的学生"能够照顾好身边的动植物"，56.9% 的学生"能够制作简单的家常餐"，而"能够运用专业知识和技能，为他人提供相关的公益性服务"的学生仅占 42.41%。

3. 具备劳动精神，但实践经验不足

问卷包含了关于奋斗、奉献、勤俭、创新等劳动精神的自我评价，结果相对比较乐观。79.66% 的学生认为自己"具备诚实守信、吃苦耐劳的品质"，78.97% 的学生认为自己"具备良好的消费习惯，珍惜劳动成果，杜绝浪费"，79.66% 的学生认为自己"喜欢探索新知识、新技术、新工艺、新方法的运用"，80% 的学生"能够在面对重大疫情、灾害时主动担当作为"。但在涉及劳动实践的问题时，84.48% 的学生"体验过种植、养殖、手工制作等简单的生产劳动"，51.38% 的学生"体验过例如木工、金工、布艺、陶艺等劳动和传统工艺制作过程"，仅有 49.31% 的学生"曾通过兼职等途径在真实的工作岗位上获得职业体验"。这一比例较低可能是由于调研对象中低年级学生占比较高，但仍在一定程度上反映了学生劳动实践经历不足。

（二）学校的劳动教育与专业教育"脱节"

1. 劳动教育必修课尚处于筹备阶段

按照相关要求，高校应当设立劳动教育必修课程，在专业人才培养方案中加入劳动教育相关内容，依托已有课程增设劳动教育模块或单独开设劳动专题教育必修课。在学时要求上，本科阶段劳动教育应当至少达到 32 学时。截至目前，由于教师配备、课程大纲设计、培养方案修订等工作需要一定时间，多数财经类高校的劳动教育必修课仍处于筹备阶段，尚未正式开课。

2. 劳动实践活动以校园内日常生活劳动为主

为推动劳动育人工作逐步落实，财经类高校相继举办各类劳动实践活动。例如，对外经济贸易大学开展"迎校庆、植新绿"校园美化劳动实践活动，主要内容包括翻耕草坪、播撒草种、栽种花卉等；中央财经大学金融学院开展"传劳动精神，谱奋斗华章"实践系列活动，主要内容包括校园道路清扫、校内长椅保洁、图书馆书架保洁等；上海财经大学开展新生宿舍"养成教育"活动，主要内容包括室内保洁、垃圾分类、物品摆放、行为习惯养成等。由此可见，目前各财经类高校劳动实践活动仍以校园内的日常生活劳动为主。

3. 劳动教育与专业教育结合度有待提高

财经类高校劳动教育在理论层面注重强化马克思主义劳动观、利用劳动模范讲座等形式弘扬劳动精神，在实践层面注重日常生活劳动的操作体验和技能培训。当前模式未能很好地实现劳动教育和专业教育、创新创业教育相辅相成、有机融合的效果。对于学生的层次阶段和技能需求而言，能力提升形式较为单一，与专业结合度不高，对于学生的专业技能提升作用有限。

（三）劳动教育效果与教学目标"偏离"

1. 缺乏科学设计，劳育活动存在"形式化"现象

根据问卷调查结果，在询问到"学生不愿意参加劳动教育活动的原因"时，77.59% 的学生认为原因包括"活动流于表面化、形式化，没有实际意义"，该选项在所有选项中排第一位。排在第二位的是"活动内容停留在简单的体力劳动层面，缺少吸引力"，57.24% 的学生选择了这一选项。通常在进行"校园保洁""植树除草"等活动时容易存在"娱乐化""体验派"的现象，劳动教育实践极易演变成学生课外"休闲娱乐活动"，使实践活动内涵与意义"肤浅化"，削弱了对学生劳动观念、意识与技能的培养。

2. 活动吸引力不足，学生参与度较低

在针对学校已经开展的劳动教育活动的参与情况调查中，39.66% 的学生"曾参与过 1 次以上学校或学院组织的劳动教育实践活动"，20.00% 的学生"曾参与过 1 次以上劳动模范讲座等劳动教育活动，没有参与过劳动实践"，25.52% 的学生"对此类活

动有一定了解,但没有实际参与过",另有14.83%的学生"不知道学校开展过相关活动"。当询问对未来学校开展的劳动教育活动的参与意愿时,多数学生表示"根据活动内容有选择地参与感兴趣的项目"。由此可见,现阶段学生对劳动教育活动参与度仍然较低,且参与的积极性与活动吸引力有较大关系。

3. 学生获得感不足,劳育效果有限

问卷结果显示,在参与过劳动教育活动的学生中,仅有50.00%的学生认为自己通过参加劳动教育"有效地培养了劳动精神,提升了劳动能力",22.41%的学生表示"有一定收获,但效果非常有限",其余学生则表示"没有任何实质收获"。这一调研结果因为样本局限性不能完全代表现阶段财经类高校劳动教育的成效,但在一定程度上反映了与高校劳动教育长期目标的较大差距。

二、财经类高校开展劳动教育面临的挑战

(一) 财经类高校学生的劳动价值观"困境"

1. 西方经济学思想的强烈冲击

在财经类高校的培养方案中,经济学类课程占据基础性和主体性地位。以西方经济学思想为基础的微观经济学、宏观经济学等课程是财经类高校中最为常见的基础必修科目,其中有一个很重要的"理性人"假设,它认为每一个从事经济活动的人都是利己的,企图用自己的最小经济代价换取自己的最大经济利益。财经类高校的经济学课程主要注重消费、投资、贸易等因素对拉动经济的贡献,强调资本积累、技术进步在经济增长中的重要性。虽然政治经济学课程涉及了马克思主义劳动价值论,但无论是课时还是篇幅都相对较小。经济学教学体系的"西化",使学生在学习西方经济学的理论的同时不可避免地会受到西方经济思想的影响。

2. "网红""明星"效应的不良导向

随着信息技术和移动互联网的发展,类型丰富的社交平台、网络直播平台兴起。随之而来的,是原本普遍的"追星"现象愈演愈烈,以及网络平台上一种新形式明星——"网红"的诞生。明星、"网红"依靠着自己的粉丝群体,仅在网络平台上发布视频、开直播互动便能赚取一大笔财富,部分"网红"的收入水平更是远高于为国家作出突出贡献的科研人员,而普通工人、农民等中低收入群体更是难以望其项背。劳动付出与收入水平的不匹配,导致越来越多的青年学生以"出名"和"当网红"为价值取向,而这种现象在财经类学生中也只增不减。以"哗众取宠"为荣,以踏实劳动为耻,以"光鲜亮丽"为荣,以扎根土地为耻的不良风气在社会中逐渐滋生,这无

疑给树立正确劳动观念带来了巨大挑战。

3. 社会主义核心价值观仍需引导

财经类高校学生对于社会主义核心价值观尚且存在认知上的偏差，对于社会主义核心价值观的自我构建还处于浅层化、表面化的阶段。结合其自身学习特点，学生往往会将名利作为衡量自身价值的标准和取向；在市场经济自由竞争、适者生存规则的影响下，学生往往会在个人利益与集体利益两者之间产生动摇甚至选择前者。社会主义核心价值观的确立是学生树立正确劳动价值观的基础和前提，高校开展劳动教育同样是弘扬社会主义核心价值观的现实需要。

（二）财经类高校开展劳动教育的专业"困境"

1. 财经类高校缺乏劳动实践类专业

与综合类高校不同，财经类高校的学科架构中经济学和管理学占据主体地位，部分高校辅以法学、文学等学科。而与劳动紧密相关的农学、工学、理学等学科极少出现在财经类高校的学科体系中。劳动类相关专业的缺乏，是财经类高校劳动氛围不浓厚、劳动教育开展困难的重要原因之一。如果单纯地为了推动学校的劳动教育，而强行引入相关学科，首先，这样做并不现实，农业、工学等学科需要具备丰富科研经验和教学经验的师资力量，需要科研仪器设备等基础设施，并非一朝一夕即可建立；其次，这样做也并无必要，以开展劳动教育、增强劳动氛围为目的，从零开始新的学科建设，投入大、产出慢、周期长，对于财经类高校的整体发展来说无疑是因小失大。

2. 财经类专业偏向理论层面，与实践联系不够紧密

以金融、经济、管理为重要学科的财经类专业，重在强化对于经济社会现象和经济热点问题的理论分析。财经类学生主修的经济学、数学、管理学类课程，也更多地偏向理论层面。久而久之，数字、代码、经济名词等理论符号在财经类高校学生的学习活动中占据主流，而动手操作、劳动实践等活动逐渐弱化。学生之间的话题也越来越多地偏向理论学术、业界研究和社会分析，这对于社会发展和经济发展来说固然有利，但反观其对于社会实践和劳动教育的影响却是消极的。与农学、化工、机械制造等学科相比，财经类学科存在"动脑不动手"的局限性。

3. 开展劳动教育的基础设施仍不完善

对各财经类高校来说，校区"小而精"是普遍特点。由于学科建设对于土地、水源、环境没有过多依赖，财经类高校大多以必要的楼房建筑搭配简单的校园绿化作为主体。校区自然资源的简单化和土地利用程度高自然会伴随着难以提供校园环境进行劳动教育的问题。另外，财经类高校如何将资源合理配置，也极大地影响着劳动教育的开展。在支持科研、校园维缮、教学运营等各项支出之余,财经类高校通常难以提供足够资金进行理想的劳动教育。在全国高校普遍加强劳动教育的背景下,相比于意识落后,如何提供配套的基础设施或许是财经类高校开展劳动教育亟待解决的现实问题。

(三) 财经类高校开展劳动教育的师资"困境"

1. 缺乏专业的劳动教育师资力量

由于学科建设的针对性,财经类高校的教师大多是以经管类学科为背景,具备相关学科经验的劳动教育领域的专业教师对于大多数财经类高校来说是极为稀缺的。由于财经类高校自身的学科局限,此类专职教师的招募难以通过本校独立培养,而不得不投入与所有高校的竞争当中。面对专业教师的不足,财经类高校要开展劳动教育,必须从其他专业教师或行政人员中进行内部挖掘,而这样的内部培养需要一定的时间成本和资金成本,短时间内同样难以支撑高校对于劳动教育师资的需求。采取何种内部培养机制和如何引进相关专业人才是财经类高校组建高水平劳动教育师资队伍必然面临的问题。

2. 劳动教育课程不系统、不完善

对于劳动教育课程的开展来说,大部分财经类高校仍处于探索阶段。部分高校只是增设了劳动教育相关理论课程,并且强调社会实践、劳动实践的重要性,而简单的理论教育和一些形式上的实践组织难以达到人才培养中劳动教育培养环节的需要。与其他课程不同,劳动教育强调理论与实践的充分结合,在形成正确的劳动价值观、学习足够劳动技能的基础上,能够正确地运用于实践中、充分地体现在生活中才是劳动教育的根本目的,学生能够掌握更多的实用技能、能切实地解决生活中面临的困难才是劳动教育的真实期待。形成系统的、完善的劳动教育体系,从理论到实践上都给予学生足够的指导与发挥空间,对于当下的财经类高校而言仍是任重道远。

3. 劳动教育理念相对落后

劳动教育,需要专门的课程作为载体,但其载体绝不仅局限于此。由于其存在的客观性和普遍性,大部分学科和专业都可以作为劳动教育的桥梁。对于财经类高校,传统的金融学、经济学、管理学都可以在满足学科自身理论要求的基础上,鼓励学生投入实践,亲身参与与其相关的社会活动中。在进行理论教育的同时,通过参与一些社会实践、公益活动同样有利于学生获取与本学科相关的、难以在书本上获得的知识。而当下财经类高校的教学模式基本固定于教室内,教学的内容多数基本局限于书本理论。更新教育理念,试着将课堂"走出去",开发多种类型、深入实践的课堂模式,不

仅是劳动教育的需要，更是所有学科建设的突破口。

三、财经类高校劳动教育实施路径

（一）注重思想性，培养正确的劳动观念

1. 在师资队伍建设中，贯彻马克思主义劳动观

马克思主义劳动观首次全面阐述了劳动在人类社会发展史上的决定性作用，它的形成在人类劳动学说史上具有重要意义，极大地推动了人类物质世界和精神世界的进步。作为劳动教育的主体之一，教师能否充分理解和运用马克思主义劳动观，是整个劳动教育能否有效进行的关键环节。对于专职开展劳动教育的教师而言，要将马克思主义劳动观与开设课程紧密结合，引导学生将其内化于心、外化于行。有重点地讲解劳动为什么、是什么的基本问题，用学生易于接受的方式讲清楚劳动的意义和价值。在劳动观念、劳动纪律、劳动相关法律法规等方面加强对学生的正面引导。

2. 在课程体系设计中，增设劳动教育必修课程

高校作为人才培养的重要基地，完善、健全的课程体系是培养全方位人才的基本要求。劳动教育作为人才培养的重要环节，将其纳入人才培养全过程，丰富多种劳动教育实践途径，设立独立的劳动教育课程势在必行。其课程内容应以马克思主义劳动观理论、满足学生职业发展需要的通用劳动科学知识和必要的实践体验为主要内容，并通过多种课堂形式，增强学生的劳动意识和增加学生的劳动技能，抓好劳动教育在思想引导上的第一关。

3. 在校园文化建设中，强化劳动文化传承

校园文化的建设，是一所高校提高学生素质、增强学校实力、塑造良好氛围的重要途径。高校应当在校园文化建设中注重劳动习惯、劳动品质的养成教育。在日常生活中，对学生进行基本的劳动要求，从自身做起，并且以社团、学生组织等形式强化劳动建设，使学生在思想上重视劳动、热爱劳动。学校同样可以利用植树节、劳动节等与劳动教育紧密相关的节日，强化劳动观念。另外，通过邀请社会先进人物进行宣讲、奖励校内劳动先进学生或教师等途径，发挥榜样作用，鼓励学生领悟劳动精神，争做新时代的奋斗者。

（二）发挥社会性，培育积极的劳动精神

1. 强化服务型劳动实践，增强学生社会责任感

高校对社会实践的重视程度越来越高，充分利用此机制，加强服务性劳动实践的开展，鼓励学生走向社会进行劳动服务，一方面有利于促进社会发展，另一方面也是劳动教育实现的重要途径。服务型社会实践是社会主义教育必不可少的一个环节，是培养"四有青年"的重要途径。在实践过程中，学生的劳动技能将得到加强、社会经验将大量积累，同时在服务社会的过程中，其社会责任感的增强是开展劳动教育更为珍贵的成果与收获。

2. 大力宣扬劳模精神与工匠精神

劳动模范与大国工匠是整个时代的先锋、民族的楷模，他们身上所承载的劳模精神与工匠精神发挥重要的引领作用，丰富了中华民族伟大精神的内涵，体现了工人阶级与劳动群体的社会奉献精神和伟大拼搏精神，是马克思主义劳动观的重要载体。劳动模范和大国工匠对于引导财经类高校学生培育践行社会主义核心价值观和树立正确的劳动观念来说是不可忽视的重要载体。通过举办"劳模进校园""大国工匠事迹报告"等劳动榜样人物进校园活动，广泛宣传劳动榜样人物和身边普通劳动者的事迹，让学生在校园里能够与劳动模范近距离互动，观摩学习劳动模范精湛技艺，切身感受勤劳敬业的劳动精神。

3. 创新教学模式，强化分工合作意识

当下高校在实践类课程的教学模式中已经开始实行小组分工、组内合作的教学模式，但尚未广泛普及，此模式的推广和创新是强化劳动观念与分工合作意识的有效途径。高效的小组分工可以最大化每个人的能力实现，各司其职、术业专攻是小组运行乃至是整个社会运行的基本规律。在劳动教育活动中强化分工合作意识，对于学生今后走向社会、实现自身价值、发挥自身才能起到助推作用。分工合作需要每个成员舍弃自身的一些小的利益，把自己的精力投入实现团队整体目标当中，这是团队的要求，更是今后走进企业、走向社会的基本要求，有利于学生深刻体会社会主义社会平等、和谐的新型劳动关系。

（三）增强实践性，提升必备的劳动能力

1. 在专业学科中有机渗透劳动精神

劳动是整个社会运行的重要动力，因此，众多学科其内在都与劳动有着密不可分的联系。以财经类专业为例，劳动是创造价值的来源，若无价值，便无经济分析的必要。在专业学科教育中渗透劳动精神，增强专业学科与劳动实践的联系，改变以往固定于书本的教学模式，督促学生更多地融入与本学科相关的实践活动当中，不仅有利于推动劳动教育的开展，更是学科全方位、实践化进步的重要动力源泉。增强劳动教育与其他学科开展有机联动，是实现劳动教育进步与学科建设完善双赢的有效途径。

2. 丰富和拓展劳动教育场所

高校作为学科教育的主体，往往缺少劳动教育的专门场所，如何丰富和拓展劳动教育场所也成为各高校实行劳动教育所面临的第一难题。首先，校内开发是拓展劳动教育场所的最直接手段，通过土地、水源、植被的开发与利用，实验室、图书馆的专职开发，功能性教室的建设，都有利于高校开展劳动教育；其次，联系校外资源，增强各企业、社区、机构与高校学生的有效互动，鼓励学生真正走入社会、进行实践，是帮助学生提早适应社会的有效途径，也是高校拓展劳动教育场所和推动劳动教育开展的另一渠道。

3. 完善劳动教育评价机制

劳动教育工作的开展，需要有效、合理、完善的评价机制来进行反馈和引导。首先，在日常教育中，及时对学生劳动行为进行评价，以自我评价为主、他人评价为辅，指导学生进行反思改进，纳入综合素质档案，作为学生整体评价的参考之一；其次，在学段结束时，依据学段目标和内容给予学生考核结果认定，综合评定主要考虑学生劳动观念、劳动能力、劳动精神、劳动习惯和品质等劳动素质发展状况，并将考核结果作为学生升学、就业的重要参考。完善的劳动教育评价机制，是对于学生劳动教育接受成果的评测，更是劳动教育自身不断积累经验、自我改进的必要环节。

习近平总书记在全国教育大会上强调："要在学生中弘扬劳动精神，教育引导学生崇尚劳动、尊重劳动，懂得劳动最光荣、劳动最崇高、劳动最伟大、劳动最美丽的道理，长大后能够辛勤劳动、诚实劳动、创造性劳动。"财经类高校应当深刻领会劳动教育的目标要求，准确把握劳动教育鲜明的思想性、突出的社会性和显著的实践性，结合自身特点探索劳动教育实施路径，使学生树立正确的劳动观念，具有必备的劳动能力，培育积极的劳动精神，养成良好的劳动习惯和品质，以"奋进之笔"谱写新时代劳动教育新篇章。

参考文献

[1] 教育部关于印发《大中小学劳动教育指导纲要（试行）》的通知 [EB/OL]. http://www.moe.gov.cn/srcsite/A26/jcj_kcjcgh/202007/t20200715_472808.html

[2] 习近平在全国教育大会上强调：坚持中国特色社会主义教育发展道路培养德智体美劳全面发展的社会主义建设者和接班人 [N]. 人民日报，2018-9-11（1）.

第三部分
合作共赢，接轨世界·入世20周年

2001年,经过中国人民的不懈努力,中国经济获得国际社会的广泛认可,中国加入世界贸易组织,以更开放包容的姿态广泛参与国际分工合作,促进了我国社会主义市场经济体制的完善和世界经济的长远增长。20年来,我国不断加快对外开放的步伐,与世界经济体系深度融合,对世界经济增长和全球贸易增长作出巨大贡献。

开放带来进步,封闭必然落后。2001年,中国加入世界贸易组织。20年来,中国推动贸易和投资自由便利化,维护多边贸易体制,坚定不移推动经济全球化朝着更加开放、包容、普惠、平衡、共赢方向发展,推动建设开放型世界经济,为世界经济增长作出了贡献。

The Extrusion Effect of State-owned Enterprises on Private Enterprises' Exports Propensity and Scale

刘舒婷[①] 张国峰[②]

Abstract: This thesis analyzes how state-owned enterprise (SOE) ratio affects private firms' export propensity and export scale. We construct a Heckman two-stage model, using a sample of manufacturing firms from the 2004—2007 Chinese Industrial Enterprise Database to examine how the industry-year SOE ratio affects the firms' export. Furthermore, we conduct a heterogeneity analysis for 31 2-digit-code industries in manufacturing. The result finds that SOEs exert an extrusion effect on the export propensity and export scale of private enterprises. Except for individual industries such as chemical raw materials and chemical manufacturing (code 26) and pharmaceutical manufacturing (code 27), the vast majority of the industries show an extrusion effect of SOE on the private enterprises' export propensity and export scale, which indicates that it is vital to effectively promote the reform of the financial system, balance the competitive relationship between state-owned enterprises and private enterprises, reduce the distortion of production factors and resource mismatch, and finally improve the export environment for private enterprises.

Keywords: export propensity; export scale; SOEs' extrusion effect

1 Introduction

Private enterprises have become an important force in China's economy. The total value of commodity export of SOEs from January to February 2021 was 23,532,814 million yuan, while the one of foreign-invested enterprises was 108,834,334 million yuan and the one of private

---

① 刘舒婷,对外经济贸易大学国际经济贸易学院国际贸易学2021级研究生。
② 张国峰,对外经济贸易大学国际经济贸易学院副教授。

enterprises reached 167,101,101 million yuan.① The value of private enterprises was 7.10 times higher than that of state-owned enterprises and 1.54 times higher than that of foreign enterprises in the same period.

Most of the existing literature focuses on analyzing the impact of SOEs on the development and financing of private enterprises, as well as the influencing factors of private enterprises' exports. However, there is less literature analyzing the impact of SOEs on private enterprises' export propensity and export scale. In this paper, we will examine the influence of SOEs on the export propensity and export volume of private enterprises after empirical regressions.

The mechanism of SOEs' influence on private enterprises in the literature can be divided into four categories of views.

The first category, from the perspective of exogenous financing constraints, argues that the state-owned financial system supports financial benefits to SOEs and SOEs have rigid dependence on this support, which leads to the financial dilemma of the private economy. As a large transition economy, China has typical ownership discrimination of financing constraints, especially on collective and private enterprises, but SOEs doesn't suffer much from such financing constraints. Further, it has been argued that under the Chinese financial system, credit and securities market financing is tilted in favor of SOEs, which results in the flowing of financial resources from private sector to the state-owned sector. Therefore, private enterprises' exogenous financing is crowded out by SOEs, and private firms are subject to greater financing constraints than SOEs. A scholar pointed out that SOEs have much easier access to credit resources than non-SOEs, while the productivity of SOEs is smaller than that of non-SOEs. There is a mismatch of credit resources among enterprises of different ownership. In addition, after classifying private enterprises into different groups according to financing dependence, the study confirmed that ownership credit discrimination significantly limits the access to exogenous financing for private firms with high financing dependence.

However, there are some opposite views arguing that such credit ownership discrimination and exogenous financing constraints are not completely harmful to private enterprises. The ownership discrimination faced by non-state-owned enterprises is an obvious obstacle to corporate financing, but at the same time, it also stimulates the investment efficiency of such enterprises. Gou et al. challenged the function of ownership discrimination, and the empirical

---

① The export commodity trade data comes from the website of General Administration of Customs of PRC.

results showed that credit rationing differences are not related to ownership differences, but to firms' own endowments and macro-financial environment. After demonstrating the extrusion effect of credit ownership discrimination, Li showed that there is a compensating effect of credit ownership discrimination through threshold regressions. When the compensating effect is greater than the extrusion effect, an increase in the share of SOEs can improve the innovation efficiency of the whole enterprises.

The second category is based on the perspective of enterprises' soft budgetary binding. When SOEs in socialist economies suffer losses, the government often needs to make additional investments, increase loans, reduce taxes, and provide financial subsidies to support SOEs, which is defined as the enterprises' soft budgetary binding. This kind of pre-event policy preferences and post-event policy subsidies given to SOEs can preferentially allocate social savings to SOEs through the state-controlled banking system. Meanwhile, non-SOEs are restricted to entry the market but the SOEs are granted to monopolize in an industry. Bai et al. argued that local government tend to protect high-taxed local enterprises and used SOE output ratio as local protection extent. State-owned enterprises themselves not only suffer from efficiency losses, but also drag down the development of private enterprises due to the soft budgetary binding. However, this soft budgetary binding may also have a positive impact on private enterprises. Li argued that there is a crowding-out effect as well as a compensating effect of the enterprises' soft budgetary binding.

The third category is based on the resource mismatch. State-owned enterprises have far greater access to resources than non-state-owned enterprises, while the degree of factor price distortion is also greater for state-owned enterprises than for non-state-owned enterprises. Resources and factors are biased toward state-owned enterprises, which to some extent discourages the flow of production factors.

The fourth category emphasizes the monopoly position of SOEs and the protection they have got in the market. There is a phenomenon called "asymmetric competition" in China's market, which means that private enterprises compete in the downstream markets while large-sized and medium-sized SOEs monopolize in some upstream markets. The profits of SOEs in the upstream monopoly are actually a kind of monopoly rent, and this administrative monopoly hinders the development of private enterprises and harms the social welfare.

There is no clear boundary between these four types of views in essence. Credit ownership and enterprise' soft budgetary binding can both lead to resource misallocation among enterprises with different ownership. However, monopoly can also be regarded as a kind of monopoly rent, which in a sense belongs to the implicit subsidies granted by the government to SOEs and therefore falls within the conceptual scope of soft budgetary binding. Generally speaking, state-owned enterprises will hold a dominant position in the market due to the unbalanced financial resource allocation and soft budgetary binding, causing an extrusion effect on private enterprises' resource acquisition as well as development.

For the private enterprises, the financing constraint is an important factor for their exports. The exogenous financing constraint of enterprises plays a significant role in their export participation, and the exports of private enterprises are more dependent on exogenous financing capacity compared to state-owned enterprises. The improvement of financing can increase the export probability and expand the export scale of enterprises. The export financing channels of enterprises of different ownership systems also differ. State-owned enterprises' export financing relies mainly on bank credit, while private enterprises' export financing relies more on commercial credit.

Therefore, we speculate that SOEs will squeeze out credit resources and production factors from private enterprises due to credit ownership and soft budgetary binding, which will put private enterprises at a disadvantage in the market competition and further affect private enterprises' export propensity and export scale.

The remainder of the thesis is organized as follows. Section 2, we conduct a statistical description of the data and set up the regression model. Section 3, we analyze the regression results, conduct a robustness test and a heterogeneity analysis. Section 4 concludes and provides policy recommendations.

2 Data Description and Regression Model

2.1 Data Sources and Descriptions

The data selected in this thesis are the unbalanced panel data of manufacturing enterprises from Chinese industrial enterprises database from 2004 to 2007, which includes all state-owned enterprises and non-state-owned enterprises above the scale (whose product sales or main business income are above 5 million yuan). The sample has a total of 1,101,777 observations before deleting. The number of enterprises increased from 259,412 in 2004 to 313,046 in 2007. Referring to general accounting standards, we removed the sample with total industrial output value, total assets, and fixed assets not more than 0. Referring to Zhang and Wang, we also removed observations with less than 8 employees and with those total assets less than fixed assets. After these treatments, the sample used in this thesis has a total of 676,702 observations and 338,959 enterprises, including 163,283 enterprises in 2004, 120,930 enterprises in 2005, 184,265 enterprises in 2006, and 208,224 enterprises in 2007. Some enterprises have entered the market, and some have exited during this period.

The statistics description of the variables is shown in Table 1.

Table 1 Descriptive Statistics

Variables	N	mean	sd	min	max
export_choice	676,702	0.275	0.446	0	1
export_value	676,693	20,910	444,921	0	1.810e+08
SOE_ratio	676,702	0.111	0.112	0	1
tfp_lp	676,690	8.303	1.078	−2.573	15.62
CI	676,702	80.75	198.4	−561.0	26,818
asset	676,699	78,154	756,880	1	1.550e+08
finace	676,702	889.1	9,597	−1.142e+06	1.556e+06
interest	676,702	811.6	9,613	−707,406	1.707e+06
subsidy	676,702	215.9	4,343	−155,840	900,000
wage_average	676,702	15.47	13.32	0.00500	842.0
age	676,594	23.23	11.91	−183	2,021
export_choice lag	252,674	0.280	0.449	0	1

2.2 Regression Model

In the sample of firms, the export value of non-exporting firms is zero. However, if we ignore non-exporting firms and only use exporting firms in the regression, randomness will be lost and therefore causes sample selection bias, which makes the estimation results not accurate. To solve this kind of sample selection bias problem, we choose the Heckman two-stage model for the regression: in the first stage, the enterprises choose export or not, i.e., the selection equation (1); in the second stage, the exporting enterprises decide the size of exports, i.e., the decision equation (2).

$$\Pr\{export\_choice_{ijpt} = 1\} = \varphi(\alpha_1 SOE\_ratio_{jt} + \alpha_2 Z'_i) \qquad (1)$$

$$export\_value_{ijpt} = \beta_0 + \beta_1 SOE\_ratio_{jt} + \beta_2 M'_i + \beta_3 \delta_i + \varepsilon_{ijpt} \qquad (2)$$

Eq. (1) uses the Probit model to estimate the probability of firm exporting, as well as the calculation of the estimated value of the inverse Mills ratio. In the Heckman second-stage regression, the estimated value of the inverse Mills ratio obtained from the calculation in (1) is added to Eq. (2) to correct the firm's export decision equation.

"i" represents the individual firm, "j" represents the 4-digit-code industry, "p" represents the region, and "t" represents the year. $export\_choice_{ijpt}$ is the export dummy variable of the firm. If the figure of $export\_choice_{ijpt}$ is 1, the firm exports and enters the foreign market; but if the figure is 0, the firm stays in the domestic market and does not export. $export\_value_{ijpt}$ is the export delivery value of the enterprise. M'_i is a set of factors that affect the size of firms' exports, including total factor productivity, capital intensity, asset size, financial cost, interest expense, subsidy, average wage of the firm, and age of the firm. Z'_i is a series of factors that affect firms' export decision. Besides the factors listed in M'_i, $export\_choice_{ijpt}$ is applied to generate a one-period lag dummy variable $export\_choicelag_{ijpt}$, which can perfectly satisfy the need for additional relevance, exclusivity, and exogeneity in the Heckman fist-stage model as an extra control variable.

We use SOE_ratio_{jt} to represent the portion of state-owned enterprises' asset in 4-digit-code industry level.

2.3 Indicator

In addition to the core variables of enterprise export propensity, enterprise export scale, and the proportion of state-owned enterprises' asset, the other control variables are selected as follows.

1. Total factor productivity (TFP)

Considering that the sample with zero investment cannot be estimated, this thesis will adopt the semi-parametric Levinsohn-Petrin (LP) method to measure the total factor productivity of enterprises. The LP method can effectively avoid the problems of endogeneity and selection bias brought by OLS regression. In this thesis, we adopt the method proposed by Lu and Lian (2012) to estimate productivity using the following variables: (1) Main business income: since the data of industrial added value of 2004 is lacked, we use main business income instead. (2) Fixed asset stock: we use total fixed assets as fixed asset stock. (3) Labor input: the average annual number of all employees is used as the indicator of labor input. (4) Intermediate inputs: we use total industrial intermediate inputs as intermediate inputs as a proxy variable for the LP method.

2. Capital intensity (CI)

We use the ratio of the average annual balance of net fixed assets (thousand yuan) to the average annual number of all employees as an indicator of capital intensity. According to the traditional factor endowment theory, countries with lower capital intensity (i.e., labor abundance) export more labor-intensive products. As a developing country with low capital intensity, China has an advantage in exporting labor-intensive products, so we expect capital intensity to have a negative relationship with exports. However, in recent years, China has gradually changed from a labor-abundant country to a capital-abundant country, so there is uncertainty about the relationship between capital intensity and export choice and export size.

3. Firm size (asset)

Firm size is directly related to a firm's export choice and export size. Due to economies of scale theory, the expansion of enterprise size will lead to lower production costs, improve market competitiveness, and thus increase the propensity to export or expand the scale of exports. Bernard and Jensen pointed out that the larger firms' size is, it will be more easier to enter the foreign market. In this thesis, the total assets (thousand yuan) is used as the indicator of enterprise size.

4. Financial cost

Finance costs refer to the costs incurred by the enterprise to raise the funds needed for production and operation, etc. The larger the number of finance cost is, the more effort it will be for the enterprise to raise production and operation. There may be a positive relationship between financial costs and firms' exports.

5. Interest expense[1]

Interest expense can measure the level of financing constraints of firms to some extent. Excessive interest expenses may affect the normal operating turnover of enterprises, thus increasing their operating costs and production costs and reducing the export amount of enterprises. However, Li and Yu point out that in the framework of Melitz general equilibrium model, the higher the success rate of a firm's project is, the easier it is for that firm to obtain

---

[1] To avoid the situation that the logarithm does not exist after taking the logarithm, we add the interest to 1 before taking the logarithm.

external financing from financial intermediaries. And the more external financing a firm can obtain, the easier it is to enter the oversea market.

6. Subsidy

Subsidy is a strategic trade policy. Subsidies to exporters can effectively reduce the production cost ratio of enterprises, improving their competitiveness and increasing their share in the international market. At the same time, in order to obtain government financial subsidies and tax benefits, enterprises are more willing to engage in export trade. However, Zhou and Sheng also point out that export subsidies may cause further mismatch of market resources. Gao and Huang point out that government subsidies can weaken the innovation incentives of exporters and make exporters fall into the "low markup rate trap", which means making exporters adopt rent-seeking behavior and increase their production costs, leading to the failure of increase of markup rate as well as the increase of exports.

7. Average wage of workers

The average wage of workers is calculated as the ratio of total wages payable (thousand yuan) to the average annual number of employees. There are many processing trade enterprises in China, which require low-skilled labor force. Thus, average worker wages may have an inverse relationship with private firms' export propensity and export size. However, according to the new-new trade theory, only firms with high productivity and better profitability will export. These firms tend to pay higher wages than firms that only make domestic sales.

8. Firm's age

There is a correlation between enterprise age and enterprise export. The age of enterprise is calculated as the figure that the current year minus the year[①] when the enterprise was founded. According to the dynamic increasing returns effect, the firm can reduce the unit production cost by increasing the cumulative output, thus having the initial advantage of the industry and facilitating the export of the firm. Traditional internationalization theory suggests that older and more mature firms will prefer to enter international markets. However, it has also been shown that there is a "u"-shaped curve between the age of Chinese firms and their propensity to export, and that young Chinese firms driven by internationalization also have a higher propensity to enter international markets.

---

① "The current year" refers to 2021.

9. One period lagged variable

$export\_choicelag_{ijpt}$ can be used to measure the fixed cost of entering the foreign market for a firm. When the figure is 1, the firm has entered the export market in the previous year. This kind of firms have their own export path and pattern and require a lower fixed cost to enter the export market than a firm with a figure of 0. This variable can be used as an exogenous variable in the Heckman first-stage regression.

3 Empirical Regression Results

3.1 Benchmark Regression Results

Table 2 shows the benchmark regressions result using the Heckman two-stage model. Column (1) is based on the export size decision equation (2) and Column (2) is based on the export choice equation (1) respectively. Considering that the mechanism of SOEs' asset proportion on private firms' exports may be influenced by the external financing constraint[①] and government subsidies, we use some interaction terms in the original equation. Columns (3) and (4) are the regression results of adding the interaction term of SOEs' assets proportion and external financing constraint on the base of the set of original equations; columns (5) and (6) are the regression results of adding the interaction term of SOEs' assets proportion and subsidy on the base of the original set of equations.

The estimation result shows that the asset proportion of SOEs is statistically significantly negative at the 1% level in both the selection equation and the decision equation, which means that in the industry-time dimension, SOEs cause crowding out of private firms' export propensity and export size.

In columns (3) and (4), the coefficient of the interaction term between SOE asset proportion and external financing constraint is significantly negative at the 1% statistical level, implying that the margin effect of SOE asset proportion depends on the value of the exogenous financing constraint. The exogenous financing constraint is a moderating variable in the extrusion effect model, and the extrusion effect on private enterprises which caused by a unit increase in both the exogenous financing constraint and the SOE asset ratio, is greater than the sum of the extrusion effect separately caused by a unit increase of the two variables.

---

① The external financing constraint of a firm is calculated as interest expense/net fixed asset value.

Similarly, in columns (5) and (6), the interaction term between SOE asset proportion and subsidy has a significantly negative coefficient in the regression of the selection equation, but the regression in the decision equation is not significant. It implies that, for enterprises' export propensity, the margin influence of the asset proportion of SOEs depends on the value of subsidy, and the subsidy is a moderating variable. However, in terms of the export volume of private enterprises, the subsidy does not affect the change in the state-owned asset ratio and thus does not affect the export size of private enterprises.

Meanwhile, the analysis of other control variables in the regression are as follows.

1. Productivity is an important factor for private enterprises' exports.

From Table 2, we can learn that the impact of productivity on private firms' export choice and export size decisions is diametrically opposed. Total factor productivity (TFP) has a significant negative correlation with export choice, but has a significant positive correlation with export size. For export choice, this negative correlation may be due to the fact that a large proportion of Chinese private enterprises are processing trade enterprises, which are mostly engaged in outsourcing work, requiring low-skilled labor and low technology, with generally low productivity levels. In contrast, for the export scale of private enterprises, the larger the scale of enterprises is, the lower the unit production cost will be, with a greater productivity, which is called scale economy. In the meantime, there is an export learning effect in the export process. Enterprises will improve their own productivity when they export due to the absorption of foreign advanced technology, management mode, etc.

2. Capital intensity is significantly negative to private enterprises' exports.

China is a labor-abundant country with an advantage in exporting labor-intensive products, while most of the private enterprises are processing trade enterprises, therefore their exports have an inverse relationship with capital intensity, which fits our expectation.

3. Enterprise size shows a significant positive relationship with private enterprises' propensity to export.

The coefficient of enterprise size (which is shown as asset in table 2) is significantly positive at 1% statistical level, which indicates that the larger the private enterprise's size is, more likely it will be for a private enterprise to participate in overseas market. It fits the viewpoints that firm's scale affects international trade in the new trade theory and the new-new trade theory, which is a crucial variable in the export of private enterprises in China.

4. Financial cost shows a significant positive relationship with private enterprises' exports,

but the impact on their export scale is not significant. The higher the financial cost of private enterprises is, the more likely they are to participate in the international trade.

5. The age of the enterprise shows a significant positive relationship with the export choice of private enterprises, and a significant negative relationship with the export volume.

The reason may be that senior private enterprises have their own export channels, so compared to the young private enterprises, it is easier for senior private enterprises to enter the foreign market. But at the same time, China's emerging private enterprises also have a certain degree of export scale advantage.

Table 2 Benchmark Regression of SOEs' Extrusion Effect on Private Enterprises' Export

Variables	(1) lnexport	(2) export_choice	(3) lnexport	(4) export_choice	(5) lnexport	(6) export_choice
export_choicelag		2.315***		2.312***		2.315***
		(224.68)		(224.26)		(224.68)
SOEratio2	-0.510***	-0.577***	-0.336***	-0.389***	-0.508***	-0.542***
	(-6.30)	(-10.97)	(-3.80)	(-6.88)	(-5.74)	(-9.70)
lntfp_lp	7.885***	-0.268***	7.894***	-0.247***	7.885***	-0.267***
	(83.81)	(-4.62)	(83.94)	(-4.23)	(83.81)	(-4.60)
lnCI	-0.011	-0.149***	-0.017**	-0.158***	-0.011	-0.149***
	(-1.54)	(-31.70)	(-2.29)	(-32.79)	(-1.54)	(-31.70)
lnasset	-0.006	0.110***	-0.010	0.105***	-0.006	0.110***
	(-0.66)	(17.66)	(-1.03)	(16.76)	(-0.65)	(17.68)
lnfinace	0.011**	0.050***	0.013**	0.053***	0.011**	0.050***
	(2.07)	(14.41)	(2.46)	(15.15)	(2.07)	(14.41)
lninterest	-0.011***	0.001	-0.008*	0.006**	-0.011***	0.001
	(-2.74)	(0.35)	(-1.89)	(2.18)	(-2.75)	(0.34)
lnsubsidy	-0.004	0.016***	-0.005	0.016***	-0.005	0.021***
	(-1.25)	(6.02)	(-1.36)	(5.97)	(-1.02)	(5.68)
lnwage_average	-0.162***	0.118***	-0.162***	0.119***	-0.162***	0.118***
	(-9.23)	(10.64)	(-9.22)	(10.74)	(-9.23)	(10.65)
age	-0.007***	0.001**	-0.007***	0.001*	-0.007***	0.001**
	(-8.33)	(2.07)	(-8.47)	(1.82)	(-8.33)	(2.09)

续表

VARIABLES	(1) lnexport	(2) export_choice	(3) lnexport	(4) export_choice	(5) lnexport	(6) export_choice
lambda		-0.665***		-0.664***		-0.665***
		(-58.54)		(-58.42)		(-58.53)
SOE_efin			-2.677***	-3.149***		
			(-4.69)	(-8.36)		
SOE_subsidy					0.001	-0.044*
					(0.03)	(-1.85)
constant	-7.204***	-1.986***	-7.195***	-1.984***	-7.204***	-1.994***
	(-39.65)	(-17.29)	(-39.63)	(-17.25)	(-39.63)	(-17.35)
observations	170,585	170,585	170,585	170,585	170,585	170,585
year	YES	YES	YES	YES	YES	YES
area	YES	YES	YES	YES	YES	YES

Note: Z-statistics are reported in the parenthesis. *, ** and *** denote the statistical significance at the 10%, 5% and 1% level, respectively.

3.2 Robust Test

The degree of SOE agglomeration varies widely across industries. Ruiming Liu, and Lei Shi (2011) point out that in a part of the upstream markets such as capital, finance, oil, electricity, and telecommunications market, a few large-sized and medium-sized SOEs take the dominant place, maintaining monopoly or oligopoly. In the downstream areas, however, private enterprises present a competitive situation. Thus, for the robustness of the results, we replace the explanatory variable state-owned enterprises' asset ratio with 4-digit-code-industry state-owned enterprises' number ratio in the time dimension. The results of the robust tests are presented in Table 3.

The regressions all control for time and region fixed effects. Columns (3) and (4) include the interaction term between the number ratio of SOEs and exogenous financing constraints, and columns (5) and (6) include the interaction term between the number ratio of SOEs and subsidy.

In the regression results, the coefficients of the number ratio of SOEs are all significantly negative. The coefficient of the interaction term between the number ratio of SOEs and exogenous financing constraint is significantly negative, indicating that the margin effect of SOE ratio is influenced by exogenous financing constraint. The results of the crowding out of state-owned enterprises on the export propensity and size of private enterprises are robust. The coefficient of the interaction term between the ratio of SOEs number and subsidy is significantly negative in the selection equation, which also indicates that subsidy is an important moderating variable for the export propensity of private firms.

Table 3　Result of the Robust Test

Variables	(1) lnexport	(2) export_choice	(3) lnexport	(4) export_choice	(5) lnexport	(6) export_choice
export_choicelag		2.295***		2.291***		2.296***
		(221.66)		(221.04)		(221.65)
SOE_ratio3	-2.432***	-2.337***	-2.113***	-1.996***	-2.727***	-2.187***
	(-13.39)	(-19.91)	(-11.17)	(-16.42)	(-13.59)	(-17.46)
lntfp_lp	7.897***	-0.285***	7.916***	-0.255***	7.900***	-0.285***
	(84.28)	(-4.90)	(84.51)	(-4.37)	(84.32)	(-4.90)
lnCI	-0.005	-0.144***	-0.014*	-0.157***	-0.004	-0.144***
	(-0.66)	(-30.47)	(-1.84)	(-32.05)	(-0.59)	(-30.51)
lnasset	-0.004	0.112***	-0.009	0.105***	-0.004	0.112***
	(-0.37)	(17.97)	(-0.93)	(16.67)	(-0.39)	(18.00)
lnfinace	0.011**	0.049***	0.014**	0.053***	0.011**	0.049***
	(1.97)	(14.05)	(2.52)	(15.10)	(2.05)	(14.00)
lninterest	-0.010***	0.001	-0.006	0.008***	-0.010***	0.001
	(-2.67)	(0.54)	(-1.39)	(3.06)	(-2.68)	(0.53)
lnsubsidy	-0.004	0.018***	-0.004	0.018***	-0.016***	0.028***
	(-0.98)	(6.90)	(-1.12)	(6.80)	(-3.18)	(7.08)
lnwage_average	-0.150***	0.124***	-0.149***	0.126***	-0.151***	0.124***
	(-8.60)	(11.16)	(-8.53)	(11.39)	(-8.64)	(11.17)
age	-0.007***	0.002***	-0.007***	0.002***	-0.007***	0.002***
	(-7.55)	(3.66)	(-7.72)	(3.36)	(7.57)	(3.69)
lambda		-0.661***		-0.660***		-0.659***
		(-57.73)		(-57.57)		(-57.54)

续表

Variables	(1) lnexport	(2) export_choice	(3) lnexport	(4) export_choice	(5) lnexport	(6) export_choice
SOE_efin			-5.518*** (-5.74)	-6.402*** (-9.87)		
SOE_subsidy					0.199*** (3.61)	-0.140*** (-3.33)
constant	-7.191*** (-39.77)	-1.856*** (-16.12)	-7.186*** (-39.78)	-1.850*** (-16.04)	-7.177*** (-39.69)	-1.869*** (-16.22)
observations	170,585	170,585	170,585	170,585	170,585	170,585
year	YES	YES	YES	YES	YES	YES
area	YES	YES	YES	YES	YES	YES

Note: Z-statistics are reported in the parenthesis. *, ** and *** denote the statistical significance at the 10%, 5% and 1% level, respectively.

3.3 Comparative Analysis Based on Different Industries

The export propensity and export scale of private enterprises differ significantly from industry to industry. After regressing each of the 31 2-digit-code industries in manufact-uring, we have the results listed in Table 4.

The majority of industries can satisfy our previous conclusion that SOEs have an extrusion effect on private firms' export propensity and export volume. However, according to Table 4, we can also find that there are some 2-digit-code industries in which SOEs have a positive effect on private firms' export propensity or export volume. For instance, in two industries, chemical raw materials and chemical products manufacturing (code 26) and pharmaceutical manufacturing (code 27), the SOEs ratio promotes both the export propensity and export scale of private enterprises. For the tobacco products industry (code 16), textile, clothing, shoes and hats manufacturing (code 18) and rubber products industry (code 29), the impact of state-owned enterprises on the export propensity of private enterprises is not significant, but it shows a significant positive effect on the export scale of private enterprises. For the waste resources and waste materials recycling industry (code 43), SOEs ratio significantly contribute to the export propensity of private enterprises, but does not affect export scale of private enterprises significantly. For the agro-food processing industry (code 13), SOEs ratio significantly promotes the export propensity of private enterprises, while they have a suppressive effect on the export volume of private enterprises.

Table 4 Results of 2-digit-code Industries①

Industry Code	lnexport	export_choice	Industry Code	lnexport	export_choice
13	-4.316***	1.472**	29	1.990***	0.440
14	-0.252	-1.032***	30	-5.318***	-3.914***
15	-1.438	-1.091**	31	-2.726***	-2.347***
16	6.042**②	-0.654	32	-1.415**	0.116
17	-2.488***	-2.468***	33	0.242	-0.131
18	3.221*	-3.230	34	-2.617***	-1.872***
19	-0.067	-1.096	35	-1.931***	-1.269***
20	-2.535***	-0.113	36	-0.848***	-0.776***
21	-0.713*	1.028***	37	0.496	-0.665***
22	-3.709*	-3.211***	38	Non③	Non
23	-0.531	-1.455***	39	-1.868***	-1.007***
24	0.659	-0.565	40	0.289	-0.527
25	-9.300	1.045	41	0.785	-0.558
26	1.796***	0.839***	42	-1.012***	-0.255
27	2.533***	1.836***	43	7.307	3.419*
28	-3.287***	-0.560			
Year	YES	YES		YES	YES

Note: Z-statistics are reported in the parenthesis. *, ** and *** denote the statistical significance at the 10%, 5% and 1% level, respectively.

4　Conclusions and Policy Recommendations

In this thesis, we conduct Heckman two-stage regressions with manufacturing data from the Chinese Industrial Enterprise Database of 2004—2007 to examine whether SOEs have an

---

① Only the regression coefficient of the proportion of state-owned enterprise assets is listed in the table. In order to make the comparison between industries more intuitive, the regression coefficients of other variables are ignored.

② The coefficients of tobacco products industry (code 16) and waste resources and scrap material recycling industry (code 43) are not referable because of the poor number of observations (97 and 830 separately) as well as multicollinearity problem, thus the number of control variables is significantly reduced.

③ The electrical machinery and equipment manufacturing industry (code 38) does not have any observations in the sample from 2004 to 2007.

extrusion effect on private firms' export propensity and export scale as well as their underlying mechanisms. The main conclusion is that the ratio of SOEs has a significant negative correlation on the export propensity and export scale of private firms. This indicates that SOEs cause an extrusion effect on the export participation and export scale of private enterprises. Also, by including the interaction term in the regression, we demonstrate that external financing constraint plays a moderating effect in the extrusion mechanism of private firms' export propensity and export size, and subsidy plays a moderating effect in the extrusion mechanism of private firms' export scale. We further analyze the heterogeneity of 31 2-digit-code industries in manufacturing and find that the vast majority of industries satisfy the extrusion effect of SOEs on private enterprises' exports, but individual industries such as chemical raw materials and chemical products manufacturing and pharmaceutical manufacturing, SOEs conversely have a facilitating effect on private enterprises' exports.

The findings of this thesis have important theoretical and practical implications: 1. Make sure to reduce unreasonable government support policies for SOEs, reduce the existence of soft budgetary binding, and help private enterprises compete more fairly in the market economy. 2. By effectively promoting the reform of the financial system, government should alleviate and solve the financing constraints on private enterprises which brought by ownership discrimination, thriving private economy, and comprehensively promoting the export of the private enterprise sector.

References

［1］张杰. 民营经济的金融困境与融资次序［J］. 经济研究, 2000 (4): 3-10.

［2］郑江淮, 何旭强, 王华. 上市公司投资的融资约束: 从股权结构角度的实证分析［J］. 金融研究, 2001 (11): 92-99.

［3］康立. 中国民营经济融资困境的理论解析及政策出路［J］. 财贸研究, 2004 (4): 42-48. DOI: 10.3969/j.issn.1001-6260.2004.04.009.

［4］卢峰, 姚洋. 金融压抑下的法治、金融发展和经济增长［J］. 中国社会科学, 2004 (1): 42-55.

［5］沈红波, 寇宏, 张川. 金融发展、融资约束与企业投资的实证研究［J］. 中国工业经济, 2010 (6): 55-64.

［6］李成, 黄友希, 李玉良. 国有企业改革和利率市场化能否改善非国有企业融资困境? ［J］. 金融经济学研究, 2014, 29 (4): 97-106.

[7] 马大来, 陈仲常, 王玲. 金融发展、所有制约束与企业资本结构: 基于省级规模以上工业企业面板数据的实证研究[J]. 经济经纬, 2015 (2): 105-110. DOI: 10.3969/j.issn.1006-1096.2015.02.018.

[8] 靳来群. 所有制歧视下金融资源错配的两条途径[J]. 经济与管理研究, 2015 (7): 36-43. DOI: 10.3969/j.issn.1000-7636.2015.07.005.

[9] 孙灵燕. 所有制信贷歧视对中国民营企业出口的影响: 基于融资的视角[J]. 南方经济, 2012 (7): 43-56. DOI: 10.3969/j.issn.1000-6249.2012.07.004.

[10] 支燕, 白雪洁, 邓忠齐. 资本约束、效率激励与所有制歧视: 中国金融发展对企业价值提升的有效性研究[J]. 财贸研究, 2014, 25 (1): 116-124.

[11] 苟琴, 黄益平, 刘晓光. 银行信贷配置真的存在所有制歧视吗?[J]. 管理世界, 2014, (1): 16-26.

[12] 李勇. 利润约束、所有制结构和自主创新[J]. 南开经济研究, 2018, (3): 100-116. DOI: 10.14116/j.nkes.2018.03.006.

[13] 林毅夫, 刘明兴, 章奇. 政策性负担与企业的预算软约束: 来自中国的实证研究[J]. 管理世界, 2004, (8): 81-89, 127.

[14] 刘瑞明, 石磊. 上游垄断、非对称竞争与社会福利: 兼论大中型国有企业利润的性质[J]. 经济研究, 2011, (12): 86-96.

[15] 史晋川, 赵自芳. 所有制约束与要素价格扭曲: 基于中国工业行业数据的实证分析[J]. 统计研究, 2007, 24 (6): 42-47. DOI: 10.3969/j.issn.1002-4565.2007.06.008.

[16] 李艳, 杨汝岱. 地方国企依赖、资源配置效率改善与供给侧改革[J]. 经济研究, 2018, 53 (2): 80-94.

[17] 孙灵燕, 崔喜君. FDI、融资约束与民营企业出口: 基于中国企业层面数据的经验分析[J]. 世界经济研究, 2011, (1): 61-66.

[18] 孙灵燕, 李荣林. 融资约束限制中国企业出口参与吗?[J]. 经济学(季刊), 2012, 11 (1): 231-252.

[19] 徐榕, 赵勇. 融资约束如何影响企业的出口决策?[J]. 经济评论, 2015, (3): 108-120.

[20] 阳佳余. 融资约束与企业出口行为: 基于工业企业数据的经验研究[J]. 经济学(季刊), 2012, 11 (3).

[21] 孔祥贞, 刘海洋, 徐大伟. 出口固定成本、融资约束与中国企业出口参与[J]. 世界经济研究, 2013, (4): 46-53.

[22] 王永进, 张国峰. 人口集聚、沟通外部性与企业自主创新 [J]. 财贸经济, 2015, (5): 132-146.

[23] 盛丹. 地区行政垄断与我国企业出口的"生产率悖论" [J]. 产业经济研究, 2013, (4): 70-80. DOI: 10.3969/j.issn.1671-9301.2013.04.008.

[24] 鲁晓东, 连玉君. 中国工业企业全要素生产率估计: 1999—2007 [J]. 经济学 (季刊), 2012, 11 (1).

[25] 李志远, 余淼杰. 生产率、信贷约束与企业出口: 基于中国企业层面的分析 [J]. 经济研究, 2013, 48 (6): 85-99.

[26] 周世民, 盛月, 陈勇兵. 生产补贴、出口激励与资源错置: 微观证据 [J]. 世界经济, 2014, 37 (12): 47-66.

[27] 高翔, 黄建忠. 政府补贴对出口企业成本加成的影响研究: 基于微观企业数据的经验分析 [J]. 产业经济研究, 2019, (4): 49-60.

[28] 杨嬛, 张学良. 天生国际化与阶段国际化: 企业年龄特征与中国企业的国际化选择 [J]. 经济管理, 2016, 38 (4): 12-23.

[29] 李春顶, 尹翔硕. 我国出口企业的"生产率悖论"及其解释 [J]. 财贸经济, 2009, (11): 84-90, 111.

[30] Cull R, Xu L C. Who gets credit? The behavior of bureaucrats and state banks in allocating credit to Chinese state-owned enterprises [J]. Journal of Development Economics, 2003, 71(2): 533-59.

[31] Brandt L, Li H. Bank discrimination in transition economies: ideology, information or incentives? [J]. Journal of Comparative Economics, 2002, 31(3): 387-413.

[32] Huang Y. Selling China: foreign direct investment during the reform era [M]. UK: Cambridge University Press, 2003.

[33] Boyreau-Debray G and Wei S J. Pitfalls of a State-dominated financial system: the case of China, CEPR Discussion Paper No. 4471. London: Centre for Economic Policy Research, 2004.

[34] Huang Y, Ma Y, Yang Z et al. A fire sale without fire: an explanation of labor intensive FDI in China, MIT Sloan School Working Paper, No. 4713-08.

[35] Kornai, Janos. The soft budget constraints [J]. Kyklos, 1986, 39(1): 3-30.

[36] Bai C, Du Y, Tao Z, et al. Local protectionism and regional specialization: evidence from China's industries [J]. Journal of International Economics, 2004, 63(2): 397-417.

[37] Hsieh C T, and Klenow P. Misallocation and manufacturing TFP in China and India

[J]. Quarterly Journal of Economics,2009,124(4):1403-1448.

[38] Levinsohn, James, Petrin, Amil. Estimating production functions using inputs to control for unobservables[J]. 2003,(2). DOI:10.1111/1467-937X.00246.

[39] Bernard A B and Jensen J B. Why some firms export[J]. The Review of Economics and Statistics,2004,86:561-56.

The Economic Effect of Hainan Pilot Free Trade Zone Policy based on PSM-DID Model

王心蕙[①]

Abstract: China announced the establishment of Hainan Pilot Free Trade Port Zone policy on April 13, 2018. This paper evaluates the impact of Free Trade Zone (FTZ) policy on economic growth via difference-in-difference (DID) model in Hainan Island. I investigate my analysis at month and provincial level. I measure economic outcomes on local GDP.

Then the paper uses propensity score matching with difference-in-difference (PSM-DID model) to ensure effectiveness. The results of both models indicate that FTZ policy shock does affect the economic outcomes positively. The FTZ policy boosts Hainan GDP growth by 21.6% at confidence level of 95%. The estimation passes parallel test, Hausman test, and placebo test.

Keywords: PSM-DID; Free Trade Zone; economic effect

1 Introduction

1.1 Free Trade Zone Policy

Free Trade Zone (FTZ) is derived from the World Customs Organization (WCO) regulations on "Free Zone". According to the *Kyoto Convention*, a Free Trade Zone is a part of the territory of a contracting party. Any goods entering this part are generally considered outside the customs territory, in the respective of import duties. FTZ is characterized by a small area within the territory of customs. It is often enacted by a single sovereign country. Generally, the imported goods into FTZ implement duty-free or bonded taxation policy, rather than tariff reduction.

Currently, representative free trade zones include Hong Kong and Singapore as the integral

---

[①] 王心蕙, 对外经济贸易大学国际经济贸易学院经济学专业(实验班)2017级本科生。

port, Hamburg of Germany and Busan of South Korea as trade port, Dubai of the United Arab Emirates as industrial port, and Rotterdam of Netherlands as logistics port.

Since September 2013, Shanghai was assigned Chinese Free Trade Policy Pioneer Zone. Until 2021, six rounds of FTZ policies have been issued, covering totally 21 provinces and direct municipals. FTZ policy is one of the most important economic upgrading policies in Chinese international trade field.

1.2 Hainan: the Free Trade Port

On April 13, 2018, the meeting was held celebrating the 30th anniversary of Hainan's establishment as a provincial special economic zone. Xi Jinping, China General Secretary, announced that "the Central Committee supports Hainan to promote the construction of Free Trade Port Zone gradually and steadily with Chinese characteristics".

On April 14, 2018, the Central Committee of the Communist Party of China (CPC) and the State Council issued the "No. 12 Document". The Article 10 discussed in detail how Hainan explored the construction of a free trade port with Chinese characteristics. It said to support Hainan with more flexible policy systems, regulatory models and management systems for both domestic and foreign trade, investment and financing, finance and taxation, financial innovation, goods import and export, etc.

On March 15, 2019, the second session of the 13th National People's Congress (NPC) voted to approve the proposal of putting legislation on the Hainan Free Trade Port on the agenda. Hainan Free Trade Zone became the only one that has been approved by national legislation. From this, we can see the high hopes that the national strategy places on Hainan.

In June 2020, the CPC Central Committee and the State Council issued the Overall Plan for the Construction of Hainan Free Trade Port. It marks the construction of Hainan Free Trade Port has entered the stage of comprehensive implementation. It established long-run strategic goals. By 2025, a system of policies and institutions for free trade ports, focusing on facilitating free trade and facilitating free investment, will be initially established. By 2035, the free trade port system and operation pattern will be more mature in aspects of investment liberalization, free cross-border capital movement, infrastructures, transportation, labor migration and data security. By 2050, fully build a high-level free trade port with strong international influence. The figure 1 below displays its long-run goals.

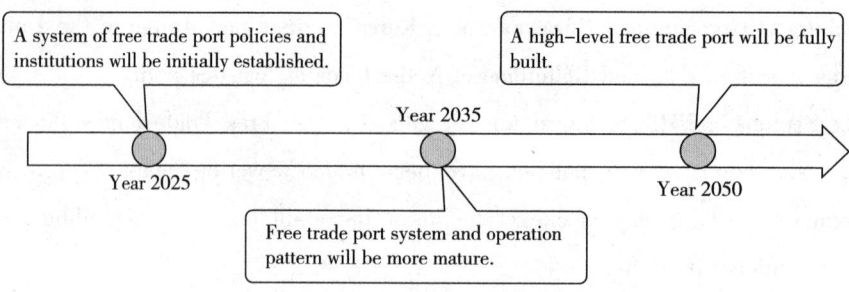

Figure 1　Hainan FTZ Goals

In compliance with FTZ policy goal, Hainan took measures to optimize its industrial structure. Firstly, Hainan speeds up the construction of airports and ferry ports in the island. Together with well-arranged high speed rail train, international airports near famous scenic spots will boost future tourism. The following Table 1 states the current construction progress.

Table 1　Airport Construction Progress

Condition	Airport	Year 2020 Departure	Transport Capacity	Maximum Departure
Operation	Meilan Airport	8,245.1	45,000	22,500
	Fenghuang Airport	7,815.8	20,000 - 25,000	10,000 - 12,500
	Qiongzhou Strait Port	5,900.0	33,000	16,500
	Bo'ao Airport	2,81.0	480	240
Construction	Danzhou Airport	/	3,600	1,800

Note: all the volume is displayed in thousand person-time.

Moreover, calm down overheated real estate to prevent economic bubbles. The charming warm weather of Hainan Island has attracted Chinese elders in the wintertime. As a traditional habit, people flocked into the real estate market for life after retirement and investment. On April 1, 2020, Hainan government implemented real estate purchase restriction policy. Non-resident families can only buy one house in Hainan province with at least 60 months transfer limitation. Besides, the lower boundary of personal first payment for commercial individual housing loans should not be less than 70%. Secondly, Hainan residential register limitations were loosed gradually to attract more labor force.

2　Literature Review

Policy effect evaluation has been a heated topic concerning free trade policy analysis. The effects cover taxation, industrial structural upgrading, legislation improvements, and the most studied economic effect. Castilho et. al. studied Brazil free trade area increases local income by promoting production. Jagdambe and Kannan analyze ASEAN-India Free Trade Agreement using gravity model and found that it has stronger trade creation effect than trade diversion effect. ASEAN-China Free Trade Agreement trade creation effects were investigated by Nie. Positive influences were found, where some bilateral countries enjoy import creation and others export creation. Lim and Breuer investigate effects of free trade agreements on market integration between South Korea and its solo and trade-bloc FTA partners. Kwark and Lim empirically estimate how much FTAs affect domestic inflation rates from analysis of 34 OECD countries.

When looking into previous studies on Chinese FTZ policies, a large proportion of literature found advantages prompt by FTZ. Xiang and He demonstrate PSM-DID model together with synthetic control method (SCM) to investigate capital flow affected by Shanghai FTZ. They found FTZ has larger effects on stimulate cross boarder investment instead of attract foreign direct investment. Song and Guo looked into how Shanghai FTZ influences local government financial power. They conducted SCM-DID model and investigated a 6%-9% positive effect with 2-year time lag. However, some literatures comment critics on FTZ policy. Zhuo et. al. argue FTZ may be "environmental policy trap". They demonstrate DID model in Guangdong provincial FTZ and put forward adverse effect on waste as GDP grow. Some scholars argued that the unbalanced development within China would aggravate social equality (Jenkins, 2013; Siroen, 2014), while others support that underdeveloped regions would be radiated by nearby free trade zones.

Since Hainan FTZ established in 2018, it has become a heated academic issue. Firstly, qualitative analysis emphasizes taxation, trade regulation, legislation, business environment, and financial openness. Liu proposed innovation path of dispute resolution mechanism to guarantee FTZ construction. To compare and contrast with other free trade zones and ports, Wang and Yang analyze Hainan financial market development by investing successful international free trade port. Guangdong and Hainan FTZs dislocation development path and Shanghai FTZ legislative innovating measure for Hainan were put forward.

However, scholars concentrate on advice proposal and comparison between free-trade-zone provinces. Previous literature lack empirical study due to the short time and delayed data upgrading. However, if we are eager to propose social political suggestions, quantitative evaluation of FTZ policy is necessary, especially on economic development. Referring to former scholars' FTZ analysis, I will investigate the economic impact of Hainan FTZ policy through PSM-DID model and monthly panel data.

3 Empirical Methodology

3.1 Model: difference-in-difference (DID)

Similar to natural experiment, Hainan was assigned the free trade port as one of China's FTZ policy series. My basic approach is DID model in the quasi-natural experiment case. First difference is between treatment group and control groups. Second difference is between prior policy time period and after shock time period. The twice difference is able to objectively and quantitatively evaluate outcomes of exogenous shock, which is the economic impact of FTZ policy on Hainan province. The formula (1) below shows my basic model framework.

$$Econgrowth_{i,t} = \beta_0 + \beta_1 Hainan \times Time_{i,t} + \beta_2 HainanFTZ_{i,t} + \beta_3 Time_{i,t} + \sum_{i=1}^{n} Control_{i,t} + \gamma_{i,t} + \varepsilon_{i,t} \tag{1}$$

Where $Econgrowth_{i,t}$ represents province s' economic growth level. $Hainan \times time_{i,t}$ is the interaction term $did_{i,t} = HainanFTZ_{i,t} \times Time_{i,t}$. $HainanFTZ_{i,t}$ is the treatment groups. It equals to one if in Hainan province. $Time_{i,t}$ is the dummy variable showing whether province i was FTZ in time t. $\sum_{i=1}^{n} Control_{i,t}$ is a series of control variables that may affect regional economic development. $\gamma_{i,t}$ is provincial and annual fixed effect. β_1 is the policy effect evaluation coefficient. If it is a positive estimation, I can conclude Hainan economy gain advantages from FTZ policy and vice-versa.

3.2 Variables Selection

Following former studies Yang et al. Huang and Zhang et al., my dependent variable is Hainan local GDP to measure economic growth.

In the DID model, the main dependent variables are dummy variables: one is treatment of affected area, the other is time of policy shock. Despite overwhelming anti-globalization trend and multilateral trade disputes, Chinese government assigned Hainan province the free trade port to further opening up in April 2018. Thus, I conduct the treatment variable at provincial level. The time variable turns positive after the announcement, indicating the long-lasting impact. Considering the time span since 2018 and delayed data update, I use monthly variables in the model. The interaction term of the two variables is what I concerning about the most. It is the DID term, whose coefficient would reveal the policy effect nearly without individual characteristics and time trend.

Despite geological differences, regional economic heterogeneities affect my model effectiveness. In previous provincial or municipal policy studies, Liu(2018) controlled average monthly wage; Tang and Xu controlled industrial structure; Yu et al. controlled the level of urbanization and globalization; Zhang and Yu(2020) controlled the level of urbanization and financial development.

Thus, my model include following control variables:

1) Monthly average income: to control living standard.

2) Monthly international trade volume: to evaluate local globalization level and openness level.

3) Monthly real estate investment: to control the spontaneous effect of real estate purchase restriction policy on local economic growth.

4) Annually variables: these include indexes of urbanization level, industrial structure, and financial market development.

3.3 Model: PSM-DID

The essence of DID estimation is to compare two groups of homogenous samples, such as twins. When exogenous shocks, the DID coefficient can perfectly reflect the effect because the two groups of samples have the same characteristics in other aspects. However, it is difficult to find completely homogeneous samples in real world. Hainan and other provinces may have inherent differences in many aspects. Therefore, I introduce propensity score matching (PSM) method to re-match the control group. I strive to keep the samples of the treated group and the control group as homogeneous as possible in more aspects. After matching, re-regress DID in order to obtain the more reliable effect. Here, I demonstrate Logit model to calculate the propensity score of every provinces. Formula (2) illustrates how propensity score calculated.

$$Logit(HainanFTZ = 1) = \beta_0 + \beta_1 aveincmonth_{i,t} + \beta_2 \ln itradex_{i,t} + \beta_3 \ln rex_{i,t} + \beta_4 fin_{i,t} + \beta_5 struc_{i,t} + \beta_6 urban_{i,t} + \varepsilon_{i,t} \quad (2)$$

After the matching using formula (2), I will use formula (1) again to accomplish the PSM-DID estimation.

4 Data

4.1 Pre-processing

4.1.1 Dependent Variable: lnGDP

The raw GDP data originally was quarterly level and in 100 mRMB (one million of RMB) units. To ensure the time span of panel data and measure monthly effect, I conduct ARIMA transform. Then I smooth it by X12 seasonal adjustment. Finally, I take log form to relieve heteroscedasticity.

4.1.2 Independent Variables

I establish the treatment variable, treat, at provincial level, where Hainan = 1 and others = 0. The monthly time variable covers January, 2014 to December, 2019. It equals t 1 since May, 2018 and 0 otherwise. The did term is the interaction of treat and time (Table 2).

Table 2 Main Variable Declaration

Variable Category	Name	Symbol	Calculation
Dependent	Economic growth	lnGDP	log form ARIMA transformed monthly GDP after X12 seasonal adjustment
Independent	DID	$Hainan \times time$	treat × time
Independent	Treat group	$treat$	$treat = \begin{cases} 1, Hainan \\ 0, others \end{cases}$
Independent	Time	$time$	$time = \begin{cases} 1, after 2018.05 \\ 0, before 2018.04 \end{cases}$

4.1.3 Control Variables

1) $aveincmonth$: monthly average income is disposable income per capita in unit of RMB.

2) ln$itradex$: monthly international trade volume is X12 seasonal adjusted from raw data, the volume of international trade both imports and exports in unit of USD, and then take log form.

3) lnrex: monthly real estate investment is X12 seasonal adjusted from raw trade volume data in unit of 100 mRMB and then take log form.

4) *urban*: index of urbanization level is the proportion of urban population to total population.

5) *struc*: index of industrial structure is the GDP proportion of service sector.

6) *fin*: index of financial market development is the GDP proportion of deposits balance of financial institutions at year-end (Table 3).

Table 3 Control Variable Declaration

Variable Category	Name	Symbol	Calculation
Control Time Effect	Average income per month	*aveincmonth*	local residence average income per month after X12 seasonal adjustment
	International trade per month	ln*itradex*	log form import and export international trade volume per month after X12 seasonal adjustment
	Real estate investment per month	ln*rex*	log form real estate investment per moth after X12 seasonal adjustment
Control Individual Effect	Economic structure	*struc*	the proportion (%) of the service sector in GDP
	Urbanization level	*urban*	the proportion (%) of urban population in total population
	Financial development level	*fin*	the proportion of deposits balance of financial institutions in GDP

4.2 Data Resources

My data covers 31 provinces and direct municipalities of China, excluding HK, Macao, and Taiwan because of missing data.

The following table 4 displayed descriptive statistics.

Table 4 Descriptive Statistics

	(1)	(2)	(3)	(4)	(5)
Variables	N	mean	S.D.	min	max
treat	2,232	0.0323	0.177	0	1
time	2,232	0.278	0.448	0	1
Hainan × time	2,232	0.00896	0.0943	0	1
aveincmonth	2,232	15,732	9,240	1,994	69,442

续表

	(1)	(2)	(3)	(4)	(5)
Variables	N	mean	S. D.	min	max
lnitradex	2,232	14.86	2.276	6.494	18.46
lnrex	2,232	7.185	1.164	-1.619	9.128
struc	2,232	50.48	8.333	36.17	83.50
urban	2,232	0.590	0.163	0.253	1.173
fin	2,097	11.45	3.025	7.083	19.62
Number of province	31	31	31	31	31

The data is mainly collected from China Economic Network Statistical Database. Several missing values due to delayed data updates are made up from China Statistical Yearbook and provincial statistical yearbook.

5 Result and Robust Test

I carried out the empirical study using STATA 15. All regressions are based on reported strongly balanced panel data. The simple regressions without control variables are reported as follow. Both random effect model (RE) and fixed effect model (FE) show negative influences of policy shock. It creates a lot of confusion against previous literature and above qualitative analysis. Thus, I double checked prerequisite conditions and added control variables to find the fittest regression with further robustness check (Table 5).

Table 5　Baseline DID Regression Results

	(1)	(2)
Variables	RE1	FE1
Hainan × time	-0.00731	-0.00731
	(-0.0587)	(-0.0587)
time	0.385***	0.385***
	(17.18)	(17.18)
treat	-1.465	
	(-1.497)	

续表

	(1)	(2)
Variables	RE1	FE1
Constant	9.138***	9.091***
	(52.01)	(783.0)
Observations	2,232	2,232
R-squared		0.122
Number of province	31	31

z-statistics in parentheses; *** $P<0.01$, ** $P<0.05$, * $P<0.1$

5.1 Stepwise Regressions

Just as mentioned above, more control variables are needed to optimize the estimation. Control variable selection referred to literature of other scholars and the underlying economic mechanics.

To answer why local economic growth under-performed with such favorable policy, I considered the international trade environment and local restriction policy. Since Sino-US trade disputes started in March 2018, Chinese substantial economy was greatly shocked. Hainan economic growth would be easily affected by international trade volume, foreign direct investment, and by upstream and downstream supply chain. Stagnant business environment hurts local people income stability. Therefore, less consumption and investment will lead to even more stagnant business. As a result, detrimental cycle damage economic development and GDP growth. To control impact of trade disputes, it is reasonable to include local residence living conditions and international trade volume into DID model.

What's more, local real estate purchase restriction was announced spontaneously with FTZ policy, which curbed the soaring housing prices of the island. The purchase restriction policy definitely has long-run advantages for local economic as a whole. But the short-run data may display adversely. Therefore, I will control real estate investment in the next step to deepen my analysis (Table 6).

Table 6 Adding Control Variables DID Regression Results

	(3)	(4)	(5)	(6)	(7)	(8)
Variables	RE2	FE2	RE3	FE3	RE4	FE4
Hainan × time	0.0592	0.0592	0.0606	0.0593	0.151**	0.130**
	(0.896)	(0.897)	(0.913)	(0.899)	(2.283)	(2.008)

续表

Variables	(3) RE2	(4) FE2	(5) RE3	(6) FE3	(7) RE4	(8) FE4
time	-0.00768	-0.00800	-0.00992	-0.00820	-0.0634***	-0.0506***
	(-0.593)	(-0.617)	(-0.754)	(-0.625)	(-4.712)	(-3.793)
treat	-1.267		-1.241*		-1.137***	
	(-1.285)		(-1.654)		(-3.327)	
aveincmonth	6.67e-05***	6.68e-05***	6.67e-05***	6.68e-05***	6.54e-05***	6.61e-05***
	(75.12)	(75.18)	(74.74)	(75.16)	(73.93)	(76.22)
lnitradex			0.0255	0.00202	0.0547***	0.00871
			(1.341)	(0.101)	(3.390)	(0.447)
lnrex					0.286***	0.225***
					(14.59)	(11.00)
Constant	8.191***	8.149***	7.812***	8.119***	5.353***	6.428***
	(46.14)	(584.1)	(24.89)	(27.30)	(19.85)	(19.60)
Observations	2,232	2,232	2,232	2,232	2,232	2,232
R-squared		0.754		0.754		0.767
Number of province	31	31	31	31	31	31

Note: z-statistics in parentheses; *** $P<0.01$, ** $P<0.05$, * $P<0.1$

Then, I added control variables step by step in both fixed effect model and random effect model as shown the above table.

When average wage is controlled, did coefficient changed sign into what we expected. As international trade environment and local real estate restriction are controlled, did coefficient estimation turns to be more significant. In order to increase the estimation significance, further heterogeneity should be controlled by group characteristics. Those control variables are not monthly based. Instead, they are annual data. The following table 7 reports the estimation.

As more control variables added into regression, the magnitude of did coefficient gradually stabilizes to a value in both random effect models and fixed effect models. It is a good signal showing the right direction. The FTZ policy gives Hainan island approximately 11%—14% increases in monthly GDP on average. Next, I will analyze whether FE model or RE model fits Hainan case to further improve my estimation.

Table 7 FE and RE DID Regression Results

Variables	(9) RE5	(10) FE5	(11) RE6	(12) RE7	(13) FE7
Hainan × time	0.150**	0.128**	0.141**	0.129**	0.117*
	(2.266)	(1.988)	(2.195)	(2.005)	(1.904)
time	-0.0680***	-0.0637***	-0.0236	-0.0214	-0.0584***
	(-4.533)	(-3.966)	(-1.557)	(-1.330)	(-3.524)
treat	-1.135***		-0.960***	-1.642***	
	(-3.303)		(-2.747)	(-4.437)	
aveincmonth	6.54e-05***	6.61e-05***	6.66e-05***	6.67e-05***	6.54e-05***
	(73.96)	(76.24)	(76.95)	(74.11)	(72.41)
lnitradex	0.0530***	0.0108	0.0472***	0.0557***	0.0414**
	(3.258)	(0.555)	(2.948)	(3.417)	(2.137)
lnrex	0.282***	0.217***	0.250***	0.240***	0.125***
	(13.83)	(10.34)	(12.47)	(11.88)	(5.862)
urban	0.173	0.441	1.925***	1.681***	1.126***
	(0.706)	(1.466)	(6.693)	(5.789)	(2.646)
struc			-0.0255***	-0.0266***	-0.0391***
			(-11.08)	(-10.58)	(-13.41)
fin				0.0957***	0.620***
				(4.632)	(9.623)
Constant	5.309***	6.192***	5.844***	4.929***	0.882
	(18.92)	(16.95)	(20.74)	(14.07)	(1.349)
Observations	2,232	2,232	2,232	2,097	2,097
R-squared		0.767			0.789
Number of province	31	31	31	31	31

z-statistics in parentheses; *** $P<0.01$, ** $P<0.05$, * $P<0.1$

5.2 Prerequisite Condition: Parallel Trend Test

The parallel trend is an essential assumption for DID model. That is, before the policy was assigned to treatment group, both control group and treatment group performed similarly. Here in Hainan case, I suppose to test whether the economic growth at similar rate comparing to other provinces before Free Trade Zone was announced. My approach is to regress dependent variable on independent variables together with dummy interaction variables. The first interaction term equals to 1 in treatment group. The second terms were specific month before and after policy shock. Since the dependent variable is transformed from quarterly data, I use 3-month time laps as the parallel test points. Note that symbol C stands for current policy period. B3, B6, A3, A6 are 3 and 6months before and after policy shock respectively.

Following figure shows a significant positive shock at policy time. It ensures to some extent that the economic develop rate differs just at the point of FTZ policy. However, the increase lasts for approximately one year. Another question arises. GDP data has a strong feature of seasonal fluctuation(Figure 2).

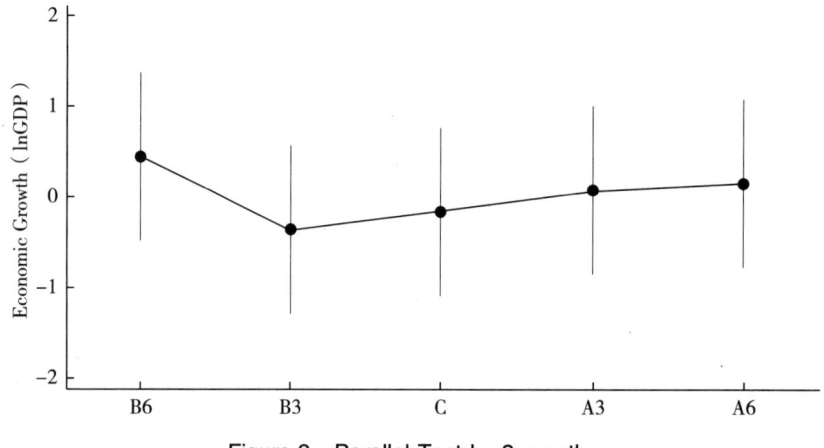

Figure 2　Parallel Test by 3 months

GDP is usually lower at the first quarter and climbing up throughout the year. To further ease quarterly data influences, I retest the parallel trend using one year time laps. Note that symbol C stands for current policy period. By1, By2, By3 and Ay1 are 1, 2, and 3 years before or after policy shock respectively.

Above Figure 3 shows a significant negative shock at policy time and a slight bounced back up one year after. The obvious deviation from zero-axis proves the homogeneity between treatment group and control group before the shock. Nevertheless, the downward effect causes a bit confusing.

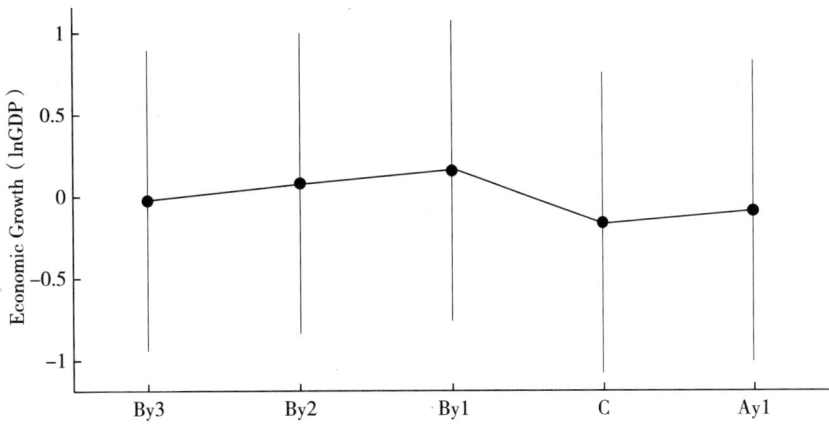

Figure 3　Parallel Test by one year

5.3　Hausman Test

Hausman test is a common method to determine FE or RE model. Once prediction method is settled, estimated coefficient can be determined. STATA reported the chi-squared value and P-value as following Table 8.

Table 8　Hausman Test

Chi-squared	177.908
P-value for the chi-squared	0.000

Thus, reject H0. Fixed Effect(FE) model fits the most, which is column (12) FE7 model in table 7.

$$\ln GDP = 0.882 + 0.117 Hainan \times treat - 0.058 time + 0.0414 \ln itradex +$$
$$0.125 \ln rex + 1.1261 urban - 0.0391 struc + 0.620 fin$$

The standard equation is reported above. The FTZ policy boosts Hainan GDP growth by 11.7% at confidence level of 90%.

5.4　Placebo Test

The region that experimented may have better conditions for policy implementation. In Hainan case, its unique geographical features and potentiality in structural upgrading may be the reason of free trade zone. If it holds, the baseline quasi-experiment assumption of DID model would fail. Therefore, I conduct placebo test to double check. GDP data has strong seasonal fluctuation.

Hence, I chose 3 months, half a year, and an entire year before the policy shock as the placebo shock time periods. According to Zhang and Yu (2020)'s method, I set up three more dummy variables at the time point 3-month, 6-month, and one-year before the actual policy announcement.

Then, I generate placebo *Hainan × time* term by timing them with policy treatment dummy variable. Rerun the difference-in-difference regression (Table 9).

Table 9 Placebo Test Result

Variables	(1) pre_yr	(2) pre_6mon	(3) pre_3mon
*Hainan × time_b*12	0.0523 (0.903)		
*b*12	0.0448*** (2.794)		
*Hainan × time_b*6		0.0660 (1.099)	
*b*6		−0.0108 (−0.694)	
*Hainan × time_b*3			0.0914 (1.477)
*b*3			−0.00932 (−0.590)
treat	−1.509*** (−4.079)	−1.623*** (−4.371)	−1.622*** (−4.379)
aveincmonth	6.57e−05*** (73.04)	6.65e−05*** (76.07)	6.65e−05*** (75.48)
ln*itradex*	0.0558*** (3.427)	0.0562*** (3.440)	0.0558*** (3.420)
ln*rex*	0.232*** (11.52)	0.237*** (11.74)	0.238*** (11.77)

续表

	(1)	(2)	(3)
Variables	pre_yr	pre_6mon	pre_3mon
urban	1.363***	1.658***	1.642***
	(4.632)	(5.655)	(5.613)
struc	-0.0292***	-0.0268***	-0.0269***
	(-11.36)	(-10.45)	(-10.58)
fin	0.0789***	0.0945***	0.0937***
	(3.786)	(4.536)	(4.521)
Constant	5.483***	4.980***	5.005***
	(15.25)	(13.82)	(14.06)
Observations	2,097	2,097	2,097
Number of province	31	31	31

Note: z-statistics in parentheses; *** $P < 0.01$, ** $P < 0.05$, * $P < 0.1$

Table 9 reports the estimations. It is shown that *Hainan* × *time_b*12, *Hainan* × *time_b*6, *Hainan* × *time_b*3 are not significant at 10% level. That is to say, in the DID model, the effect of Hainan economic growth is brought about by the Free Trade Zone. It is a robust conclusion.

5.5 PSM-DID model

The DID model requires high similarities before policy implementation. In addition to parallel trend, propensity score matching (PSM) model could eliminate the impacts of undetectable variables and show more detailed quantitative results.

The match is done by STATA commands *psmatch*2, including all control variables of model 7 in table 7, which are average income per month, log form of international trade volume, log form of real estate investment, urbanization level, economic structural index, and financial openness index.

The matching method in PSM may vary the regression results. Therefore, I changed different matching method to test which matching method fits the most and the robustness of PSM-DID estimation. I include one-to-one neighborhood matching, one-to-four neighborhood matching, 0.03 caliper one-to-four matching, and kernel matching. If no significant matching differences appeared, PSM-DID regression should not be affected by matching different logarithms (Table 10).

Table 10 Matching Robust by Different Logarithms

Matching Logarithm	ATT	t-value	Matched	Unmatched
one-to-one, neighbor	7.761	5.00	72	2025
one-to-four, neighbor	7.761	6.19	72	2025
0.03 *caliper*	7.768	5.96	72	2025
kernel	7.761	5.95	72	2025

The above Table 10 concludes several matching methods. We can see no large deviation of ATT-value and matched sample number. In addition, t-values are large enough to satisfy 10% confidence level.

Then I test whether matching could reduce bias of one-to-four kernel method. Figure 4 and 5 show the standardized bias cross variables in percentage and propensity score between groups. We can observe an obvious reduction in sample bias from figure 4.

In below Figure 5, Treated group means samples from Hainan island and Untreated means other provinces'. On support means data is matched in common range and will be include in later difference-in-difference regression. Off support means data will be eliminated by from sample pool. We can see a large amount of samples are in blue and yellow, color of off support.

Therefore, I redo the stepwise regression under PSM-DID to determine most appropriate control variables. I use kernel matching method, which is embedded into PSM-DID command, *diff*, in STATA.

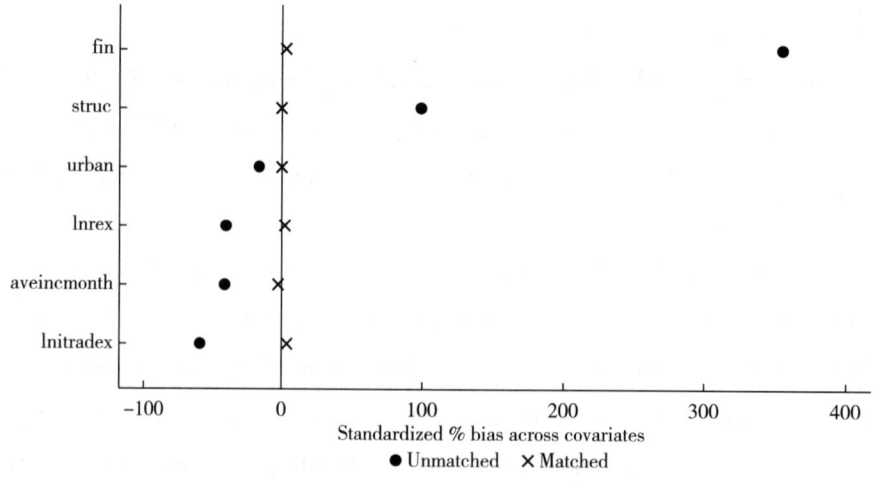

Figure 4 Standardized bias

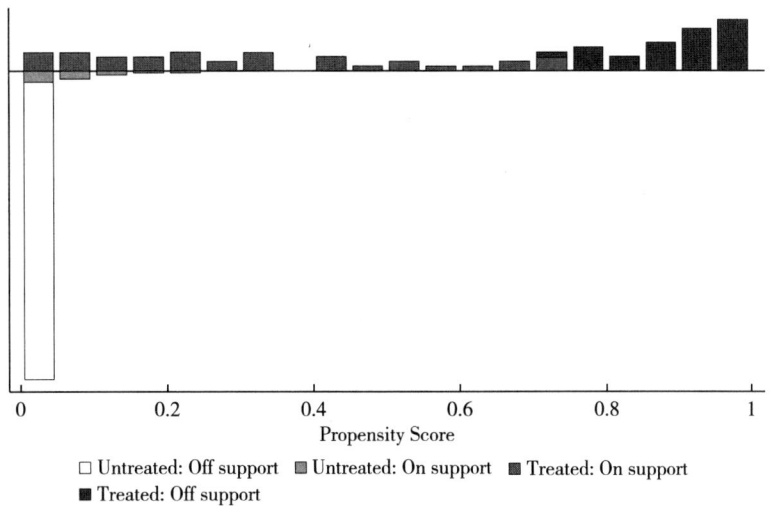

Figure 5 PSM Group Score

As adding more control variables, the propensity score matching will eliminate more samples, reduce observation number, and thus lower the accuracy of my estimation. Most PSM-DID estimation results show a positive effect of Hainan FTZ policy on local GDP growth (Table 11).

Table 11 PSM DID Regression Results

Variables	(1)	(2)	(3)	(4)	(5)	(6)
Hainan × treat	0.142	0.208*	0.103	0.261**	0.014	0.000***
	(1.13)	(1.62)	(0.74)	(1.97)	(0.11)	(942)
lnitradex	-0.154***	-0.152***	-0.162***	-0.567***	-0.628***	-2.076***
	(0.049)	(-2.72)	(-2.77)	(-4.13)	(-3.99)	(-5.48)
lnrex		-0.012	-0.038	0.727**	0.672**	1.532***
		(-1.32)	(-0.29)	(2.43)	(2.49)	(4.71)
urban			0.566	6.240***	7.738***	1.126***
			(0.53)	(3.61)	(4.31)	(4.81)
fin				0.729***	0.787***	1.886***
				(3.61)	(7.36)	(6.33)
aveincmonth					-1.224e-04***	1.795e-04***
					(-5.61)	(-3.84)
struc						0.430***
						(5.58)

续表

Variables	(1)	(2)	(3)	(4)	(5)	(6)
Constant	-1.176*	-1.126	-1.126	-14.973***	-14.118***	-46.58
	(-1.67)	(-1.32)	(-1.32)	(-5.42)	(-5.61)	(-6.56)
Observations	757	754	730	216	217	158
Treated	71	71	72	72	70	37
Control	686	683	658	144	147	121
R-squared	0.11	0.10	0.12	0.73	0.72	0.36

Note: z-statistics in parentheses; *** $P<0.01$, ** $P<0.05$, * $P<0.1$

Considering the number of observations and significance as table 11 states, the coefficient after matching is 26.1%, slightly higher than original DID estimation with the P-value of 5%. The result gives strong evidence supporting original model: FTZ policy have positive influences in Hainan case.

6 Conclusion and Avenues for Future Research

In my paper, I study the economic effect on Hainan of China's serial Free Trade Zone policy. Gathering and analyzing provincial monthly data between 2014 and 2019, I conduct the PSM-DID model to estimate the growth rate of local GDP in percentage caused by the policy. A relatively significant positive economic effect has been found. The FTZ policy boosts Hainan GDP growth by 11.7% at confidence level of 90%.

To ensure the effectiveness of my prediction, I introduced several methods for robustness check. My DID data passed parallel trend test. The fixed effect estimation is chosen from stepwise control variable regressions and hausman test. Then, I chose one quarter, half year, and one year prior to the policy shock to run placebo tests. No significant results were found. Placebo test passed.

Furthermore, I conduct kernel propensity score matching and run DID regression again. I test different matching logarithms and find out the matching results not much differs. The robustness of kernel match ensured. The PSM-DID result still shows a positive ecnomic affect at about 26.1% with a significance level of 95%.

Finally, I give the result that FTZ policy in Hainan province stimulates its economic development. I report an average 12.9% monthly GDP increase estimated by DID model and an average 21.6% increase estimated by PSM-DID model. These results are partially driven by data and model limitations. Further research is necessary to investigate the relationship between free trade policies and economic outcomes. The estimation is only roughly studied in the empirical model. It can be further improved as more reliable data can be collected in the future.

References

［1］崔兴华，林明裕．FDI 如何影响企业的绿色全要素生产率？——基于 Malmquist-Luenberger 指数和 PSM-DID 的实证分析［J］．经济管理，2019，41（03）：38 – 55.

［2］符大海，鲁成浩，秦伊伦．国内税收优惠促进企业出口了吗？——基于"准自然实验"的经验证据［J］．中央财经大学学报，2021（02）：3 – 17 + 54.

［3］刘瑞明，赵仁杰．西部大开发：增长驱动还是政策陷阱——基于 PSM-DID 方法的研究［J］．中国工业经济，2015（06）：32 – 43.

［4］聂飞．中国 – 东盟自贸区战略的贸易创造效应研究：基于合成控制法的实证分析［J］．财贸研究，2017，28（07）：36 – 47.

［5］宋丽颖，郭敏．自贸区政策对地方财力的影响研究：基于双重差分法和合成控制法的分析［J］．经济问题探索，2019（11）：14 – 24.

［6］王利辉，刘志红．上海自贸区对地区经济的影响效应研究：基于"反事实"思维视角［J］．国际贸易问题，2017（02）：3 – 15.

［7］项后军，何康．自贸区的影响与资本流动：以上海为例的自然实验研究［J］．国际贸易问题，2016（08）：3 – 15.

［8］杨经国，周灵灵，邹恒甫．我国经济特区设立的经济增长效应评估：基于合成控制法的分析［J］．经济学动态，2017（01）：41 – 51.

［9］张阿城，于业芹．自贸区与城市经济增长：资本、技术与市场化——基于 PSM – DID 的拟自然实验研究［J］．经济问题探索，2020（10）：110 – 123.

［10］张军，闫东升，冯宗宪等．自由贸易区的经济增长效应研究：基于双重差分空间自回归模型的动态分析［J］．经济经纬，2019，36（04）：71 – 77.

［11］张颖，逯宇铎．自贸区建设对区域经济增长及创新能力影响研究：以辽宁自贸区为例［J］．价格理论与实践，2019（03）：130 – 133.

［12］Allcott H. Site selection bias in program evaluation［J］. Quarterly Journal of Economics,2015,130（3）：1117-1165.

［13］Castilho M，Menéndez. Marta，Sztulman A. Poverty changes in Manaus：Legacy of a Brazilian FTZ［J］？ Review of Development Economics 2018,23（23）：102-130.

[14] Chauffour J, Maur J. Preferential trade agreement policies for development: A handbookm. World Bank Publications,2011.

[15] Jenkins G P,Kuo C Y. Taxing mobile capital in FTZs to the detriment of workers[J]. Development Discussion Papers,2013:88 - 96,412 - 413.

[16] Ravkumar S. The study of free trade zone policy in India:A make in India Initiative [J]. International Journal of Multidisciplinary Management Studies,2016,6(2):10 - 18.

[17] Schweinberger A G. Special economic zones indeveloping and/or transition economies:A policy proposal[J]. Review of Internaitona Economics,2003,11(4):619 - 629.

[18] Siroen J,Yücer A. Trade performance of FTZs[J]. Working Paper,2014.

[19] Siriwardana M. The Australia-United States free trade agreement: an economic evaluation[J]. North American Journal of Economics & Finance,2007,18(1):117 - 133.

[20] Wang J. The economic impact of special economic zones: Evidence from Chinese municipalities[J]. Journal of Development Economics,2013,10(1):133 - 147.

[21] ZHENG W, YANG Z, WANG X. Policy and politics behind Shanghai's Free Trade Zone Program[J]. Journal of Transport Geography,2014(34):1 - 6.

Explore the Influence Factors of International Competitiveness of Intellectual Property Trade
——Based on the Competitive Advantage Theory

王可欣[①]

Abstract: With the development of global trade and the general trend of economic globalization, intellectual property trade plays an increasingly significant role in international competition as an important part of service trade. This paper first selects relevant literature as a strong support. Then we analyze the development situation of international intellectual property trade and compared the international competitiveness of international intellectual property trade of countries. Also, this paper applies the theory of national competitive advantage for theoretical analysis and establishes a fixed-effect regression model with 20 years' data from 36 countries to conduct an empirical study based on the competitive advantage theory. The empirical results show that the total trademark applications, GDP per capita, foreign direct investment and international patent application acceptance all have a significant positive impact on intellectual property trade. Finally, the article puts forward some suggestions to improve the international competitiveness of intellectual property trade, including strengthening scientific and technological research and development, enhance protection, attracting foreign investment and creating a good environment.

Keywords: intellectual property trade; international competitiveness; competitive advantage theory

1 Introduction

The intellectual property trade first developed from the developed countries in Europe and

---

① 王可欣,对外经济贸易大学国际经济贸易学院西方经济学 2021 级硕士研究生。

America. As early as the birth of Berne Convention in 1886, the trade of intellectual property began to appear gradually. After the Second World War, intellectual property trading activities developed on a large scale and reached a climax in the late 1970s. Uruguay Round of negotiations from 1986 to 1994 included intellectual properties as a subject of trade negotiations. In the last ten years, the world intellectual property trade has been fully developed, and now the intellectual property trade has risen to one of the three pillars that have the same status as trade of goods and services.

Intellectual property is the concentrated expression of human creativity and wisdom. It is an important resource of social production and economic development. With the development of global trade and the general trend of economic globalization, intellectual property trade plays an increasingly prominent role in international competition as an important part of service trade. It permeates into the trade of goods and services, reflecting the innovation ability of a country to some extent. And it is also the key to measure the international competitiveness of a country. Due to the advanced nature of science and technology and the dominant position in the international division of labor and the global industrial chain, developed countries have always been in a monopoly position in intellectual property trade. Although the developing countries started slowly and the share of intellectual property trade is small, they have always maintained a good momentum of development.

Intellectual property is the result created by people through intellectual work, which is essentially a kind of intangible wealth. According to the WTO's "Trade-Related Intellectual Property Agreement", the scope of intellectual property includes patents, trademarks, copyrights and so on.

Intellectual property trade can be divided into broad sense and narrow sense: From a broad perspective, it refers to the trade of intellectual property products, especially some high-tech products like computer software. From a narrow perspective, it is a trade behavior of selling or buying the right to use intellectual property including intellectual property license and intellectual property transfer, etc. This paper measures the volume of intellectual property trade using the charges for the use of intellectual property. It is from a narrow sense.

From 1961 to 1985, the change of international intellectual property trade was only 9.7 billion dollars. From 1985 to 2000, the average annual increased about 11 times of the increase in 1961 to 1985. From 2000 to 2019, the trade volume has increased by 311 billion dollars, with an average annual growth rate of 9.29%.

As intellectual property is indispensable in economic development, it is particularly important to improve the intellectual property trade and increase its international competitiveness. Therefore, it is of great theoretical and practical significance to analyze the influence factors of the international competitiveness of intellectual property trade. This paper selects relevant literature as a strong support, analyzes the development situation of international intellectual property trade and compared the international competitiveness of international intellectual property trade among countries. Also, this paper applies the theory of national competitive advantage for theoretical analysis and conducts an empirical study by establishing a multiple regression analysis model. Finally, some suggestions are put forward to enhance the international competitiveness of intellectual property.

2 Literature Review

Since the late 18th century, many major capitalist countries in the West have successively carried out the industrial revolutions. Technology and national economy have developed rapidly, the intellectual property trade has also gradually risen, and the demand for intellectual property protection is also increasing. After the end of World War II, issues in the field of intellectual property trade began to be gradually studied by scholars. This part will review the literature on international competitiveness of intellectual property trade. Comparatively speaking, domestic scholars have done more research on intellectual property trade. This paper will classify and review the different aspects involved in the literature.

2.1 Literature on Competitive Advantage of Intellectual Property

Cheng proposed to create and cultivate China's intellectual property or intellectual property-based competitive advantage. This viewpoint highlighted the importance of economic or competitive advantages with technology and brand as the core, which provided a theoretical basis for the development of intellectual property trade in China. Guo improved the "intellectual property advantage". They believed that the intellectual property advantage was embodied in four aspects: system advantage, rule advantage, intellectual property resource advantage and intellectual property operation advantage. Dai used the TC index to compare the competitive advantages of intellectual property trade and conducted a quantitative study on the development of intellectual property trade. He believed that the development degree of a country's intellectual property trade can reflect the country's independent innovation ability, so the rapid development of intellectual property trade is an indispensable condition for a strong country.

2.2 Literature on the Importance of Intellectual Property

Li pointed out the importance of intellectual property trade to the development of international trade. Increasing the development of intellectual property trade is very important to improve the trade environment. He also discussed ways to develop China's intellectual property trade. Ye believed that intellectual property trade not only promotes the world economy and trade. With the enhancement of the level of intellectual property protection, the intellectual property trade barriers have increased, which has also caused more frequent intellectual property disputes in international trade. Titus used panel data from 38 countries from 1992 to 2005 in order to study the impact of strengthening China's intellectual property protection on China's foreign direct investment (IFDI). The results found that the improvement of the level of intellectual property protection has a significant role in promoting inward direct investment, and that FDI from different regions has different performances. Pawel found that intellectual property-intensive products accounted for the share of exports and imports in most developed countries, and their share in emerging economies increased rapidly. Cui carried out a comparative analysis of the indicators related to the trade in intellectual property services between China and the United States, and proposed that under the background of current trade frictions, the cooperation between China and the United States in the field of intellectual property should be promoted and the development of intellectual property trade should be promoted in an all-round way.

2.3 Literature on Influence Factors of Intellectual Property Trade

Neil empirically found that intellectual property trade in developing countries and countries with high imitation ability has the strongest positive impact on imports. Akinori studied the impact of international migration and business networks on income from intellectual property trade. This paper uses Japan's bilateral trade flows data, and the results show that the income from intellectual property trade is positively affected by the number of immigrants while it is not influenced by FDI. Li comprehensively used a number of trade competitiveness indicators to compare the international competitiveness of intellectual property trade between China and Japan. Then it selected relevant indicators based on the competitive advantage theory, analyzed and studied the factors affecting the intellectual property trade between the two countries, and put forward countermeasures and suggestions such as strengthening the input of senior production factors.

2.4 Literature on the International Competitiveness of Intellectual Property Trade

Balassa proposed that the international competitiveness of a country's specific industries can be measured by explicit comparative advantage index. Wang analyzed China's intellectual property trade competitiveness from the international comparison of export market share, annual export growth rate and trade competitiveness index. Xu used the international market share and TC index to analyze and compare intellectual property trade competitiveness of China, South Korea and the United States. China's comprehensive competitiveness of intellectual property trade is very weak. She suggested strengthening the adjustment of the intellectual property trade's structure, continuing to increase investment in scientific research. Liu conducted a comparative study on the international competitiveness of China's intellectual property trade based on 20 major economies through multiple trade competitiveness indicators and found that the competitiveness of China's intellectual property service trade is extremely weak. However, it is a necessary stage. Whether it can develop later depends on whether it can improve its innovation ability.

3 Development Situation of Intellectual Property Trade

Under the trend of economic globalization, with the continuous development of science and technology, the focus of international trade is shifting from goods trade to service trade. As an important part of service trade, intellectual property trade is also developing rapidly. The global economy is transforming from industrial economy to knowledge economy, and intellectual property trade is becoming another important growth point of international trade and world economy. The intellectual property trade has the following characteristics in its development:

3.1 The Scale Continues to Expand

Since the third scientific and technological revolution in the middle of the 20th century, the tertiary industry has been developing and its proportion in the national economy has been rising. The invention of electronic computers has made the development of science and technology more and more important. People has paid more and more attention to the development of science and technology. At the end of the 20th century, the Internet and other emerging technologies developed rapidly. Thus, the knowledge-based economy emerged gradually, and intellectual property continued to develop and expand in scale. In the 21st century, intellectual property trade continues to develop rapidly, and the growth rate is also increasing. But the growth rate has slowed down until recent years (Figure 1).

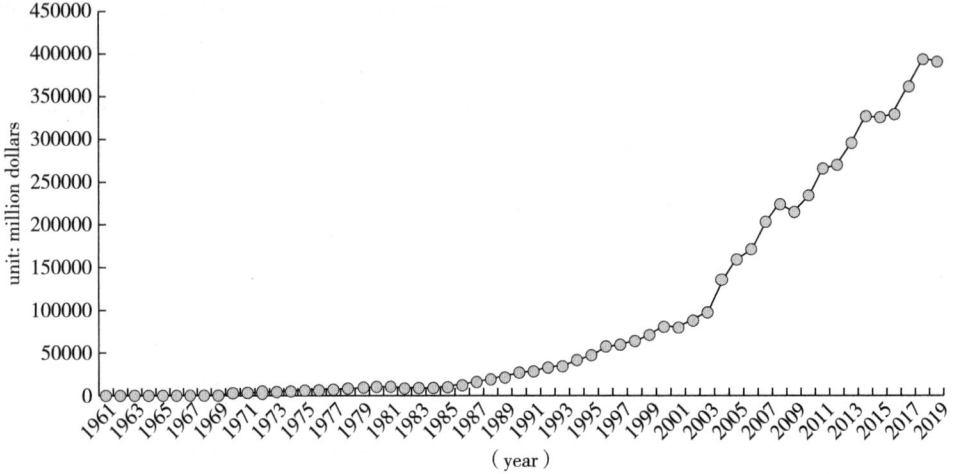

Figure 1　Exports of International Intellectual Property Trade from 1962 to 2019

Source: World Bank database.

As shown in the figure above, we can see:

The period from 1961 to 1985 was the embryonic stage of the development of international intellectual property trade. The intellectual property trade was developing at a slow speed. The change of international intellectual property trade was only 9.7 billion dollars, with an average annual increase of 404 million dollars.

The period from 1985 to 2000 was the growth stage of international intellectual property trade. The development speed of intellectual property trade was constantly accelerated. The trade volume increased by 70.78 billion dollars, with an average annual increase of 4.42 billion dollars, which was about 11 times of the average annual increase from 1961 to 1985.

From 2000 to 2019, the international intellectual property trade witnessed a rapid development stage. The growth rate of the trade volume reached a very high level. The trade volume has increased by 311 billion dollars, with an average annual increase of 15.55 billion dollars and an average annual growth rate of 9.29%.

3.2 The Development Trend is Similar to the Trend of Foreign Trade

In order to reflect the development of the world intellectual property trade more clearly, this paper makes statistics on the relevant data of world trade in goods, service and intellectual property from 2000 to 2019. The results are shown in the Figure 2:

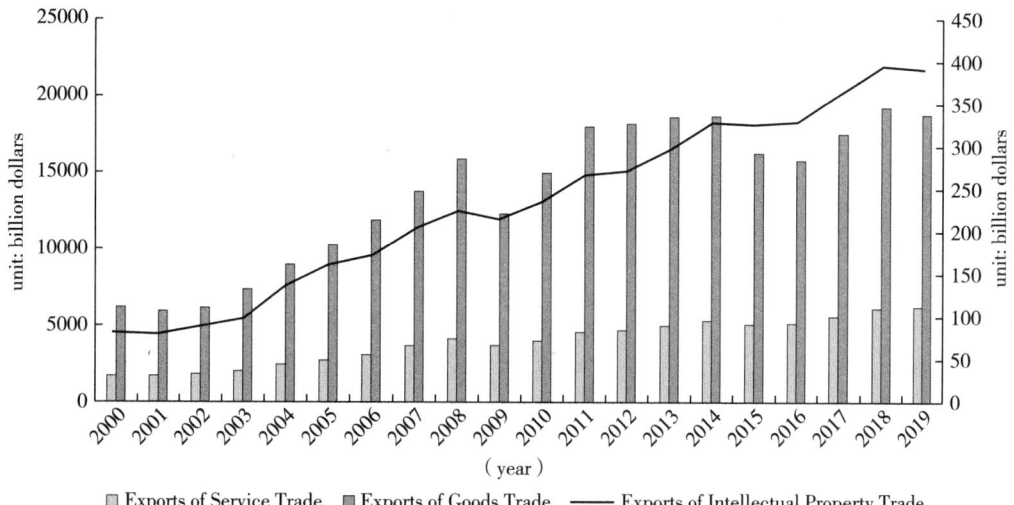

Figure 2　Development of World Trade in Services, Goods and Intellectual Property

Source: World Bank database.

Note: Exports of goods trade and exports of service trade is shown on the left vertical axis, and exports of intellectual property trade is shown on the right vertical axis.

Through the Figure 2, we can easily find that the development trend of international intellectual property trade is similar to the trend of foreign trade. From 2000 to 2007, trade in goods, services and intellectual property all showed an overall growth trend, especially the trend of trade in services and trade in intellectual property was more similar. Due to the impact of the global financial crisis in 2008, the trade volume of goods, services and intellectual property had been negatively affected to varying degrees. From 2009 to 2019, intellectual property trade has been rising steadily. In some years, the growth rate has slowed down although the trade volume did not decline.

From the similarity of the three development trends, we can see that the development of foreign trade can increase the demand for intellectual property, stimulate the creation of domestic intellectual property, and drive the development of intellectual property trade. At the same time, the development of intellectual property trade can improve the level of science and technology, and is more conducive to the development of trade in goods and services, so as to achieve the effect of mutual promotion.

3.3 The Regional Distribution is Unbalanced

For a long time since the end of World War II, the developed countries have been the main participants of international intellectual property trade by virtue of their advanced science and technology and relatively perfect intellectual property protection system. As shown in table 1, the world's top 15 countries of intellectual property trade in 2000 and 2009 were all developed countries. Until recent years, the intellectual property trade of developing countries has developed rapidly due to the strengthening of scientific and technological strength of developing countries and the gradual improvement of their ability to create, protect and apply intellectual property. Although the development speed of developed countries is not as fast as that of developing countries in recent years, they still occupy the main position and dominant position in intellectual property trade. Because they have a solid enough foundation and a leading position in science, technology and innovation. What's more, we can see from the chart that there is only one developing country-China, which ranks among the top 15 in the world intellectual property trade, ranking 12th.

Table 1 The Top 15 Exporters in Intellectual Property Trade and Corresponding Exports in 2000, 2009 and 2019

Year 2000			Year 2009			Year 2019		
Ranking	Country Name	Exports ($ million)	Ranking	Country Name	Exports ($ million)	Ranking	Country Name	Exports ($ million)
1	United States	43476	1	United States	85730	1	United States	117401
2	Japan	10227.4	2	Netherlands	26701.9	2	Japan	46853.1
3	United Kingdom	6748.82	3	Japan	21698.0	3	Netherlands	41842.1
4	France	3973.97	4	United Kingdom	13816.5	4	Germany	36170.6
5	Germany	2535.82	5	France	12671.4	5	United Kingdom	25257.1

continued

Year 2000			Year 2009			Year 2019		
Ranking	Country Name	Exports ($ million)	Ranking	Country Name	Exports ($ million)	Ranking	Country Name	Exports ($ million)
6	Canada	2323.90	6	Switzerland	12083.8	6	Switzerland	23906.3
7	Switzerland	2203.99	7	Germany	7212.87	7	France	15960.5
8	Netherlands	2170.47	8	Sweden	4599.53	8	Ireland	11868.2
9	Sweden	1414.42	9	Canada	3604.95	9	Singapore	8472.84
10	Italy	1317.49	10	Italy	3270.32	10	Sweden	8246.58
11	Finland	886.37	11	Korea	3255.40	11	Korea	7742.00
12	Korea	701.50	12	Denmark	2607.87	12	China	6604.71
13	Israel	496.10	13	Belgium	2557.96	13	Canada	5396.14
14	Australia	394.19	14	Finland	1734.93	14	Italy	4515.73
15	Norway	160.59	15	Hungary	1701.29	15	Belgium	3725.36

Source: World Bank database.

4 Comparison of International Competitiveness of Intellectual Property Trade

4.1 Compare by Export Volume

According to the ranking of intellectual property trade and export volume in table 1, we can compare the economic strength of various countries in terms of absolute amount. It can be clearly seen from the figure that the United States remains the first, while Japan, the United Kingdom and Sweden remain in the top 15. It indicates that these developed countries have a very strong international competitiveness in the intellectual property trade. The ranking of Netherlands is increasing, but the ranking of Canada is decreasing. While China and Ireland are at the forefront of development, countries such as Finland and Australia have been pushed out of the top 15. South Korea and Singapore which are two members of the "Asian Tigers" are also on the list. On the whole, the international competitiveness of intellectual property trade in developed countries is relatively high, especially in big knowledge countries such as the United States. The international competitiveness of intellectual property trade in developing countries is constantly improving. However, apart from China, no other developing countries rank in the forefront of the development of intellectual property trade at present. And there is still a big gap between developed countries and developing countries in international competitiveness in this respect.

4.2 Compare by International Market Share

International Market Share (IMS) refers to the proportion of a certain product's total export volume in a country or a region in the similar product's total international export volume, namely the share of such product in the international market of the country or the region.

The calculation formula of international market share is as follows:

$$IMS_{ci} = X_{ci} / X_{ci}$$

Where IMS_{ci} is the international market share of product i in country c; X_{ci} is the export volume of product i in country c; X_{ci} is the total export volume of product i in the world.

The larger the IMS_{ci} is, the higher the international market share of such products in country c is and the stronger the international competitiveness is. On the contrary, the smaller the IMS_{ci} is, the lower the international market share of such products in country c is, and the weaker the international competitiveness is.

In this paper, we can compare the international competitiveness of intellectual property trade by comparing the international market share of intellectual property trade. The Table 2 shows the international market share of the world's leading intellectual property exporters from 2010 to 2019:

Table 2　The International Market Share of the World's Leading Intellectual Property Exporters from 2010 to 2019 (%)

Country	2010	2011	2012	2013	2014	2015	2016	2017	2018	2019
United States	40.55	40.28	39.97	38.51	35.63	34.14	34.34	32.69	30.21	30.06
Canada	1.20	1.26	1.46	1.55	1.46	1.26	1.37	1.35	1.40	1.38
Switzerland	5.70	5.93	6.58	6.46	5.72	5.35	6.70	6.37	6.57	6.12
Germany	3.53	4.04	3.81	6.10	7.19	7.40	8.73	8.61	9.23	9.26
France	5.82	5.77	4.72	4.46	4.45	4.68	4.71	4.66	4.50	4.09
United Kingdom	6.06	5.58	4.98	5.98	6.08	6.36	5.83	6.32	6.67	6.47
Japan	11.39	10.91	11.82	10.69	11.43	11.21	11.90	11.54	11.58	12.00

continued

Country	2010	2011	2012	2013	2014	2015	2016	2017	2018	2019
Korea	1.36	1.66	1.45	1.47	1.70	2.01	2.11	2.02	1.97	1.98
Netherlands	10.66	10.42	10.61	10.11	11.68	11.52	8.10	9.00	9.77	10.71
Brazil	0.08	0.11	0.10	0.12	0.11	0.18	0.20	0.18	0.21	0.16
China	0.35	0.28	0.39	0.30	0.21	0.33	0.35	1.33	1.41	1.69
India	0.05	0.11	0.12	0.15	0.20	0.14	0.16	0.18	0.20	0.22
Russia	0.16	0.21	0.25	0.25	0.20	0.22	0.17	0.20	0.22	0.26

Source: World Bank database.

As can be seen from the table 2, the IMS index of the United States shows an overall downward trend from 2010 to 2019, but the international market share of intellectual property in the United States in 2019 still far higher than that of other countries. Japan's IMS index ranks second in the world and maintains a stable level all the time. Among the developed countries, Germany, Switzerland and the United Kingdom shows a rising trend, while France shows a decreasing trend. Among developing countries, Brazil, China, India and Russia all show an overall upward trend, but the IMS index is all lower than 2%. Among them, China has the fastest growth rate, increasing from 0.35% in 2010 to 1.69% in 2019, an increase of 3.83 times, which is the country with the fastest growth rate in the IMS index of developing countries. The international competitiveness of intellectual property trade is compared from the perspective of international market share.

Overall, from the perspective of the international market share of intellectual property trade, the international competitiveness of the developed countries is always in monopoly position in the field of intellectual property trade, and the international competitiveness of intellectual property trade is very strong; the international competitiveness of intellectual property trade in developing countries is weak, but it is developing with a good momentum and its international competitiveness has been constantly improving.

5 The Theoretical and Empirical Analysis

In the previous section, we analyzed the development situation of international intellectual property trade and compared the international competitiveness of international intellectual property trade among countries. This section will first carry out theoretical analysis, and then establish an empirical study on the influence factors of international competitiveness of intellectual property trade by establishing a multiple regression analysis model.

5.1 Theoretical Analysis

In 1817, the British classical economist David Ricardo put forward the comparative advantage theory. He pointed out that each country should produce and export products with "comparative advantage" and import products with "comparative disadvantage". In 1933, Swedish economists Ohlin and Heckscher proposed the factor endowment theory. The factor endowment theory believes that a country should export those commodities that need to intensively use the country's relatively abundant and cheap factors and import commodities that need to intensively use relatively scarce and expensive factors.

Based on comparative advantage theory and factor endowment theory, developed countries completed the three industrial revolutions earlier. They have accumulated abundant capital and technology and have significant comparative advantages in intellectual property trade. The developing countries have a short development time and a low starting point in intellectual property trade, so they do not have comparative advantages. As a result, developed countries are in a monopoly position in the global intellectual property export market while most developing countries can only rely on importing intellectual property-related products to meet the needs of their economic development. However, intellectual property is created by human beings rather than the natural endowment of a country. Therefore, developing countries can increase their comparative advantage by creating intellectual property through technological development.

In 1990, American professor Michael Porter put forward the national competitive advantage theory. Porter believed that the national competitive advantage is produced under the comprehensive effect of various factors within the economy. The national competitive advantage theory summarizes the factors that affect a country's competitive advantage into four domestic determinants and two external factors. The four domestic determinants include factors of production, demand conditions, related supporting industries, enterprise's strategic structure and competition. And the two external influence factors are opportunity and government respectively.

Based on the national competitive advantage theory, this paper will analyze the influence factors of international competitiveness of intellectual property trade from four domestic determinants and two external influence factors.

5.2 Variables and Data

Based on the theory of national competitive advantage and considering the degree of influence on the international competitiveness of intellectual property trade, this paper analyzes the factors affecting the international competitiveness of intellectual property trade from four domestic determinants and two external factors so as to determine the explanatory variables:

1. Factors of production. The accumulation of intellectual property such as trademarks, will affect the supply of intellectual property trade and may have an impact on its international competitiveness. In this paper, the total trademark applications is selected as a variable reflecting the factor conditions. Total trademark applications data comes from the WIPO database.

2. Demand conditions. A country's demand for the development of intellectual property trade depends on the quality of life of its people to a certain extent. In this paper, GDP per capita is selected as a variable reflecting demand conditions. The GDP per capita data comes from the World Bank.

3. Related supporting industries. In this paper, monetary freedom was selected as a variable reflecting this aspect. Monetary freedom combines a measure of inflation with an assessment of various activities that distort prices. The monetary freedom index comes from the American Think Tank Heritage Foundation.

4. Enterprise's strategic structure and competition. When enterprises adopt overseas expansion strategies and conduct foreign direct investment, the export of intellectual property of related industries will often be driven. In this paper, foreign direct investment is selected as a variable reflecting this aspect. The foreign direct investment data comes from the World Bank.

5. Opportunity and government. In international trade, countries have reached a consensus to strengthen the protection of intellectual property. Therefore, this paper chooses the number of international patent application acceptance to reflect the protection degree of intellectual property and takes it as a variable in terms of opportunities and governments. The data on the number of international patent application acceptance comes from the WIPO database.

As for the selection of explained variables, this paper selects the export volume of intellectual property trade as the embodiment of its trade competitiveness based on the previous literature review. The data is the charges for the use of intellectual property (receipts) provided by the World Bank.

This paper selects the exports of intellectual property trade (IPT) as the explained variable, the total trademark applications (TA), GDP per capita (PGDP), monetary freedom index (MF), foreign direct investment (FDI) and international patent application acceptance (PG) as the explanatory variables. Due to the availability and completeness of the data, this paper selects data from 36 countries from 2000 to 2019 for analysis. Among them, the unit of IPT is million dollars, the unit of PGDP is dollar, the unit of FDI is million dollars, and the unit of TA and PG is thousand. The variable information is shown in the following Table 3.

Table 3 Variable Information

Variable	Meaning	Data source	Unit
IPT	the exports of intellectual property trade	World Bank	million dollars
TA	the total trademark applications	WIPO	thousand
PGDP	GDP per capita	World Bank	dollar
MF	monetary freedom index	Heritage Foundation	[0,1]
FDI	foreign direct investment	World Bank	million dollars
PG	international patent application acceptance	WIPO	thousand

Next, we will use scatter charts to predict the relationship between influence factors and intellectual property trade.

As can be seen from the scatter diagram, total trademark applications, GDP per capita, foreign direct investment and international patent application acceptance are all expected to be positively correlated with the explained variables. But monetary freedom does not seem to have a high correlation with the variable being explained.

5.3 Empirical Analysis

This paper adopts panel data for multiple regression analysis. In this paper, we use the fixed-effect model to make regression. And the model is as follows:

$$IPT_{it} = \lambda_i + \gamma_t + \beta_1 TA_{it} + \beta_2 PGDP_{it} + \beta_3 MF_{it} + \beta_4 FDI_{it} + \beta_5 PG_{it} + u_{it}$$

Where IPT_{it} is exports of intellectual property trade in country i at time t; TA_{it} is total trademark applications in country i at time t; $PGDP_{it}$ is GDP per capita in country i at time t; MF_{it} is monetary freedom in country i at time t; FDI_{it} is foreign direct investment in country i at time t; PG_{it} is international patent acceptance in country i at time t.

First we do the Hausman's test. We assume that H0 represents the coefficients estimated

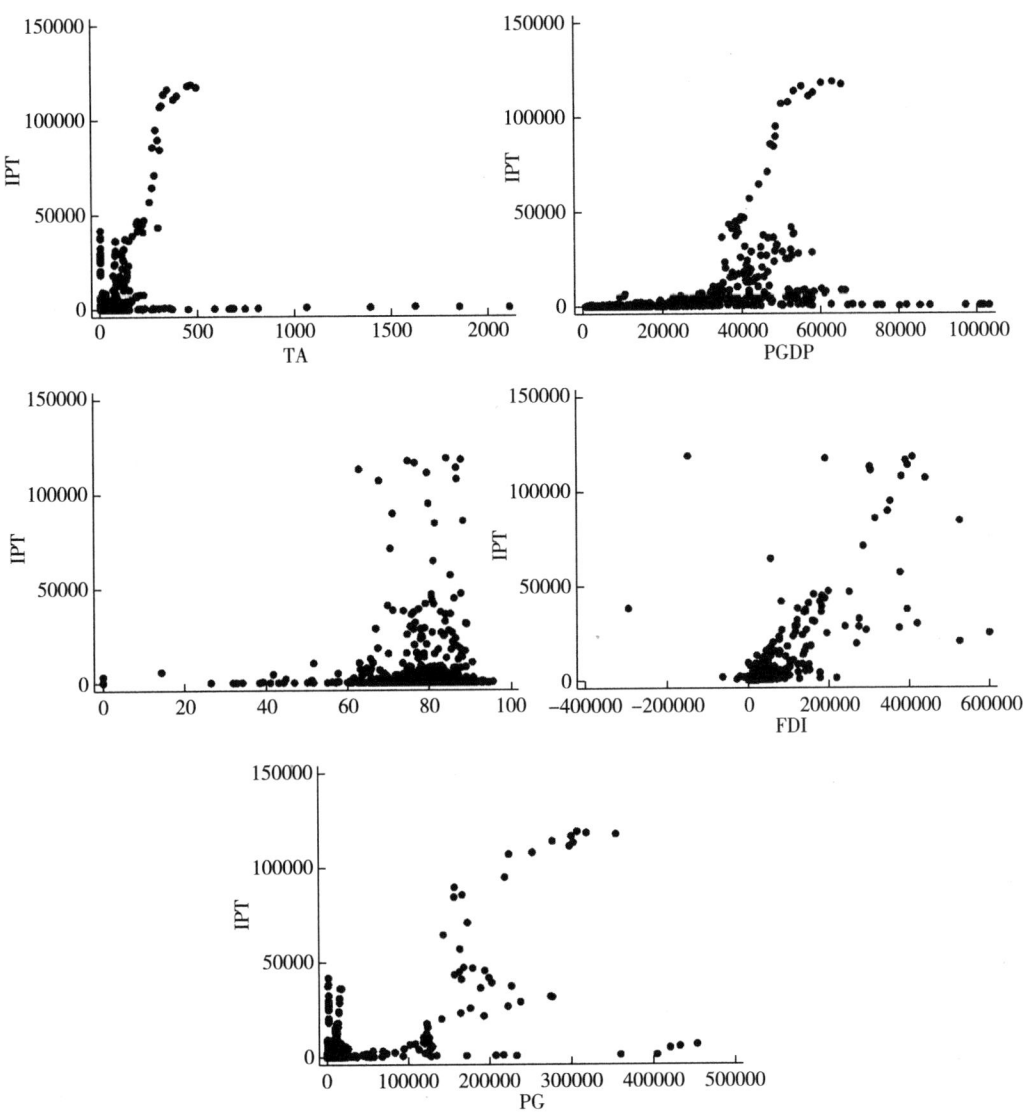

Figure 3 Scatter Plots between Explained Variable and Explanatory Variables

under fixed-effect model and random effects model are the same, and the coefficients estimated under random effects model are the most effective. And we assume that H1 represents the estimated coefficients of fixed-effect model are still consistent while the estimated coefficients of random-effect model are inconsistent. Then we conduct this test. The result is Prob > chi2 = 0.0000 which reject H0. And we can draw the conclusion that fixed-effect model is more suitable rather than random effects model. The following table 4 shows the results of the Hausman's test:

Table 4 Hausman (1978) Specification Test

	Coef.
Chi-square test value	36.611
P-value	0

Using 20 years' data from 36 countries, we perform the fixed-effect model's regression. The regression results are as follows (Table 5):

Table 5 Regression Results

	(1)	(2)
	IPT	IPT
TA	6.005***	5.9***
	(1.867)	(1.899)
PGDP	0.224***	0.181***
	(0.029)	(0.04)
MF	8.972	12.083
	(19.07)	(21.662)
FDI	0.019***	0.021***
	(0.004)	(0.005)
PG	0.06***	0.054***
	(0.007)	(0.007)
_cons	-2433.759	-2436.965
	(1495.075)	(1891.606)
Observations	720	720
R-squared	0.25	0.27
Standard errors are in parentheses		
*** $P<0.01$, ** $P<0.05$, * $P<0.1$		

The result (1) is the regression result using the individual fixed-effect model. The result (2) is the regression result using the bidirectional fixed-effect model. The regression results show that the bidirectional fixed model with time fixed effect and individual fixed effect is the most effective estimation method. Next, we analyze the variables after regression:

Total trademark applications (TA): In terms of its sign, the coefficient of TA is positive. It means that the increasing of total trademark applications can help the increasing of the exports of the intellectual property trade. The coefficient is 5.9 which means that the total trademark application increases by 1, the import volume will increase by 5.9. When it comes to the significance, TA is statistically significant at 1% significance level.

GDP per capita (PGDP): The coefficient of this variable turns out to be positive. It represents the influence of the GDP per capita on the exports of intellectual property trade is positive. Every increase in it will contribute to the increase of the export value by 18.1%. PGDP is statistically significant at 1% significance level.

Monetary freedom(MF) index: Although the empirical results show that the coefficient is positive, it is not statistically significant, which means that there is no significant relationship between the increase of monetary freedom and the improvement of international competitiveness of intellectual property trade. This may be because this variable cannot well represent the influence of related supporting industries on the international competitiveness of intellectual property trade. Therefore, we need to improve some things in the whole model. We are expected to re-choose one which can better represent the impact of the related supporting industries.

Foreign direct investment (FDI): The coefficient of this variable is positive, signifying that the foreign direct investment may accelerate the exports. When the foreign direct investment increases by 1, the import volume will increase by 2.1%. And this variable is statistically significant at 1% significance level.

International patent application acceptance (PG): The coefficient is positive, indicating that the international patent application acceptance encourages exports. That is what we expected. Every increase in PG will increase the export value by 5.4%. When it comes to the significance, PG is statistically significant at 1% significance level.

Next, we conduct empirical regression from the perspectives of developed countries and developing countries. The regression results are as follows(Table 6, Table 7):

Table 6 Regression Results of Developed Countries

IPT	Coef.	St. Err.	t-value	P-value	[95% Conf	Interval]	Sig
TA	147.761	20.94	7.06	0	106.552	188.97	***
PGDP	-0.092	0.056	-1.65	0.099	-0.202	0.017	*
MF	-16.159	31.917	-0.51	0.613	-78.97	46.652	
FDI	0.028	0.005	5.40	0	0.018	0.038	***

continued

IPT	Coef.	St. Err.	t-value	p-value	[95% Conf	Interval]	Sig
PG	0.107	0.02	5.32	0	0.068	0.147	***
Constant	−5489.75	3147.939	−1.74	0.082	−11684.673	705.173	*
Mean dependent var		10922.496		SD dependent var		22441.815	
R-squared		0.612		Number of obs		340.000	
F-test		19.656		Prob > F		0.000	

***$P<0.01$, **$P<0.05$, *$P<0.1$

Table 7 Regression Result of Developing Countries

IPT	Coef.	St. Err.	t-value	P-value	[95% Conf	Interval]	Sig
TA	−0.556	0.078	−7.13	0	−0.71	−0.403	***
PGDP	0.023	0.007	3.26	0.001	0.009	0.036	***
MF	0.466	1.328	0.35	0.726	−2.147	3.079	
FDI	−0.019	0.001	−13.70	0	−0.021	−0.016	***
PG	0.016	0.001	27.28	0	0.015	0.017	***
Constant	−80.884	116.18	−0.70	0.487	−309.414	147.646	
Mean dependent var		152.238		SD dependent var		534.632	
R-squared		0.809		Number of obs		380.000	
F-test		59.535		Prob > F		0.000	

***$P<0.01$, **$P<0.05$, *$P<0.1$

From the perspectives of developed countries and developing countries, the total trademark applications, GDP per capita, foreign direct investment and international patent application acceptance all have a positive impact on the international competitiveness of intellectual property trade. Among them, the positive impact of GDP per capita on developed countries is statistically significant at the 10% level. Others are statistically significant at the 1% level.

6 Conclusions and Suggestions

According to the regression results above, the total trademark applications, GDP per capita, foreign direct investment and international patent application acceptance all have a positive impact on the international competitiveness of intellectual property trade, especially the positive impact of the total trademark applications is most significant.

The increase of the total trademark applications represents that the country's innovators will pay more attention to trademarks in the international market, which is conducive to domestic intellectual property to participate in international competition and improve the possibility of intellectual property trade. GDP per capita can reflect the demand of consumers to some degree. The increase of per capita GDP will drive people's demand for intellectual property products, which is the driving force for the development of intellectual property trade. The relationship between foreign direct investment and intellectual property trade is complementary. Increasing FDI can boost trade in intellectual property. Meanwhile, the increase of intellectual property trade can also attract foreign investment. International patent application acceptance is the quantification of the degree of intellectual property protection. The improvement of the degree of intellectual property protection can encourage the export of intellectual property trade, thereby enhancing the international competitiveness of intellectual property trade.

The shortcoming of this paper lies in that there is not a significant correlation between monetary freedom index and the exports of intellectual property trade. Therefore, more appropriate variables should be selected to represent the influence of related supporting industries on the international competitiveness of intellectual property trade.

Next, we will put forward suggestions to improve the international competitiveness of intellectual property based on the above research conclusions:

1. Strengthen scientific and technological research and development. Most intellectual property rights are tied to technology and innovation. Strengthen scientific and technological research and development, increase investment in scientific research funds, increase scientific research results, and improve the quality of intellectual property rights, thereby enriching the supply of intellectual property trade.

2. Enhance protection. Increasing the protection of intellectual property is not only reflected in the importance of international patent application acceptance, but should also improve the legal system, regulate market order, and impose severe penalties on violations of intellectual property rights. People should also be encouraged to apply for patents and trademarks.

3. Attract foreign investment. Foreign direct investment is conducive to promoting intellectual property trade. While attracting foreign investment, the country should also actively invest abroad, seize the favorable development opportunities, conform to the trend of economic

globalization, and constantly improve the international competitiveness of intellectual property trade.

4. Create a good environment. In order to accelerate the development of intellectual property trade, corresponding measures should be taken in terms of monetary regulation and market intervention to promote intellectual property trade and create a favorable macroeconomic environment for the development of intellectual property trade.

Reference

［1］程恩富, 丁晓钦. 构建知识产权优势理论与战略：兼论比较优势和竞争优势理论［J］. 当代经济研究, 2003（09）：20-25+73.

［2］郭民生, 郭铮."知识产权优势"理论探析［J］. 知识产权, 2006（02）：16-23.

［3］代中强. 比较优势、竞争优势与我国知识产权贸易发展［J］. 现代经济探讨, 2007（02）：60-63.

［4］李浩. 我国知识产权贸易存在的问题及对策［A］. 中国《资本论》研究会. 第十二次资本论学术研讨会论文集［C］. 中国《资本论》研究会：中国《资本论》研究会, 2004：7.

［5］叶留娟, 赵有广. 国际知识产权贸易在世界经济发展中的作用［J］. 黑龙江对外经贸, 2008（04）：53-55.

［6］Awoke T O, Yin D. Intellectual property rights protection and the surge in FDI in China[J]. Journal of Comparative Economics, 2010, 38(2):217-224.

［7］Awoke T O, Yin D, Does stronger intellectual property rights protection induce more bilateral trade[J]? Evidence from China's Imports, World Development, 2010, 38(8).

［8］PAWELF, ANDZELIKAK. International trade in intellectual property-intensive goods [J]. Warsaw School of Economics, 2013 (8):1-14.

［9］崔艳新. 中美知识产权服务贸易发展战略研究［J］. 国际贸易, 2019（04）：68-77.

［10］Bela B. Trade liberalization and revealed comparative advantage [J]. Manchester School, 1965, 33:99-123.

［11］NEILF. Intellectual property rights and the margins of international trade[J]. The Journal of International Trade & Economic Development, 2014, 23(1):1-30.

［12］Akinori Tomohara. Migrant and business network effects on intellectual property trade:Evidence from Japan,Economic Analysis and Policy,2019,62:131-139.

［13］李显显. 中日知识产权贸易竞争力影响因素比较研究［J］. 特区经济，2019（08）：104-108.

［14］王小溪，白远. 从知识产权贸易竞争力的国际比较看我国的创新能力［J］. 商场现代化，2009（05）：5-8.

［15］徐娴丽，李雁玲. 我国知识产权贸易的国际竞争力分析［J］. 价格理论与实践，2011（05）：83-84.

［16］刘艳，王诏怡. 中国知识产权服务贸易的国际竞争力分析：基于20个主要经济体的比较［J］. 上海商学院学报，2015，16（03）：76-83.

An Empirical Study on the Impact of the "Belt and Road" Initiative on the Overseas Business Revenue of Chinese Enterprises

何 娟[①] 蒋灵多[②]

Abstract: The "Belt and Road" ("B & R") initiative provides a breakthrough for China's comprehensive deepening reform, it also opens a new window to develop overseas business for Chinese enterprises and promotes the increase of Chinese enterprises' overseas business revenue. From the perspective of quasi-natural experiments, and based on the panel data of A-share listed enterprises in China from 2011 to 2019, this study empirically examines the impact of the implementation of "B & R" initiative on the overseas business revenue of enterprises in China's provinces along the route by using difference in difference method. The regression results show that "B & R" initiative has significantly contributed to the increase of overseas business revenue of enterprises in China's provinces along the route, and the reliability of the conclusions has been proved by various robustness tests. From the analysis of the heterogeneity of enterprise property rights, the positive impact of "B & R" initiative on the increase of overseas business revenue of non-state-owned enterprises is more significant than that of state-owned enterprises; from the analysis of the heterogeneity of enterprise scale, "B & R" initiative has a significant impact on the increase of overseas business revenue of large enterprises, but the policy effect for small and medium-sized enterprises is not significant. Finally, after the analysis of the results, this study proposes corresponding policy enlightenments for the continuous promotion of the "B & R" construction to develop overseas business and increase overseas business revenue of Chinese enterprises.

Key words: the "Belt and Road" initiative; overseas business revenue; difference in

---

① 何娟,对外经济贸易大学国际经济贸易学院金融专业2021级研究生。
② 蒋灵多,对外经济贸易大学国际经济贸易学院讲师。

difference model

1 Introduction

From September to October 2013, Chinese President Xi Jinping successively proposed a cooperation on the "Silk Road Economic Belt" and the "21st-Century Maritime Silk Road". In March 2015, "B & R" initiative entered the formal implementation stage. As a highly valued cooperative initiative, "B & R" initiative has become more effective after more than six years of development. According to the Ministry of Commerce of China, in 2020, Chinese enterprises directly invested $17.79 billion in 58 countries along "B & R", year-on-year growth is 18.3%, accounting for 16.2% of the total in the same period. In addition, Chinese enterprises signed 5,611 foreign contracts in 61 countries along "B & R" and the value of newly signed contract is $141.46 billion, accounting for 55.4% of the newly signed contract value of my country's foreign contracting projects in the same period; and completed turnover of $91.12 billion, accounting for 58.4% of the total amount. With the continuous deepening of "B & R" construction, economic cooperation between China and countries along the route has also been further developed.

Under the trend of increasingly close economic links over the world and the active guidance of the opening-up policy of China, Chinese enterprises actively participate in international competition and cooperation, relying on the national macroeconomic policies' support to enhance international competitiveness in order to gain international market share. However, when Chinese enterprises are faced with the highly competitive international market, more complexity and uncertainty will affect the overseas business revenue of enterprises at different levels. "B & R" initiative proposed by China conforms to the globalization of the world economy and brings new opportunities and challenges for Chinese enterprises to develop overseas business, and whether this initiative will help Chinese enterprises increase their overseas business revenue and achieve high-quality development is an issue of great practical significance, which is worthy of discussion.

There are comprehensive qualitative research results on "B & R" initiative in academic circles. The subjects of quantitative studies are mostly China and countries along "B & R", and the data are mainly concentrated at the macro level, but quantitative research on the micro-enterprise level for "B & R" initiative is relatively lacking. This paper selects Chinese A-share listed enterprises from 2011—2019 as the research object, and adopts the DID method to explore the impact of "B & R" initiative on the overseas business revenue of Chinese listed enterprises. The possible innovations and marginal contributions are: First, the research on the role of "B & R" initiative in promoting the increase of Chinese enterprises' overseas business revenue has been enriched. At present, few studies have explored the relationship between "B & R" initiative and the overseas business revenue of Chinese enterprises, but this paper uses the quasi-natural experiment of "B & R" initiative to analyze the different impacts of "B & R" initiative on the overseas business of enterprises in different provinces in China, and to supplement the studies on the breakdown of the impact of "B & R" initiative in different provinces in China. Second, this paper examines the contribution of "B & R" initiative to the overseas business revenue of Chinese enterprises from the micro level. Enterprises are the main participants in "B & R" construction, but due to the limited availability of micro-level data, existing quantitative researches are mostly based on the national macro-level. Therefore, this paper collects and organizes the relevant data of listed enterprises to examine the positive effects of the "B & R" to make up for the shortage of micro-level studies. Third, this study adopts the DID method to assess the policy effects of "B & R" initiative on the overseas business revenue of Chinese enterprises, which overcomes the policy endogeneity problems that may exist in other empirical methods, and objectively and effectively assess the net effect of "B & R" initiative.

The content structure of the rest of this paper is as follows: Section 2 is the review of literatures; Section 3 is a theoretical rationale and research hypothesis; Section 4 is a difference in difference model construction with variables and data description; Section 5 is an empirical study of the impact of "B & R" initiative on Chinese enterprises' overseas business revenue and a robustness test; Section 6 is a heterogeneity analysis; and Section 7 is a conclusion and policy implications.

2 Related Literature

The current literature is rich in qualitative studies on the "B & R" initiative. First, the impact of "B & R" initiative on economic and trade relations of China. Yu (2020) points out that "B & R" initiative has facilitated the construction of bilateral and multilateral trade mechanisms between China and countries along "B & R" and promoted the restructuring of the global economic and trade pattern; while Yang (2020) analyzes that the overseas economic and trade cooperation zones (COCZ) under the "B & R" initiative in China have political, economic and cultural problems; Miao et al. (2020) discusses the problems of international financial cooperation under "B & R" construction of China, and proposes deepening economic cooperation and improving the investment and financing and credit system. Second, the influence of the "B & R" initiative on China's "go globally" strategy. Peng (2016) points out that "B & R" initiative provides a new opportunity for China's manufacturing industry to go globally and also puts forward new requirements, and then puts forward corresponding suggestions to improve supporting policies; Zheng et al. (2019) propose the new opportunities, challenges and risks faced by Chinese enterprises going globally under "B & R" initiative, and point out that measures should be taken at different levels, including the government, professional institutions, social organizations and enterprises themselves; Zhang et al. (2020) elaborate on the connotation and manifestation of high-quality development of "B & R", and on the basis analyzed the advantages of Chinese enterprises in participating in "B & R" infrastructure projects as well as the problems and challenges in talents, investment coordination and management experience, and proposes a new development path for Chinese enterprises to "go globally".

Quantitative studies on "B & R" are generally divided into macro-level studies on China and the countries along the "B & R", and micro-level investigations based on enterprise data. First, macro-level researches based on data from countries along "B & R" include the impact of outward foreign direct investment (OFDI), import and export trade, PPP projects and COCZ. There are many studies on the influence of China's foreign direct investment and export and import trade. Zhang (2020) uses a time-varying stochastic frontier model to investigate the efficiency of China's FDI in countries along "B & R" initiative and concludes that "energy saving and emission reduction" situation and political environment of the host country have significantly influenced China' direct investment efficiency and risk; Zeng et al. (2021) use an extended investment gravitational model and concluded that the business environment of the countries along "B & R" play an important role in promoting Chinese outward FDI, with an inverted U-shaped relationship; Wang et al. (2021) investigate the factors affecting the efficiency of China's agricultural exports to Asian countries along the "B & R" using the stochastic frontier gravity model, and the results show that institutional distance, tariffs and exchange rates have a hindering effect on export efficiency, while the signing of FTA agreements between the two trading parties and the fact that the country to which the trade is directed is a member of WTO or APEC has a catalytic effect on export efficiency; Wu et al. (2020) analyze the impact of trade facilitation on China's imports from "B & R" countries based on the trade gravity model, and the results indicate that trade facilitation has a catalytic influence on China's imports, while in the trade facilitation index, the customs environment and port efficiency have a more significant role in promoting China's imports. In addition, Shao (2021) studies the effects of psychological distance and risk sharing on the investment effect of PPP projects, and the results indicate that psychological distance has a hindering influence on the investment impact of PPP projects, and risk sharing is the mechanism of action between psychological distance and the investment effect of PPP projects; Li (2020) uses the progressive DID method to study the impact of the establishment of COCZ on the countries along "B & R", and the study shows that the economic benefits of COCZ are prominent in 5—12 years after their establishment, and the microscopic mechanism of action of overseas industrial parks and agricultural parks is slightly different.

Second, the current research at the micro-level of enterprises examines the effect of "B & R" initiative on different aspects of enterprise financing, investment, cross-border M&A, financialization, enterprise value and the internationalization. Li et al. (2020) uses the difference in difference method to find that "B & R" initiative has a important expansion impact on the financing scale of enterprises and can reduce financing cost and financing transaction cost of enterprises effectively; Zhao (2020) studies the effect of "B & R" initiative on the investment of listed enterprises in China's manufacturing industry and the results show that the investment of listed manufacturing enterprises in provinces along the route increased significantly more than other provinces after the implementation of "B & R" initiative, and "B & R" initiative has a more obvious promotion effect on listed manufacturing enterprises in China; Tong et al. (2020) use the PSM-DID method to study that "B & R" initiative has a significant inhibitory influence on the financialization level of supported enterprises, and the inhibitory effect on non-nationalized enterprises is stronger than that on nationalized enterprises, and the geographical differences have a more inhibitory influence on the financialization level of enterprises with a lower degree of marketization; Jung et al. (2020) finds that the cultural export of "B & R" initiative has a significant impact on the earnings of cross-border M&As based on 192 cross-border M&As from 2011—2015; Yang (2019) et al. find that "B & R" initiative has a positive influence on enterprise value, and has a significant effect on the enterprise value of private listed enterprises, but not on the enterprise value of overcapacity enterprises; Wang et al. (2018) study the impact of "B & R" initiative on the internationalization of Chinese manufacturing listed enterprises, and the results show that "B

& R" initiative significantly improves the internationalization of manufacturing enterprises, and the degree of improvement is higher for non-nationalized enterprises than nationalized enterprises, and corporate resources are the path to enhance the internationalization of enterprises.

Most studies on enterprises' overseas business revenue concentrate on the level of overseas subsidiary overseas operating revenue. Liu et al. (2016) study the effect of environmental risks on overseas subsidiary overseas business revenue and find that industry risks negatively affect subsidiary performance by reducing the level of the localization of investment and marketing in overseas subsidiaries, political risks have not influenced marketing localization and investment localization, but directly affect the subsidiary overseas business revenue; Makino et al. (1998) study the impact of local ownership restrictions by host governments on the choice of foreign entry model and its performance, and show that local ownership restrictions have a significant passive effect on the wholly owned subsidiaries' financial performance, but don't directly affect the financial performance of joint ventures; Han (2020) study the impact of home country risk prevention mechanism on the overseas business revenue of overseas subsidiaries, and the results show that the overseas business revenue of overseas subsidiaries is positively related to the establishment of a risk prevention mechanism in the home country, and the effect of this mechanism depends on the legitimacy of the enterprise in the host country; Wu et al. (2016) analyze the effect of inward and outward international diversification on enterprises' overseas business revenue, and the study shows that enterprises enhance overseas business revenue through inward country diversification, but inward regional diversification reduces overseas business revenue, and outward country and regional diversification weaken the effect of inward country diversification on overseas business revenue; Li et al. (2017) studies the impact of overseas parallel strategies on enterprises' overseas business revenue, and the results show that balanced overseas parallel strategies has a passive effect on enterprises' overseas business revenue, the degree of internationalization has a positive effect on this effect, and compound overseas parallel strategies has a positive effect on overseas business revenue of the enterprises, and the breadth of corporatization has a negative effect on this impact; Wang (2020) explores the impact of bilateral diplomatic relations on MNEs' overseas market performance and shows that bilateral diplomatic relations promote MNEs' overseas market performance by increasing MNEs' legitimacy in the host market.

In general, qualitative studies on "B & R" initiative are abundant, and quantitative studies are mostly focused on the macro-level of China and countries along "B & R", while micro-level studies of enterprises are mostly on the impact on enterprise financing, foreign investment and enterprise value. The research on overseas business revenue of enterprises is mostly focused on the overseas operating revenue of overseas subsidiaries, but less research has been conducted on the effect of "B & R" initiative on the overseas business revenue of Chinese enterprises in difference provinces. This paper takes Chinese listed enterprises as the main study subjects and provides micro experiences to prove the positive impact of "B & R" initiative on the overseas business revenue of enterprises in China's provinces along the route, in order to enrich the research on the "B & R" construction and the overseas business revenue of Chinese enterprises.

3 Research Hypothesis

The current global situation is complex and changeable, the deep-rooted influence of the economic crisis continues to emerge, the global economy is still in a volatile state. And the economic development of China has entered a new state, the beginning of structural deceleration, from high-speed development to high-quality development stage (Liu et al., 2020). However, the imbalance in regional development, industrial structure is unreasonable, and some enterprises have problems with the product structure, excess capacity is difficult to resolve and other issues have restricted economy's further development of China. In such a domestic and international economic situation, China propose "B & R" initiative to promote opening up to the world, and deepen economic and trade exchanges between China and countries along "B & R", promote common development, reach common prosperity, and reach mutual benefit and win-win.

Firstly, "B & R" initiative is a regional cooperation initiative with openness and inclusive that aims to promote macro policy coordination between China and countries along "B & R", develop a good trade dispute settlement mechanism, reduce trade frictions, and promote the economic factors to flow orderly and free, efficient allocation of resources and deep market cooperation (Shen, 2019). Therefore, "B & R" initiative can reduce trade frictions between Chinese enterprises and countries along "B & R", reduce costs and expenses of export trade and overseas business for enterprises, open up international markets and new sales channels for enterprises, expand the scale of Chinese enterprises' overseas business, increase foreign trade, and promote the increase of enterprises' overseas business revenue.

Secondly, "B & R" initiative provides a huge market for enterprises with excess capacity to directly export excess products, transfer domestic production capacity, resolve excess capacity (Yang et al., 2019). In addition, entering the international market means more fierce competition, thus forcing enterprises to transform and upgrade, improve innovation and R&D, enhance enterprise value and core competitiveness, thus meeting market demand and opening up international markets. Therefore, "B & R" initiative has a positive impact on the increase of overseas business revenue of Chinese enterprises.

Finally, on the one hand, the central government will give policy preference to the provinces along the "B & R", on the other hand, as an essential national policy, the "B & R" initiative is bound to receive positive responses from local governments and all sectors of society. In particular, local governments will develop lots of supporting measures to boost the implementation of national policies, and enterprises will directly benefit from the series of measures. For example, subsidies, special support, tax incentives and other measures from local governments in provinces along the "B & R" will play a positive role in supporting enterprises (Li et al., 2020), providing them with financial support, reducing corporate taxes and fees, thereby helping them to expand their overseas business and promoting enterprises' overseas business revenue in China's provinces along the route. Based on the analysis above, this study puts forward the following hypotheses:

H1: The "B & R" initiative has a catalytic impact on the overseas business revenue of enterprises in China's provinces along the route.

The nature property rights and size of Chinese enterprises may have different effects on the increase of their overseas business revenue. First, China is a public ownership-based economy with multiple ownership systems, and the different ownership systems of enterprises may cause differences in the effect of "B & R" initiative on Chinese enterprises' overseas business revenue between state-owned enterprises (SOEs) and non-state-owned enterprises (non-SOEs) (Du et al., 2017). In general, non-SOEs have inherent weaknesses, not only facing regional administrative barriers in their development, but also often suffering from stronger financing constraints, but SOEs have policy and resource advantages, thus crowding out the survival and development space of many non-SOEs. "B & R" initiative provides policy support and financing convenience for non-SOEs, and reduces the transaction risks with countries along "B & R", and lifts the constraints on non-SOEs that SOEs do not have, creating development opportunities for non-SOEs, and is more conducive to the increase of non-SOEs' overseas business revenue. In addition, it is easier for non-SOEs to fully unleash their development energy under

"B & R" initiative. Because SOEs are state-owned assets and are subject to strict domestic regulation and foreign scrutiny when conducting overseas business, in contrast, non-SOEs are more market-oriented, neither subject to strict domestic regulation in foreign investment and trade nor subject to foreign access restrictions due to the nationalized nature, and non-SOEs have higher flexibility and can more easily conduct trade transactions with countries along "B & R". Therefore, they can fully unleash their vitality under "B & R", which is more conducive to increasing their overseas business revenue (Yang et al., 2019).

Second, there are lots of differences in the effect of different enterprise sizes on the overseas business revenue. Large enterprises have special advantages in the process of overseas business, as they have strong financial backing and higher reputation, and have financing advantages. "B & R" initiative provides enterprises a window for Chinese enterprises to the outside world, which means more investment opportunities and larger markets. In participating in "B & R" construction, large enterprises can take advantage of their marketing expenses to focus on expanding overseas markets, and they can take advantage of the economies of scale to share their market expansion costs and reduce overseas marketing costs. In addition, large enterprises can also rely on their strong economic strength to increase investment in product development, they can produce more new products more rapidly, thus they have a stronger competitive advantage in the market. However, small and medium-sized enterprises have weak capital and face the dilemma of "difficult and expensive financing", and have limited ability to bear transaction risks when trading with countries along "B & R". Therefore, "B & R" initiative is more beneficial to the overseas business revenue of large enterprises than small and medium-sized enterprises. Thus this paper proposes following hypothesis:

H2: The "B & R" initiative has a more significant impact on the increase of overseas business revenue of non-state-owned enterprises than state-owned enterprises.

H3: The "B & R" initiative has a more significant impact on the increase of overseas business revenue of large enterprises compared to small and medium-sized enterprises.

4 Data and Methodology

4.1 Data Sources and Variable Descriptions

This paper chooses the relevant annual data of A-share listed enterprises for a total of 9 years from 2011-2019, and makes the following exclusions from the initial data: (1) exclude the samples of ST and ＊ST listed enterprises with financial abnormalities;(2) exclude the samples of listed enterprises with significant absence of core data and control variables such as overseas business revenue, etc. After the above exclusions, this study obtains a total of 579 sample data of Chinese enterprises, and the data sample size is 5211. The sample data are obtained from WIND database and CSMAR database.

In this paper, the overseas business revenue① of enterprises is used as the explanatory variable, and the core explanatory variable is the policy effect cross term, whose coefficient represents the net policy effect, and the control variables are enterprise age, equity concentration, director and supervisor remuneration, enterprise size, total assets net profit margin, enterprise value, supervisory board size, and market power, etc. The meanings and calculation methods of relevant variables are shown in Table 1.

Table 1 Description of Relevant Variables and Their Meanings

Category	Variable Name	Variable Symbol	Variable Meaning
Explained variables	Corporate overseas business revenue	FInc	The overseas revenue obtained through exports and overseas business revenue obtained through the overseas branches or subsidiaries
Explanatory variables	The "Belt and Road" initiative policy dummy variable	$Treat_{j,t}$	Registered places are the 18 provinces included in the "B & R" initiative is assigned a value of 1, while registered places are other provinces is assigned a value of 0
	The "Belt and Road" initiative time dummy variable	$Post_{i,t}$	It is assigned a value of 1 in 2015 and beyond, and a value of 0 before 2015
Control variables	Enterprise age	Age	Number of years of business establishment
	Shareholding concentration	Herf10	The sum of the squared shareholdings of the top ten outstanding shares of the enterprise
	Shareholding checks and balances	Balance	The largest shareholder's shareholding ratio / Total shareholding ratio of the 2nd-5th largest shareholder

---

① The "overseas business revenue" included in this study only includes overseas business revenue obtained through exports and overseas business revenue obtained through the overseas branches or subsidiaries, and does not include investment revenue from foreign investment by enterprises. In addition, due to the availability of data, it is not possible to obtain the revenue of each company's business in each country, but only the overall overseas business revenue of the company, including exports.

continued

Category	Variable Name	Variable Symbol	Variable Meaning
Control variables	Two powers in one	Dual	If the chairman and general manager are one person, the value is 1, otherwise it is 0
	Remuneration of directors and supervisors	Salary	Total remuneration of directors, supervisors and senior management
	Enterprise size	Size	Total assets of the enterprise
	Net profit margin of total assets	ROA	Net income / Average balance of total assets
	Enterprise value	TobinQA	Market value A/Total assets
	Supervisory board size	SupBoard	Total number of supervisory board
	Market power	Market	Operating revenue/Operating cost
	Cash flow	CFlow	Net cash flow from operating activities
	Comprehensive tax rate	Tax	(Sales tax and surcharge + income tax expense)/Total operating income
	Fixed assets ratio	Fasset	Net fixed assets/total assets
	Cost of sales growth rate	SFee	(Selling expenses for the current year-Selling expenses for the same period of the previous year) / (Selling expenses for the same period of the previous year)
	Increase in cash and cash equivalents	Cash	Net increase in cash and cash equivalents of the enterprise for the period
	Impairment loss on assets	AssetLoss	Losses resulting from the provision for impairment of various assets of the enterprise
	Monetary funds	Currency	Total cash on hand, deposits in bank settlement accounts, foreign deposits, deposits in bank drafts, deposits in cashier's checks, deposits in credit cards, deposits in letter of credit deposits, etc. of the enterprise

4.2 Model Construction

In order to assess the net policy effects of "B & R" initiative objectively and effectively, this paper proposes to evaluate the impact of "B & R" initiative on the overseas business revenue of Chinese enterprises using the difference in difference method. First, this study chooses A-share listed enterprises from 2011 to 2019 as the study observation sample, while the "Vision and Actions for Promoting the Construction of the Silk Road Economic Belt and the 21st-Century Maritime Silk Road" includes 18 provinces along the "B & R", including Northwest 6 provinces which are Xinjiang, Shaanxi, Gansu, Ningxia, Qinghai, Inner Mongolia; Northeast 3 provinces which are Heilongjiang, Jilin, Liaoning; Southwest 3 provinces which are Chongqing, Guangxi, Yunnan, Tibet; coastal 5 provinces and cities which are Shanghai, Fujian, Guangdong, Zhejiang and Hainan. The "B & R" initiative identifies the above provinces based on the economic functions and roles of different regions, which have more location advantages than other provinces, and the "B & R" initiative has more obvious policy effects on the increase of overseas business revenue of enterprises in these 18 provinces along the route (Zhao, 2020). Therefore, in this paper, registered places are the above 18 provinces involved in the "B & R" initiative is used as the experimental group, while registered places are other provinces is used as the control group, which is also in line with the nature of a "quasi-natural experiment". The "B & R" initiative was proposed in 2013, and it was formally implemented in March 2015. Therefore, this paper establishes 2015 and beyond as the implementation period of "B & R" initiative, and before 2015 as the non-implementation period of "B & R" initiative. Based on this, the following difference in difference model is constructed in this paper:

$$Y_{ijt} = \beta_0 + \beta_1 Treat_j \times Post_t + \gamma X_{it} + \theta_i + \mu_t + \varepsilon_{ijt} \qquad (1)$$

Among them, Y_{ijt} is the explanatory variable, indicating the overseas business revenue of Chinese enterprises, $Treat_j$ is the dummy variable for the implementation policy of "B & R" initiative, registered places are the 18 provinces involved in the "B & R" initiative is assigned a value of 1 for the experimental group, while registered places are other provinces is assigned a value of 0 for the control group. $Post_t$ denotes a dummy variable for the implementation time of "B & R" initiative, with a value of 1 for 2015 and beyond and 0 for before 2015. $Treat_j \times Post_t$ is the policy effect cross term, and its coefficient β_1 represents the net policy effect. X_{it} denotes a series of control variables, μ_t denotes time fixed effects, θ_i denotes individual fixed effects, ε_{ijt} is a random disturbance term, and this paper also incorporates the standard error of clustering at the enterprise level. The subscripts i, j, t denote enterprise, province and year, respectively.

5 Empirical Analysis and Robustness Test

5.1 Parallel Trend Test

The premise of the policy assessment adopting the DID model is that the experimental and control groups share a common trend of change prior to the implementation of the policy, and so as to test the applicability of the DID model in the policy evaluation, this paper conducts a parallel trend test on the overseas business revenue of enterprises in the experimental and control groups, i. e., to test whether the overseas business revenues of the two samples have a common trend before the implementation of "B & R" initiative. If the difference in variation exists before the establishment of "B & R" initiative, the policy effect estimated by the model may be caused by the difference between the experimental and control groups, and the policy assessment results of the difference in difference method are not credible. In this paper, the regression method is used to conduct parallel trend tests, and the test model is constructed as follows:

$$Y_{ijt} = \alpha_0 + \beta Treat_j \times \sum_{t=2012}^{2019} Year_t + \gamma X_{it} + \theta_i + \mu_t + \varepsilon_{ijt} \qquad (2)$$

In model (2), $Treat_j$ is still a dummy variable for the implementation of "B & R" initiative, which is assigned as 1 for the experimental group and 0 for the control group, while $Year_t$ is a dummy variable for the year in model (2), which assumes that "B & R" initiative was implemented between 2011 and 2019. According to the result in column (3) of Table 2, the regression coefficients of $Treat \times Year2012$ to $Treat \times Year2014$ are insignificant while the regression coefficients of $Treat \times Year2015$ to $Treat \times Year2019$ are significant, therefore, the regression coefficients of the overseas business revenue of the experimental group and the control group do not vary with the year before the implementation of "B & R" initiative, and the growth trend of the overseas business revenue only differs after the implementation of "B & R" initiative in 2015. In addition, as shown in Figure 1, the regression coefficients of the policy effect interaction term fluctuate around 0 before 2014, while the regression coefficients are significantly positive in 2015 and after, indicating that the model passes the parallel trend test.

5.2 Standard Regression Results

This paper estimates the impact of the implementation of "B & R" initiative on the

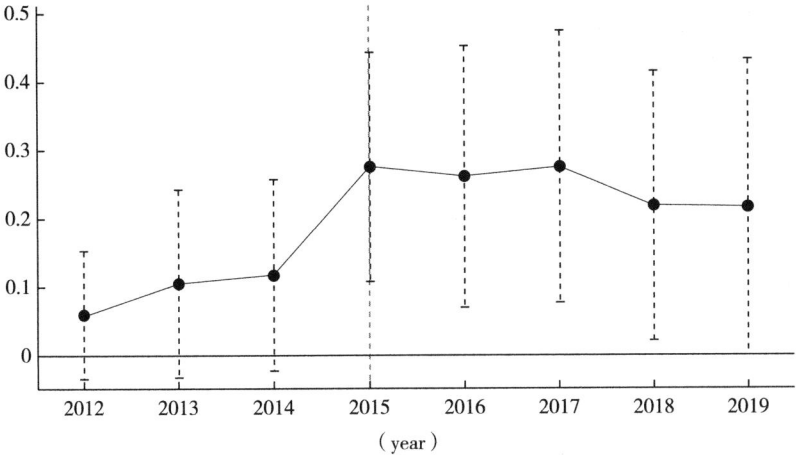

Figure 1　Parallel Trend Test

overseas business revenue of Chinese enterprises through the difference in difference method, firstly, this paper apply Stata15 software to perform the least squares regression on the standard model (1), and Table 2 shows the estimation results. The interaction term (*Treat* × *Post*) between "B & R" listed enterprises (*Treat*) and "B & R" initiative shock (*Post*) is added in column (1) to test the effect of "B & R" initiative on Chinese enterprises' overseas business revenue. The regression results show that the coefficients are significant at the confidence level of 1% and coefficient is positive, which indicates that the implementation of "B & R" initiative can positively promote the overseas business revenue of Chinese enterprises. In order to control the omitted variable bias, the regressions in column (2) include control variables such as enterprise age, equity checks and balances, and enterprise size, as well as fixed effects of individual and time, and the results indicate that the magnitude of the coefficient of the interaction term of the policy effect changes slightly, but is still significantly positive at the confidence level of 1%, which indicates that "B & R" initiative has a positive impact on the overseas business revenue of enterprises in China's provinces along the route. In addition, the coefficient is 0.179, which indicates that the implementation of "B & R" initiative increases the average overseas business revenue of the experimental group by 17.9 percentage points compared to the control group, while other conditions remain unchanged. Hypothesis 1 is verified. The main reason for the "B & R" initiative to increase the overseas business revenue of enterprises in China's provinces along the route is that, on the one hand, the central government will provide policy inclination to the 18 provinces along the route, on the other hand, local governments in the provinces along the route, in response to the national call, will also develop a series of supporting measures to promote the implementation of national policies, such as government subsidies, special support, and tax incentives for local enterprises, thus providing financial support to enterprises and reducing their costs, which will help them to develop overseas business and increase their overseas business revenue.

Table 2 Standard Regression Results of the Policy Effects of the "Belt and Road" Initiative

Variables	(1) lnFInc	(2) lnFInc	(3) lnFInc
Treat × Post	0.619*** (0.0539)	0.179*** (0.0690)	
Treat × Year 2012			0.0592 (0.0474)
Treat × Year 2013			0.105 (0.0696)
Treat × Year 2014			0.117 (0.0714)
Treat × Year 2015			0.276*** (0.0852)
Treat × Year 2016			0.261*** (0.0974)
Treat × Year 2017			0.276*** (0.101)
Treat × Year 2018			0.219** (0.100)
Treat × Year 2019			0.217** (0.110)
Controls	No	Yes	Yes
Time Fixed	No	Yes	Yes
Individual Fixed	No	Yes	Yes
Constant	1.155*** (0.0159)	−5.265*** (0.918)	0.790*** (0.0544)
Observations	5,211	5,196	637
R^2	0.087	0.305	0.079

Robust standard errors in parentheses *** $P<0.01$, ** $P<0.05$, * $P<0.1$

5.3 Robustness Tests

5.3.1 Counterfactual Test

This paper divides the research sample into an experimental group and a control group, and the control group is not influenced by "B & R", i.e., except for the listed enterprises registered in 18 provinces along the "B & R", other listed enterprises are not affected by "B & R" initiative. This paper constructs a counterfactual test to verify whether the control group is affected by the implementation of "B & R" initiative. This paper selects 40 listed enterprises with the highest number of times of 100 times random sampling, and assume that the implementation of "B & R" initiative also has an impact on the above 40 enterprises, and test whether the control group is affected by "B & R" initiative by determining the coefficient of the policy effect interaction term on the basis of equation (1). If the coefficient of the policy effect interaction term does not pass the significance test, then the control group is not affected by the implementation of "B & R" initiative. The result in column (1) of Table 3 indicates that the coefficient of the interaction term of "B & R" policy effects do not pass the significance test, indicating that DID method is used to assess the policy effects of the implementation of "B & R" initiative, which satisfies the hypothesis that the control group is not affected by the implementation of the initiative.

5.3.2 Exclusion of Extreme Values Test

In order to avoid the impact of the large differences between enterprises with strong overseas business development and those with insufficient overseas business development on the validity of the policy assessment, this paper adopts the method of excluding extreme values by removing 1% of the sample of enterprises at each end of the sample with the most and least overseas business revenues. The regression result is shown in column (2) of Table 3, where the interaction term of the policy impact on the overseas business revenue of Chinese enterprises is significantly positive at the confidence level of 5% with the coefficient of 0.168, indicating all else being equal, the implementation of "B & R" initiative increases the average overseas business revenue of the experimental group by 16.8 percentage points compared to the control group. The results show that the policy effect of "B & R" initiative still passes the significance test after excluding the influence of extreme disturbance values, and the regression results of the policy effect are robust.

5.3.3 One Period Lagged Test for Control Variables

The implementation of "B & R" initiative may not affect enterprises immediately, and they may not be able to respond immediately. Because of the continuous activities of enterprises and the need to plan ahead, the policy effects of "B & R" initiative have a certain time lag, so this paper uses a one-period lag for the control variables in the model to test the policy effects. The results in column (3) of Table 3 show that the policy effect interaction term of overseas business revenue is significantly positive at the 5% confidence level, and its sign and significance don't change substantially, which proves that the regression results of this paper are robust.

Table 3 Robustness Tests

Variables	(1) lnFInc	(2) lnFInc	(3) lnFInc
Treat × Post	0.0396 (0.0705)	0.168** (0.0690)	0.140** (0.0682)
Controls	Yes	Yes	Yes
Time Fixed	Yes	Yes	Yes
Individual Fixed	Yes	Yes	Yes
Constant	-5.265*** (0.929)	-5.273*** (0.919)	-5.099*** (0.985)
Observations	5,196	5,089	4,625
R^2	0.302	0.310	0.281

Robust standard errors in parentheses *** $P<0.01$, ** $P<0.05$, * $P<0.1$

6 Heterogeneity Analysis

6.1 Analysis of Enterprise Property Rights Heterogeneity

In China, enterprises with different nature of property rights vary greatly, and the implementation of "B & R" initiative will also have different effects on enterprises with different nature of property rights. In order to further investigate the impact of heterogeneity in property rights on the overseas business revenue of enterprises under "B & R" initiative, this paper examines the differences through group regression. On CSMAR database, the property rights of enterprises are divided into many types, such as private enterprises, SOEs, Sino-foreign joint ventures etc. In this paper, the property rights of sample enterprises are divided into SOEs and non-SOEs to test the effect of policy implementation of different types of enterprises, Table 4 shows the regression results. In Table 4, the coefficient of the interaction term of the policy effect of SOEs in column (1) is positive but it is not significant, indicating that the impact of the implementation of "B & R" initiative on the SOEs' overseas business revenue is not significant, but the coefficient of the interaction term of the policy effect of non-SOEs in column (2) is significantly positive at the confidence level of 5%, indicating that the implementation of "B & R" initiative significantly promoting the increase of overseas business revenue of non-SOEs. The coefficient is 0.19, indicating that because of the implementation of "B & R" initiative, the average increase of overseas business revenue of non-SOEs in the experimental group is 0.19 higher than that in the control group. Hypothesis 2 is verified. The reason why "B & R" initiative has a more significant impact on the increase of overseas business revenue of non-SOEs is that because of SOEs' nationalized nature, they are often subject to both strict domestic regulation and foreign scrutiny when engaging in overseas investment and trade with foreign enterprises, which has a negative effect on the overseas business of SOEs, but non-SOEs are easier to release their vitality under "B & R" initiative because of their market-oriented nature and flexibility. Therefore, "B & R" initiative provides development opportunities for non-SOEs and promotes their increase of overseas business revenue more significantly.

Table 4　Regression Results by Enterprise Ownership Grouping

	(1)	(2)
	State-owned Enterprises	Non-state-owned Enterprises
Variables	lnFInc	lnFInc
Treat × Post	0.0326	0.190**
	(0.109)	(0.0871)
Controls	Yes	Yes
Time Fixed	Yes	Yes
Individual Fixed	Yes	Yes
Constant	-4.671**	-4.690***
	(1.917)	(1.011)
Observations	1,845	3,351
R^2	0.234	0.376

Robust standard errors in parentheses　***$P<0.01$, **$P<0.05$, *$P<0.1$

6.2 Analysis of Enterprise Size Heterogeneity

The policy dividends that enterprises of different sizes receive in response to "B & R" initiative may also vary, so as to further investigate the effect of enterprise size heterogeneity on the overseas business revenue of enterprises in response to "B & R" initiative, in this paper, the sample enterprises are divided into large enterprises and small and medium-sized enterprises to test the effect of the initiative on the implementation of different sizes of enterprises, and Table 5 shows the regression results. The results indicate that the interaction term of the policy effect for large enterprises in column (1) is positive at the significance level of 5%, which indicates that the implementation of "B & R" initiative more significantly affect the overseas business revenue of large enterprises. The coefficient is 0.183, indicating that the average increase of overseas business revenue of large enterprises in the experimental group is 18.3% higher than that of the control group because of the implementation of "B & R" initiative. The coefficient of the interaction term of the policy effect for small and medium-sized enterprises in column (2) is not significant, indicating that the effect of the implementation of "B & R" initiative on the overseas business revenue of small and medium-sized enterprises is not significant. Hypothesis 3 is tested. The reason why "B & R" initiative more significantly influence the increase of overseas business revenue of large enterprises compared to small and medium-sized enterprises is that large enterprises have strong capital advantages and are more competitive in developing business in overseas markets, while the "B & R" construction projects are characterized by large investment scale and high risk factor, and large enterprises are able to bear higher risks, but small and medium-sized enterprises have limited ability to bear risks, which makes it difficult for them to fully obtain the policy dividends brought by the "B & R" initiative.

Table 5 Regression Results by Enterprise Size Grouping

	(1)	(2)
	Large Enterprises	Small and Medium-Sized Enterprises
Variables	lnFInc	lnFInc
Treat × Post	0.183** (0.0884)	0.135 (0.0890)
Controls	Yes	Yes

continued

	(1)	(2)
	Large Enterprises	Small and Medium-Sized Enterprises
Time Fixed	Yes	Yes
Individual Fixed	Yes	Yes
Constant	-4.849***	-1.880
	(1.111)	(1.348)
Observations	3,589	1,607
R^2	0.333	0.323

Robust standard errors in parentheses *** $P<0.01$, ** $P<0.05$, * $P<0.1$

7 Conclusion

The implementation of "B & R" initiative provides a broader market for Chinese enterprises to conduct overseas business, helps reduce trade frictions between Chinese enterprises and countries along "B & R", pushes enterprises to transform and upgrade, and promotes their competitiveness. This paper empirically examines the effect of the implementation of "B & R" initiative on the increase of overseas business revenue of enterprises in China's provinces along the route using the DID method and conducts the analysis of enterprise property rights heterogeneity and enterprise size heterogeneity based on the panel data of 579 listed enterprises in China from 2011 to 2019, the results of which show that, "B & R" initiative significantly influence the overseas business revenue of enterprises in China's provinces along the route, indicating that the policy effect of "B & R" initiative is significant, and the results are tested by parallel trend tests, counterfactual tests, tests excluding extreme values, and control variables lagged by one period. From the heterogeneity analysis, firstly, the heterogeneity test of enterprise property rights shows that compared with SOEs, "B & R" initiative has a significant contribution to the overseas business revenue of China's non-SOEs; while the heterogeneity analysis of enterprise size shows that compared with small and medium-sized enterprises, "B & R" initiative has a more significant positive impact on the overseas business revenue of large enterprises.

Based on research conclusions above, there are following policy implications:

First, the empirical research in this study proves that "B & R" initiative, as the top-level design of China, has already produced positive policy effects on Chinese micro enterprises and promoted the increase of the overseas business revenue of enterprises in China's provinces along the route, so the construction of "B & R" should be promoted more firmly and comprehensively, starting from these 18 provinces, giving full play to the comparative advantages of domestic regions, implementing a more proactive open strategy, strengthening the interaction and cooperation between East and West, and comprehensively upgrading the level of open economy. For one thing, the government should actively guide enterprises and improve relevant supporting measures. In addition, the government should enhance multi-faceted cooperation with countries along "B & R" to reduce trade frictions and effectively mitigate political risks, and enhance the confidence of domestic enterprises in conducting overseas business. For another, enterprises should actively respond to the call of national policies, effectively use the development opportunities of "B & R" initiative, and actively seek strategic opportunities to improve the increase of overseas business revenue under the condition that resources and market factors are satisfied.

Second, the government should take corresponding measures, such as relaxing regulation under permissible conditions to encourage state-owned enterprises to conduct overseas business so that they can better fulfill their public functions and social responsibilities; likewise, the key role of non-SOEs in building the pattern of openness to the world should not be ignored, and the state should give more attention to non-SOEs and provide more resources to solve the financing problems of non-SOEs, and can also encourage SOEs and non-SOEs to cooperate and develop together, integrate the advantages of enterprises with different property rights, jointly develop international markets and cultivate global competitiveness.

Third, as the construction of "B & R" continues to develop in depth, small and medium-sized enterprises are becoming more and more active factors in the implementation of "B & R". The government should pay more attention to the overseas business development of small and medium-sized enterprises, help solve the problem of "difficult and expensive financing" for them, stimulate their development vitality, encourage them to actively join in international competition and cooperation, as well as build a more influential Chinese enterprise brand by driving small and medium-sized enterprises to enter overseas markets together with large enterprises.

References

[1] Yu T. China-foreign economic and trade relations and the reconstruction of global

economic and trade pattern under the "Belt and Road" initiative[J]. Business and Economic Research,2021,3 149-151.

[2] Yang F. Operational risks and countermeasures of cross-border economic and trade cooperation zone based on the background of the "Belt and Road" initiative[J]. Business Economics Research 2021,3 144–148.

[3] Miao Q, Asmussen C. Discussion on "One Belt One Road" construction and international financial cooperation[J]. Proceedings of Business and Economic Studies, 2020,3(3) 61-64.

[4] Peng P. Policy suggestions on "Go globally" of manufacturing industry under the background of the"Belt and Road" Initiative[J]. Climbing,2016, 35(4) 46-50.

[5] Zheng X P, Lu W Z. The basic idea of speeding up the "Go globally" of enterprises under the "Belt and Road" Initiative[J]. Journal of Hebei University (philosophy and Social Sciences Edition),2019,44 (2) 87-93.

[6] Zhang X, Wang C, Li J, S et al. Strategic thinking on "Go globally" of Chinese enterprises under the background of the "Belt and Road" Initiative's high-quality development[J]. International Trade 2020,1 15 – 21.

[7] Zhang S. A study on the efficiency and risk of China's Direct Investment in the "Belt and Road Initiative" countries[J]. Research the World,2020,12 23 – 30.

[8] Zeng H, Qiao L L, Jia L N, et al. An empirical study on the impact of Business Environment on China's OFDI in countries along the "Belt and Road" Initiative—from the perspective of national differences[J]. Research on the World,2021,2 38 – 45.

[9] Wang R Y, Xiao H F. Institutional distance and China's Agricultural Export efficiency—based on an empirical study of Asian countries along the "Belt and Road" Initiative[J]. Journal of China Agricultural University 2021,26 (1):176 – 184.

[10] Wu D, Wu Y. The impact of Trade Facilitation on China's imports from the "Belt and Road Initiative" countries—an empirical analysis based on trade gravity model[J]. Industrial Technical Economy,39 (2):73-81.

[11] Shao Y H, Wang J M, Shao S Y. Psychological distance, risk sharing and PPP Project Investment effect—A study based on the "Belt and Road" Initiative's empirical data of 39 countries[J]. Soft science,2021 1 – 11.

[12] Li J Y, Li C Y. A study on the Economic benefits of overseas Economic and Trade Cooperation Zone to the countries along the "Belt and Road" Initiative[J]. Business Economics

Research,2020(2):147-151.

[13] Li J J,Li J C. The "Belt and Road" Initiative, Enhancement effect of Corporate Credit financing and Heterogeneity[J]. World economy,2020,43(2):3-24.

[14] Zhao K J. The impact of the "Belt and Road" initiative on the investment of listed enterprises in China's manufacturing industry[J]. Journal of Shanghai Jiao Tong University (philosophy and Social Sciences Edition),2020,28(4):47-56.

[15] Tong F F,Zhao X Y. The impact of the "Belt and Road" initiative on the financialization of enterprises—an empirical test based on PSM-DID[J]. Guizhou Social Science,2020(5):141-148.

[16] Jung J Y,Wang W,Cho S W. The role of confucius institutes and one belt,one road initiatives on the values of cross-Border M & A:empirical evidence from China[J]. Sustainability,2020,12(24):1-20.

[17] Yang B,Huang Z J,Wei J J. The "Belt and Road" initiative, corporate financial characteristics and corporate value[J]. Finance and Accounting Newsletter,2019(33):56-61.

[18] Wang W,Yang R. The impact of the "Belt and Road" initiative on the internationalization of Chinese manufacturing enterprises:an estimation based on the difference in difference model[J]. Business Economics,2018,37(11):70-77.

[19] Liu J,Yao Z J,Wang L. The "Belt and Road" initiative and the competitiveness of China's listed manufacturing enterprises[J]. Finance and Accounting Monthly,2020(16):153-160.

[20] Makino S,Beamish P W. Local ownership restrictions, entry mode choice, and FDI performance:Japanese overseas subsidiaries in Asia[J]. Asia Pacific Journal of Management,1998,15(2):119-136.

[21] Han X. Risk management, legitimacy, and the overseas subsidiary perfor-mance of emerging market MNEs[J]. International Business Review,2020:1-14.

[22] Wu B,Li W Y,Yan H F. A study on the multi-level impact of international diversification on enterprises' overseas business revenue-an integrated analysis of inward and outward internationalization[J]. Science and Technology Management 2016,37(7):3-14.

[23] Li Z J,Gao Q L,Qi M J. The impact of Chinese enterprises' overseas concurrent strategies on overseas business revenue[J]. China Economic Issues,2017(6):60-71.

[24] Wang T,Jia Y,Cui P P,et al. How diplomatic relations affect multinational enterprises' performance in overseas markets[J]. China Industrial Economics,2020(7):

80-97.

[25] Shen M H. "One Belt, One Road", trade costs and new international development cooperation-A perspective on constructing regional economic development conditions[J]. Foreign Affairs Review (Journal of Foreign Affairs Institute),2019,36(2):1-28.

[26] Du D Y, Tang X J, Li W. Has the "Belt and Road" strategy enhanced corporate value? —Empirical evidence from listed enterprises of the "Belt and Road" concept stocks[J]. Finance and Accounting Newsletter,2017(32):16-18+129.

[27] Zhou J, Liu Y J, Zeng X M. Can the "Belt and Road" initiative improve the profitability of OFDI enterprises[J]? Business Economics and Management,2020(2):69-83.

[28] Yu Z J, An J. Discussion on the integration of small and medium-sized enterprises into the "Belt and Road" construction relying on financial technology[J]. Foreign Economic and Trade Practice,2018(2):57-60.

[29] Liu X H, Gao L, Lu J Y, et al. Environmental risks, localization and the overseas subsidiary performance of MNEs from an emerging economy[J]. Journal of world business, 2016,51(3):356-368.

[30] Jiang G L, Jung J C, Makino S. Parent firm corporate social responsibility and overseas subsidiary performance: a signaling perspective[J]. Journal of World Business,2020, 55(6):1-13.

[31] Zhang H B, Li Y Z. Research on the impact of ODI entry model on multinational enterprises' overseas business performance[J]. Scientific Research Management,2020,41(9): 209-218.

探讨营商环境对出口增加值的影响

——以"一带一路"沿线国家为例

蒲海霞[①]

摘 要：随着经济全球化成为趋势及全球价值链体系学说趋于完善，本文开展营商环境对出口增加值的影响的研究。本文使用固定效应模型，以"一带一路"沿线35个国家为研究对象，时间跨度为2008—2017年，进行面板数据的实证分析。本文采用的数据来自世界银行公布的营商报告、世界发展指标数据库和全球价值链与中国贸易增加值核算数据库。结果显示：营商环境与出口增加值成显著正相关关系；在营商环境的细分指标中，执行合同、登记财产和保护少数投资者3项指标都与出口增加值负相关，获得电力及办理施工许可证对于出口增加值的促进作用比较显著，而包括开办企业、办理破产、获得信贷、纳税的国内指标比包含跨境贸易的国外指标对出口增加值的正面影响更大。本文可以为"一带一路"沿线各国政府实现经济转型升级、提升出口增加值提供新思路。

关键词：营商环境 出口增加值 "一带一路"

一、引言

自中国提出构建"一带一路"经济带后，世界的目光便无法从横跨亚欧非三大洲的这片地区移开视线。一方面，从历史角度看，"一带一路"地区山水相连，彼此之间的贸易往来已有数千年之久；另一方面，从经济角度看，"一带一路"地区有众多经济体，沿线各国的出口贸易占据世界总出口贸易额的很大一部分。对"一带一路"地区进行经济研究，既是顺应了经济全球化大趋势，也是对中国政府构建"一带一路"经济带的积极响应。

在经济全球化浪潮下，全球价值链体系中出口增加值成为更加值得注意的经济指标。

[①] 蒲海霞，对外经济贸易大学国际经济贸易学院国际经济与贸易专业2017级本科生。

相比出口量，出口增加值更能直观反映出国家或部门在全球价值链中的地位，帮助一国政府更清晰地认识到其在国际贸易中的真实获益。而营商环境与企业发展息息相关。人们逐渐意识到，经济发展除了依赖劳动力、资本等传统经济要素外，营商环境所涵盖的制度等要素也起着重要作用。世界银行响应各国的呼声，自2004年开始，逐年推出世界各国的《营商环境报告》。本文便在此背景下，开展营商环境与出口增加值的研究。

本文的研究意义：第一，过往文献对于出口增加值的研究主要集中于核算方法、影响因素等，而本文对营商环境和出口增加值的关系可以提供一定的理论支撑；第二，国家正在大力建设"一带一路"，将研究对象定为"一带一路"，有利于加深我国对于"一带一路"沿线各国的认识，促进彼此的贸易往来；第三，对于营商环境的细分指标如何影响出口增加值展开研究，可以帮助政府精准化制定相关政策，并为此提供实证分析和数据支持。

本文内容如下：第一，对现有文献进行梳理、评述；第二，设定计量模型，说明选取的变量和数据；第三，展示基准回归结果并针对性地进行分析，第四，对模型进行稳健性检验和内生性探讨；第五，针对营商环境的一级指标展开拓展分析；第六，提出本文结论和政策建议。

二、文献综述

（一）出口增加值

自出口增加值的概念出现后，出口增加值的核算方法一直在被探讨并逐步得到完善。郑丹青和于津平利用企业生产增加值与国家贸易增加值的关系，由微观指标推导宏观指标。随着时代发展，全球贸易主要构成变为中间品贸易。王直等突破了经典里昂惕夫方法的局限性，观察不同国家及部门从中间品贸易中获得的贸易增加值。Lianling, Y. 和 Cuihong, Y. 将中国的出口分为三类，即加工贸易、正常货物贸易和正常服务贸易，并基于中国的非竞争性投入产出表（包含加工贸易）计算出口增加值。

本文欲建立出口增加值与营商环境的计量模型，在这之前需要探讨出口增加值受何因素影响。一些学者从双边贸易角度进行了研究。例如，李文秀和姚洋洋针对中美双边贸易，发现要素比例与相对生产率对出口增加值的相关关系成立。江希和刘似臣也同样针对中美双边贸易展开研究，并区分了长短期效果。结果显示，长期来看，对出口增加值的影响从高到低为：垂直专业化程度、比较优势、规模经济。短期效果与长期正好相反。另外刘培青从多边贸易角度，以中国、印度、日本为例，得出结论：出口规模对出口增加值有举足轻重的地位，而产业关联、出口商品结构和出口目的地的效应都不显著，行业增加值率与出口增加值则呈现负相关关系。Olczyk 和 Kordalska 在对 7 个中东欧经济体研究时，结果表明劳动生产率、垂直专业化和就业结构（按照劳动力技能高低划分）都对出口增加值有显著影响。

另有一些研究从企业微观角度入手，研究企业出口增加值。郭晶和刘菲菲研究中国的企业出口增加值，将影响因素分为 3 个方面：①外部要素（FDI、出口倾向）；②内部要素（要素禀赋、行业结构）；③政府作用（政府补贴）。另外鉴于企业的主体特殊性，还在模型中加入了企业年龄、企业性质这些变量，与主体为国家的实证分析有不同之处。此研究还在要素禀赋中加入了研发、服务这些高端非传统要素。

在对现有文献进行梳理之后，我们可以发现：第一，对出口增加值的研究集中于核算方法、影响因素等方面，而对于其他方面的探讨还比较少；第二，出口增加值的核算方法在随着时代不断更新完善，不适应当今世界贸易形势的测算方法终究会被淘汰；第三，需要从多个维度考虑出口增加值的影响因素，如双边贸易与多边贸易、宏观（国家）与微观（企业）等。

（二）营商环境

世界银行自 2003 年起，每年都会发布《全球营商环境报告》，其指标体系围绕企业生命周期，包含开办企业、获得电力、办理破产等 10 个一级指标和诸多二级指标。但世界银行采取的评价指标不一定适用于各国。杨涛从中国实际出发，以鲁、苏、浙、粤四省为样本，将影响企业经营的营商环境分为 3 个方面：市场环境、政策政务环境和法律环境。另外，在海南省市场监管局的报告中提到，应参考经合组织服务贸易限制性指数，增加反映服务贸易规制环境的指标，以弥补世界银行营商环境评估体系对服务业的评价之欠缺。娄成武和张国勇认为应将市场主体满意度引入营商环境评估指标设计，以避免评估的自由主义取向。彭向刚和马冉构建了以政府质量为评价主体的指标体系，认为在经济表现之外，政府质量也不容忽视。

营商环境的重要性日渐被人们所认知，而它对众多经济要素的影响已有众多文献开展研究。为了促进私营部门的增长，许多国家实施了旨在使经商更容易、成本更低的改革。众多研究结果也表明，做生意的总体容易程度和成本确实与营商环境有关。而针对企业如何受到营商环境影响已有诸多文献开展研究。杨亚平和李腾腾在我国企业积极"走出去"的大背景下，研究对外投资选址时是如何受到当地营商环境影响的，并将企业按照资源、商贸、技术等投资偏好划分，通过实证分析各自对于营商环境的独特偏好。周泽将等根据企业所有制将企业划分为国有企业与非国有企业，并发现营商环境对非国有企业的信贷成本影响更加明显。许志端等的研究是关于技术创新、企业绩效受到的营商环境的影响,并重点关注了企业异质性,包括所有制和是否为制造业。

除此之外,一些文献是研究营商环境与宏观经济要素的联系。史长宽和梁会君从我国不同省份入手,研究营商环境与进口的联系,结果表明,地区差异巨大,中西部地区营商环境亟待改进。魏泊宁利用引力模型,研究了"一带一路"沿线国家的口岸营商环境与我国产品出口的关系,并分别研究了不同种类产品、不同收入水平国家、地理距离等详细情况。Nketiah 和 Sarpong 以撒哈拉以南非洲的 45 个国家为研究对象,构建了营商环境与外国直接投资的计量模型,并得到结论:营商环境对外国直接投资有重要影响。

综上所述,一方面,世界银行《营商环境报告》评估体系趋于成熟完善,公信力较高。但也存在不可忽视的缺陷,如对于各国适用度不同、忽视服务贸易、带有自由主义倾向、轻视政府质量等,也由此涌现出诸多学者构建出其他指标体系以改进完善。另一方面,营商环境对一些宏微观经济指标的影响已有研究。

相对于以往研究,本文的创新之处有以下几个方面。第一,本文研究了营商环境对于出口增加值的影响,为政府提升出口增加值提供新思路、新方法。第二,过往许多文献对出口增加值的测度方法基于里昂惕夫经典方程,但随着中间品贸易成为世界贸易主流,里昂惕夫方法已不适用于当今世界贸易态势。本文出口增加值的数据测算跳出里昂惕夫框架,更能够准确反映全球价值链上国际分工的重要特征。第三,已有众多文献研究了出口增加值的影响因素。在此基础之上,本文创新性地构建了营商环境与出口增加值之间的计量模型。

三、模型设定及变量、数据说明

(一) 模型设定

依照前文所述,在已有研究基础之上我们设定以下计量模型:

$$\ln VAXF_{it} = \alpha_0 + \alpha_1 \ln DB_{it} + \alpha_2 \ln VAXFS_{it} + \alpha_3 \ln EXPORT_{it} + \alpha_4 \ln FDI_{it} + \alpha_5 \ln GDP_{it} + v_{it} \tag{1}$$

其中,i 代表国家,t 代表年份,α_0 代表常数项,α_1、α_2、α_3、α_4、α_5 为待估参数。被解释变量为 $VAXF$,代表出口增加值。核心解释变量为 DB,代表总体营商环境。控制变量为出口增加值率($VAXFS$)、出口规模($EXPORT$)、外国直接投资(FDI)、国民生产总值(GDP)。v_{it} 为随机扰动项。

在世界银行的营商环境报告中,营商环境的细分指标有 10 个。我们在进行拓展分析时,将这些细分指标代替总体营商环境加入到回归模型中来,变形后的回归模型如下所示:

$$\begin{aligned}
\ln VAXF_{it} = {} & \alpha_0 + \alpha_1 \ln START_{it} + \alpha_2 \ln CONS_{it} + \alpha_3 \ln ELE_{it} + \alpha_4 \ln PROP_{it} + \\
& \alpha_5 \ln GRE_{it} + \alpha_6 \ln MIN_{it} + \alpha_7 \ln TAX_{it} + \alpha_8 \ln TRA_{it} + \\
& \alpha_9 \ln CONT_{it} + \alpha_{10} \ln INSOL_{it} + \alpha_{11} \ln VAXFS_{it} + \\
& \alpha_{12} \ln EXPORT_{it} + \alpha_{13} \ln FDI_{it} + \alpha_{14} \ln GDP_{it} + \upsilon_{it}
\end{aligned} \quad (2)$$

其中,START 代表开办企业,CONS 代表办理施工许可证,ELE 代表获得电力,PROP 代表登记财产,GRE 代表获得信贷,MIN 代表保护少数投资者,TAX 代表纳税,TRA 代表跨境贸易,CONT 代表执行合同,INSOL 代表办理破产。通过以上 10 个营商环境细分指标,我们可以从更详细的视角研究我们的主题。

(二) 变量、数据说明

1. 被解释变量:出口增加值(VAXF)

根据王直等对于全球价值链的研究,出口增加值共有 3 种衡量指标:基于产业部门前向关联计算的出口增加值(VAXF),基于产业部门后向关联计算的出口增加值(VAXB),一国到另一国出口中隐含的被外国吸收的国内贸易增加值(DVA)。而在多国家(≥3 国)的模型中,也就是适用于我们的"一带一路"沿线国家的模型中,3 种指标在计算总出口时是完全相同的。因此,我们选取 VAXF 作为出口增加值的代理变量。时间跨度为 2008—2017 年。

截至 2020 年,"一带一路"沿线国家共有 64 个,但受限于数据的可获得性,我们最后选取了 35 个国家[①]作为样本参与计量模型中。数据来自 UIBE GVC Indicators 数据库[②]。

2. 解释变量:营商环境(DB)

营商环境这一变量由营商环境便利度分数代表,而纳税等 10 个一级指标也由各自二级指标经过相应计算得到的分数来表示。分数区间为 0 ~ 100 分,分数越高,代表营商环境越好。数据来自世界银行《营商环境报告》(Doing Business)[③]。

3. 控制变量

(1) 出口增加值率(VAXFS)。根据 UIBE GVC Indicators 数据库中的 UIBE GVC index system,出口增加值率(VAXFS)等于出口增加值(VAXF)与国家/部门层面的增加值或 GDP(SVA)的比值,即 VAXFS = VAXF/SVA。数据来自 UIBE GVC

---

① 35 个国家包括:中东欧,波兰、立陶宛、爱沙尼亚、拉脱维亚、捷克、斯洛伐克、匈牙利、斯洛文尼亚、克罗地亚、罗马尼亚、保加利亚、希腊、俄罗斯;南亚和中西亚,哈萨克斯坦、吉尔吉斯斯坦、土耳其、塞浦路斯、印度、巴基斯坦、孟加拉、斯里兰卡、马尔代夫、尼泊尔、不丹;东亚、东南亚,蒙古国、中国、新加坡、马来西亚、印度尼西亚、泰国、老挝、柬埔寨、越南、文莱、菲律宾。
② 数据来源:http://rigvc.uibe.edu.cn/index.htm
③ 数据来源:http://www.doingbusiness.org/

Indicators 数据库。

（2）出口规模（EXPORT）。出口规模由货物和服务出口这一指标来表示。数据来自世界银行的世界发展指标数据库[①]（World Development Indicators，WDI）。

（3）外国直接投资（FDI）。外国直接投资由外国直接投资净流入这一指标来表示。数据来自世界银行的世界发展指标数据库。

（4）国民生产总值（GDP）。本文衡量的是以国家为个体的规模经济，而从国家层面来看，国民生产总值是比较合适的反映规模经济的代理变量。数据来自世界银行的世界发展指标数据库。

变量说明见表1。

表1 变量说明

变量类型	变量名称	变量符号	变量说明
被解释变量	出口增加值	$VAXF_{it}$	基于产业部门前向联系计算的出口增加值
解释变量	总体营商环境	DB_{it}	各国整体营商环境的得分情况
	开办企业	$START_{it}$	各国开办企业的得分情况
	办理施工许可证	$CONS_{it}$	各国办理施工许可证的得分情况
	获得电力	ELE_{it}	各国获得电力的得分情况
	登记财产	$PROP_{it}$	各国登记财产的得分情况
	获得信贷	GRE_{it}	各国获得信贷的得分情况
	保护少数投资者	MIN_{it}	各国保护少数投资者的得分情况
	纳税	TAX_{it}	各国纳税的得分情况
	跨境贸易	TRA_{it}	各国跨境贸易的得分情况
	执行合同	$CONT_{it}$	各国执行合同的得分情况
	办理破产	$INSOL_{it}$	各国办理破产的得分情况
控制变量	出口增加值率	$VAXFS_{it}$	出口增加值率 = 出口增加值/国家或部门层面的增加值或 GDP（SVA）
	出口规模	$EXPORT_{it}$	各国的货物和服务出口额
	外国直接投资	FDI_{it}	各国 FDI 净流入
	国民生产总值	GDP_{it}	各国的国民生产总值

[①] 数据来源：http://datatopics.worldbank.org/

（三）描述性统计

表2为本文各变量的描述性统计结果。如表所示，出口增加值的均值较低，说明"一带一路"沿线各国在全球价值链中总体获益较少。出口增加值的最小值与最大值存在较大差距，这可能是因为"一带一路"涉及亚非欧三大洲，地理区域广阔，涉及国家情况复杂，在全球价值链中所处地位不同。

表2 变量的描述性统计

变量	均值	标准差	最小值	最大值
VAXF	10.50	2.004	6.061	15.22
DB	4.174	0.146	3.711	4.485
VAXFS	−1.238	0.492	−3.170	−0.459
EXPORT	24.47	1.811	20.20	28.53
FDI	21.82	1.971	15.68	26.40
GDP	25.30	1.859	21.16	30.14

注：描述性统计已进行对数运算。

四、实证结果及分析

首先，我们经过 Hausman 检验和似然比检验，结果显示拒绝了混合效应和随机效应，因此我们采用固定效应模型。

（一）多重共线性检验

模型可能存在多重共线性，因此采用数据的方差膨胀因子（VIF）进行多重共线性检验。如表3所示，核心解释变量营商环境的 VIF 值为2.03，未超过10。此外，出口增加值率和外国直接投资的 VIF 值也都未超过10。VIF 的总体平均值为15.80，虽然超过10，但这是因为国民生产总值与出口规模的 VIF 值远超于10，分别为41.14、40.47。为了防止这两个变量导致模型有多重共线性，我们采取逐步回归法。

表3 各变量的 VIF 检验结果

变量	VIF	1/VIF
GDP	41.14	0.024308
EXPORT	40.47	0.024712

续表

变量	VIF	1/VIF
VAXF	3.99	0.250674
VAXFS	3.94	0.254094
FDI	3.27	0.305748
DB	2.03	0.492995
Mean VIF	15.80	

(二) 基准回归结果

本文使用 stata 13.0 对数据进行回归分析。模型（1）到模型（5）为个体固定效应。模型（1）只对核心解释变量营商环境进行回归，模型（2）至模型（5）逐渐加入更多控制变量并进行逐步回归。而模型（6）则对所有变量进行个体、时间双固定效应回归。所有模型都通过了 F 检验，说明模型较为显著。

如表 4 所示，所有模型中，核心解释变量营商环境的系数均为正数。另外，除模型（6）以外，其余所有模型中，核心解释变量营商环境的系数都在 10% 的水平下显著。这表明"一带一路"沿线国家的营商环境与出口增加值拥有显著正相关关系，一个国家的营商环境越好，出口增加值就会越高。这可能是因为：一个国家的营商环境优秀，一方面有利于本国企业发展，出口规模扩大，也会促进许多高附加值企业发展，最后导致出口增加值增加；另一方面，会吸引更多高附加值外资企业进入，进而扩大出口增加值。

观察各控制变量。出口增加值率在所有模型中的系数都在 5% 的水平下显著为正，表明"一带一路"沿线国家的出口增加值率与出口增加值拥有显著正相关关系。出口增加值率越高，出口增加值越高。从前文出口增加值率的计算公式也可以推测出两者的正相关关系。

出口规模在模型（3）和（4）中的系数为正，而在模型（5）和（6）中系数为负。这在一定程度上说明出口规模大的国家，并非一定有高额的出口增加值，反而有时是负相关关系。这可能是因为一些国家经济体量大，出口规模大，但位于全球价值链体系的低端，因而出口增加值少。

外国直接投资和国民生产总值的系数都在 5% 的水平上显著为正，表明两者都对出口增加值起到正向促进作用。外国直接投资流入能带动高附加值企业发展，国民生产总值高代表经济发展水平高，最终都会导致高出口增加值。

表 4　营商环境与出口增加值的基准回归结果

	（1） lnVAXF	（2） lnVAXF	（3） lnVAXF	（4） lnVAXF	（5） lnVAXF	（6） lnVAXF
DB	8.510*** (2.82)	7.217** (2.50)	6.672** (2.37)	5.214* (1.98)	6.290*** (3.02)	2.376 (0.86)
VAXFS		2.494*** (4.95)	2.327*** (3.79)	2.170*** (3.42)	2.195*** (3.75)	1.576** (2.42)
EXPORT			0.959 (1.53)	0.993 (1.48)	−0.534 (−0.61)	−0.295 (−0.42)
FDI				0.180*** (3.63)	0.154*** (3.59)	0.070** (2.18)
GDP					2.362** (2.59)	1.505** (2.36)
常数项	−25.157* (−2.00)	−16.794 (−1.38)	−38.046** (−2.30)	−36.875** (−2.14)	−62.948*** (−3.74)	−29.767** (−2.30)
国家固定效应	是	是	是	是	是	是
时间固定效应	否	否	否	否	否	是
R^2	0.075	0.302	0.319	0.318	0.344	0.558
N	35	35	35	35	35	35
F 检验	0.00789	3.42e−06	5.94e−10	3.43e−09	0	0
F	7.970	18.64	31.64	22.66	39.67	44.59

注：（ ）内为稳健标准误，***、**和*分别表示1%、5%和10%的显著性水平。

（三）稳健性检验

为了检验营商环境对于出口增加值的效应是否稳健，我们分别从"一带一路"沿线的不同地区来进行回归。我们将所选取样本中的35个国家划分为中东欧、南亚和中西亚、东亚和东南亚三类。实证结果如表5所示。3个模型的实证结果显示，核心解释变量营商环境的系数均为正，而中东欧地区的系数在1%的水平上显著，东亚和东南亚营商环境的系数在5%的水平上显著，说明即使在不同地区，营商环境与出口增加值仍呈正向相关关系。而观察各自系数，东亚和东南亚地区系数最高，为18.226，表示营商环境对于出口增加值的促进作用最强。中东欧次之。南亚和中西亚地区系数最低，为0.075，表示营商环境对于出口增加值的促进作用最弱。综上所述，本文结论有高度稳健性。

表5　分地区回归结果

	（7）	（8）	（9）
	中东欧	南亚、中西亚	东亚、东南亚
DB	9.750***	0.075	18.226**
	(5.19)	(0.03)	(2.86)
其他控制变量	已控制	已控制	已控制
常数项	-102.165***	-10.653	-53.137**
	(-5.44)	(-0.25)	(-2.71)
R^2	0.638	0.573	0.582
N	13	11	11
F检验	2.21e-06	2.03e-05	0.000734
F	29.97	25.87	11.31

注：（）内为稳健标准误，***、**和*分别表示1%、5%和10%的显著性水平。

（四）内生性问题的探讨

本文模型可能存在双向因果关系。一方面，营商环境及其他控制变量能够通过一定作用机制导致出口增加值的变化；另一方面，出口增加值变化也会导致营商环境变化。例如，一国出口增加值增加，说明该国在全球价值链体系中地位上升，经济发展水平提高，促进政府更加注重营商环境建设。除了双向因果关系，本文模型因受限于数据可获得性问题，只选取了"一带一路"沿线部分国家进行回归分析，因此可能还存在样本选择偏误。

以上问题都会导致模型存在内生性。为了解决内生性，借鉴崔鑫生的做法，本文采取了两种方式来应对。第一种方法如表6中模型（10）所示，将核心解释变量营商环境滞后一期进行回归；第二种方法如模型（11）所示，将滞后一期的营商环境作为工具变量进行回归。第一阶段回归的F统计量为2575.38，远大于10，故认为不存在弱工具变量。

表6　自变量滞后一期与工具变量回归结果

	（10）	（11）
	自变量滞后一期	工具变量
DB		0.722
		(-0.688)

续表

	(10)	(11)
	自变量滞后一期	工具变量
L. DB	7.818***	
	(3.62)	
其他控制变量	已控制	已控制
常数项	-91.925***	-15.26***
	(-4.73)	(-2.59)
N	35	35
R^2	0.306	0.75

注：( )内为稳健标准误，***、**和*分别表示1%、5%和10%的显著性水平。

五、进一步分析

采用张会清的分类方法，将营商环境的10个一级指标分为四类。第一类为要素市场（factor）：含义为企业能够获得的资金、劳动力等要素支持，包括获得信贷1项指标。第二类为税制环境（tax）：包括纳税1项指标。第三类为贸易便利（facility）：含义为企业面临的贸易环境，包括获得电力、执行合同、跨境贸易3项指标。第四类为政法环境（political）：含义为企业面临的政法制度环境，包括开办企业、办理施工许可证、登记财产、保护少数投资者、办理破产5项指标。以上四类指标分别对应模型（12）至模型（15），模型（16）则是对10个一级指标全部进行回归。

采用数据的方差膨胀因子（VIF）对以上模型进行多重共线性检验。如表7所示，营商环境的10个细分指标的VIF值均小于10，变量总体的VIF值为6.14，也小于10。因此，模型不存在多重共线性问题。

表7 营商环境细分指标的 VIF 检验结果

变量	VIF	1/VIF
EXPORT	30.54	0.032745
GDP	26.60	0.037587
CONT	5.08	0.196973
VAXFS	3.77	0.265512
PROP	3.07	0.325456
FDI	2.95	0.338997

续表

变量	VIF	1/VIF
GRE	2.06	0.485459
START	1.98	0.505116
INSOL	1.96	0.518500
ELE	1.85	0.541054
TAX	1.83	0.546922
TRA	1.53	0.654489
CONS	1.45	0.687486
MIN	1.34	0.747829
Mean VIF	6.14	

如表8所示，在进行四类指标的分类回归后，结果显示：政法环境类指标对于出口增加值的影响最显著，要素市场类指标对于出口增加值的影响最弱。除此之外，无论是四类指标分别回归，还是十个指标一起回归，执行合同、登记财产和保护少数投资者3项指标都与出口增加值负相关。这可能是因为从边境内制度和边境上制度两个维度来考量，上述3个指标倾向于国内的规则制度，有利于国内的经济变量，但对于进出口的影响并不明显。

在模型（16）中，获得电力和办理施工许可证系数较大且比较显著，说明这两个变量对于出口增加值的促进作用比较明显。其余变量中，除去执行合同、登记财产和保护少数投资者3项与出口增加值负相关的指标，其他变量虽都不显著，但系数大小不同也能说明一定问题。根据各变量政策效应的偏向，我们将其分为国内指标和国外指标。国内指标包括开办企业、办理破产、获得信贷和纳税，表8模型（16）显示，4项国内指标系数较大。国外指标包括跨境贸易，系数较小，仅为0.002。结果说明，国内指标比国外指标对出口增加值的正面影响更大。可能是因为国内指标发展优秀，代表着国内产业的逐步升级及在向全球家价值链更高端的迈进。

表8 营商环境细分指标与出口增加值的回归结果

	（12）	（13）	（14）	（15）	（16）
	要素市场	税制环境	贸易便利	政法环境	全部变量
ELE			2.281**		1.576*
			(2.54)		(1.92)

续表

	（12）	（13）	（14）	（15）	（16）
	要素市场	税制环境	贸易便利	政法环境	全部变量
CONT			-0.247		-1.362
			(-0.15)		(-0.79)
TRA			0.301		0.002
			(0.93)		(0.01)
GRE	0.378				0.606
	(0.80)				(1.09)
TAX		0.585			0.457
		(1.25)			(0.91)
START				2.569	2.347
				(1.53)	(1.36)
CONS				1.544*	1.715*
				(1.90)	(1.70)
PROP				-0.184	-0.504
				(-0.21)	(-0.66)
MIN				-0.449	-0.406
				(-0.92)	(-0.88)
INSOL				0.868	0.682
				(1.08)	(0.69)
其他控制变量	已控制	已控制	已控制	已控制	已控制
常数项	-35.922**	-35.510*	-46.280**	-49.056**	-51.066**
	(-2.24)	(-2.01)	(-2.23)	(-2.68)	(-2.57)
R^2	0.302	0.303	0.307	0.334	0.357
N	35	35	34	33	33

注：（）内为稳健标准误，***、**和*分别表示1%、5%和10%的显著性水平。

六、结论及政策建议

（一）结论

本文利用固定效应计量模型对各变量进行实证分析，得到以下结论：首先，核心解释变量营商环境与出口增加值成显著正相关关系。一个国家拥有良好的营商环境，能够促进出口增加值增长，而恶劣的营商环境会阻碍出口增加值的增长。其次，在控制变量中，对外直接投资、国民生产总值和出口增加值率也都是激励出口增加值增长的重要因素。最后，在营商环境的 10 个一级指标中，执行合同、登记财产和保护少数投资者 3 项指标都与出口增加值负相关，获得电力和办理施工许可证对于出口增加值的促进作用比较显著，而包括开办企业、办理破产、获得信贷和纳税的国内指标比包含跨境贸易的国外指标对出口增加值的正面影响更大。

（二）政策建议

通过前文的实证分析，我们可以得到以下政策启示。第一，沿线各国要想真正的从"一带一路"中获益，不仅要重视出口贸易量，还要看到出口增加值的重要性，粗放型经济虽然能够带来短期利益，但长期来看，还是要努力实现经济转型升级，获取价值链高端利益。第二，良好的营商环境有利于出口增加值增长。而要打造优秀营商环境，需要"一带一路"沿线各国政府承担起责任。针对获得电力和办理施工许可证这 2 项对于出口增加值促进作用比较显著的指标，政府应采取措施加以改善，如大力建设电力基础设施、提高行政审批效率等。第三，对中国来说，作为"一带一路"的发起者与倡导者，可利用亚洲基础设施投资银行等政府间机构，重点支持"一带一路"沿线各国的营商环境建设。

参考文献

［1］郑丹青，于津平. 中国出口贸易增加值的微观核算及影响因素研究［J］. 国际贸易问题，2014（08）：3-13.

［2］王直，魏尚进，祝坤福. 总贸易核算法：官方贸易统计与全球价值链的度量［J］. 中国社会科学，2015（09）：108-127+205-206.

［3］Lianling Y, Cuihong Y. Changes in domestic value added in China's exports: A structural decomposition analysis approach［J］. Journal of Economic Structures，2017；6（1），1-12.

［4］李文秀，姚洋洋. 要素比例、技术差异与出口增加值：基于中美两国双边贸易出口的实证研究［J］. 财贸经济，2015（06）：98-111.

［5］江希，刘似臣. 中国制造业出口增加值及影响因素的实证研究：以中美贸易为例［J］. 国际贸易问题，2014（11）：89-98.

［6］刘培青. 全球价值链中出口增加值的影响因素：以中、印、日为例［J］. 湖

南财政经济学院学报,2016,32(04):143-151.

[7] Olczyk M, Kordalska A. Gross exports versus value-added exports: Determin-ants and policy implications for manufacturing sectors in selected CEE countries [J]. Eastern Eur Econ, 2017, 55 (1): 91-109.

[8] 郭晶,刘菲菲. 中国出口国内增加值提升的影响因素研究 [J]. 世界经济研究,2016(06):43-54+135.

[9] 杨涛. 营商环境评价指标体系构建研究:基于鲁苏浙粤四省的比较分析 [J]. 商业经济研究,2015(13):28-31.

[10] 娄成武,张国勇. 基于市场主体主观感知的营商环境评估框架构建:兼评世界银行营商环境评估模式 [J]. 当代经济管理,2018,40(06):60-68.

[11] 彭向刚,马冉. 政务营商环境优化及其评价指标体系构建 [J]. 学术研究,2018(11):55-61.

[12] Canare T, Francisco J P, Morales J F. Long- and short-run relationship between firm creation and the ease and cost of doing business [J]. Int J Econ Bus, 2019, 26 (2): 249-275.

[13] 杨亚平,李腾腾. 东道国营商环境如何影响中国企业对外直接投资选址 [J]. 产经评论,2018,9(03):129-147.

[14] 周泽将,高雅萍,张世国. 营商环境影响企业信贷成本吗 [J]. 财贸经济,2020,41(12):117-131.

[15] 许志端,阮舟一龙. 营商环境、技术创新和企业绩效:基于我国省级层面的经验证据 [J]. 厦门大学学报(哲学社会科学版),2019(05):123-134.

[16] 史长宽,梁会君. 营商环境省际差异与扩大进口:基于30个省级横截面数据的经验研究 [J]. 山西财经大学学报,2013,35(05):12-23.

[17] 魏泊宁. 口岸营商环境对我国产品出口的影响:基于"一带一路"沿线国家的实证研究 [J]. 经济经纬,2020,37(02):77-85.

[18] Nketiah-Amponsah E, Sarpong B. Ease of doing business and foreign direct investment: Case of Sub-Saharan Africa [J]. International Advances in Economic Research, 2020, 26 (3): 209-223.

[19] 崔鑫生. "一带一路"沿线国家营商环境对经济发展的影响:基于世界银行营商环境指标体系的分析 [J]. 北京工商大学学报(社会科学版),2020,35(03):37-48.

[20] 张会清. 地区营商环境对企业出口贸易的影响 [J]. 南方经济,2017(10):75-89.

The Pilot Policies of Cross-border E-commerce and New Opportunities for China's Import Trade

杨 静[①]

Abstract: With the in-depth development of electronic information technology and economic globalization, the status and important role of e-commerce in international trade has become increasingly prominent, which has injected new impetus into the development of China's foreign trade. This paper uses the data of China customs from 2007 to 2018, takes the setup of cross-border e-commerce pilot cities as experimental event, and uses the multi-period Difference-in-Difference model to estimate the role of pilot policies of cross-border e-commerce in promoting China's import trade. The study shows that: (1) The pilot policies of cross-border e-commerce promote a significant increase in the value of China's import by 11.73%, the quantity of import increases significantly by 11.65%, and the price of import does not change significantly. In other words, the trade promotion effect of pilot policies of cross-border e-commerce is driven by quantity. (2) The pilot policies of cross-border e-commerce promote the import of general trade and its proportion, and the structure of import trade is optimized. Besides, it has a more significant promotion effect on consumer goods. (3) The pilot policies of cross-border e-commerce have a more obvious role in promoting the import trade from countries along the "Belt and Road". This paper affirms the strategic significance of the pilot policies of cross-border e-commerce and provides important theoretical guidance for the further development of cross-border e-commerce in China.

Keywords: cross-border; e-commerce pilot city; import trade

---

① 杨静,对外经济贸易大学国际经济贸易学院国际经济与贸易专业2017级本科生。

1 Introduction

For a long time, China's economy has relied on investment and export-driven, but import trade also plays an important role in the development of a country or region. It is not only conducive to improving the production efficiency of enterprises, but also helps to promote technological innovation, export scale expansion and export quality upgrade. The State Council's guiding opinions on strengthening imports to promote the balanced development of foreign trade also pointed out that further strengthening imports and promoting the balanced development of foreign trade have important strategic significance to coordinate the use of both domestic and foreign markets, alleviate bottleneck pressure on resources and the environment, accelerate scientific and technological progress and innovation, improve residents' consumption levels, promote economic structural upgrading, reduce trade friction, and improve international competitiveness. This is an inevitable requirement for achieving scientific development and transforming the economic development mode. And it is a basic task of China's foreign trade at present and in the future. However, it is worth noting that although China's import management laws and regulations are improving and the degree of market opening is increasing, imports still have some issues, like imperfect trade systems and policies, low trade facilitation, low import organization, incomplete import structure, and so on.

As the Chinese government attaches more and more importance to the development of import trade, import trade research has attracted more and more scholars' attention. The scholars conducted research on trade liberalization, trade potential, and trade effects. In the study of trade effects, scholars mainly examined the impact of import trade in terms of cost plus, employment changes, innovative research and development, value chain reshaping, etc. Some scholars examined their impact on imports from the perspective of trade policies implementation. Mao found that the decline in trade policy uncertainty not only significantly promotes the expansion of the import scale of enterprises, but also helps to increase the probability of enterprise imports, extend the duration of imports and improve the quality of imported products. Cao et al. found that the "Belt and Road" initiative generally improves China's international pricing power in the import market, especially for the import of labor-intensive products. Although many scholars have conducted research on import trade, they have not investigated the impact of cross-border e-commerce policies on China's import trade.

In recent years, China's economic development is entering a "new normal", the old economy is showing signs of weakness, and the new economy, which is based on "Internet +", is flourishing. In the context of digital trade, fragmented orders and personalized demand have made cross-border e-commerce, such a new trade format flourish. Cross-border e-commerce has become an important means for Chinese enterprises to carry out international trade, and has become a driving force for the steady growth of China's foreign trade and structural adjustment. According to the statistics from the General Administration of Customs, the total value of retail import and exports of goods through the customs cross-border e-commerce management platform reached 134.7 billion yuan in 2018, increased by 50% compared to 2017. From a structural point of view, the proportion of cross-border e-commerce export trade is always higher than the proportion of import trade. The development of China's cross-border e-commerce takes exports as the main goal, aiming to support traditional foreign trade enterprises to use the Internet platform to achieve transformation and upgrading, and explore new overseas market. With the changes in China's economic strength and position in international division of labor, China has gradually shifted from "one-way opening" that initially focused on exports and introduction of foreign capital, to "two-way opening" that focused on the balance of import and export、introduction of foreign capital and overseas investment. In the context of weakening traditional competitive advantages, cross-border e-commerce, as a new trade format and new model, is conducive to the transformation and upgrading of traditional foreign trade enterprises, helps to strengthen China's import and export competitive advantage in terms of cost efficiency, and provides new opportunities for enterprises to build international brand and enhance international competitiveness. At the same time, cross-border e-commerce responds to domestic consumers' demand for a higher quality of life, which is conducive to improving the welfare of domestic consumers. In addition, it is also a new impetus to promote the upgrading of industrial structure and create economic growth points, which is of great significance for improving China's opening to the outside world and promoting the formation of a new pattern of comprehensive opening.

With the vigorous development of cross-border e-commerce, the Chinese government has paid more attention to the positive role of cross-border e-commerce imports, and has issued a series of policy measures. For example, in December 2012, the National Development and Reform Commission and the General Administration of Customs jointly established Zhengzhou, Shanghai, Chongqing, Hangzhou and Ningbo as the first batch of cross-border e-commerce pilot cities. Since then, the Ministry of Commerce and other departments have expanded pilot scope of cross-border e-commerce retail import many times. In June 2015, the General Office of the

State Council issued the "Guiding Opinions on Promoting the Healthy and Rapid Development of Cross-Border E-Commerce", which pointed out that it is necessary to increase imports reasonably and expand domestic consumption, and put forward measures to optimize customs supervision, and improve inspection and quarantine supervision. Also clearly regulated import and export tax policies, and improve e-commerce payment settlement management and other measures. On March 24, 2016, the Ministry of Finance, the General Administration of Customs, and the State Administration of Taxation jointly announced that from April 8, 2016, cross-border e-commerce retail import will no longer be subject to postage taxes on postal items, but on goods collect tariffs, import value-added tax and consumption tax to promote the healthy development of cross-border e-commerce. On April 7, 2016, 11 departments, including the Ministry of Finance, the Development and Reform Commission, the Ministry of Industry and Information Technology jointly released the "Cross-border e-commerce retail import list" to the society. On April 18, 2016, in order to implement cross-border e-commerce retail import tax policy, the Ministry of Finance, the Development and Reform Commission, the Ministry of Industry and Information Technology and other three departments announced the "Cross-border e-commerce retail import list (second batch)". On November 30, 2018, in order to promote the healthy development of cross-border e-commerce retail imports, the Ministry of Finance, the Development and Reform Commission and other 13 departments announced the "Cross-border e-commerce retail import list (2018 version)", and implements from January 1, 2019. In November 2017, the "Notice of the Customs Tariff Commission of the State Council on Adjusting the Import Tariffs of Certain Consumer Goods" stated that from December 1, 2017, the import tariffs of some consumer goods will be reduced at a provisional tax rate. According to the decision and deployment of the Party Central Committee and the State Council, China will adjust the import tax policy for cross-border e-commerce retail import from January 1, 2019, increase the upper limit of commodity limits for tax preferential policies, and expand the scope of the list. With the development of Internet technology and the support of policy measures, cross-border e-commerce may promote the growth of China's import trade and respond to the call of China's foreign trade development plan.

  Then, can the pilot policy of cross-border e-commerce promote the development of China's import trade? Is the impact on China's import trade driven by volume or price? Can the pilot policy of cross-border e-commerce improve China's import trade structure? In the face of growing consumer demand, can the pilot policy of cross-border e-commerce promote the import of consumer goods, and meet effective demand? Under the "Belt and Road" initiative, does the pilot policy of cross-border e-commerce promote the import from countries along the "Belt and Road", and inject a new engine into the implementation of the "Belt and Road" strategy?

Answering the above questions is critical to the evaluation of the trade effect of the cross-border e-commerce pilot policy. For this reason, this paper uses the data from 2007 to 2018 of China Customs and the "Chinese City Statistical Yearbook", takes the establishment of cross-border e-commerce pilot cities as experimental event, and uses the multi-period Difference-in-Difference model to evaluate the impact of the cross-border e-commerce pilot policy on China's import trade. This paper examines the recognition conditions of the difference-in-difference model from parallel trend test and expected effect test these two aspects, so as to ensure the unbiasedness of the estimation results. On this basis, this paper further analyzes from the aspects of general trade import and its proportion, import of consumer goods, and imports from countries along the "Belt and Road", as well as examines the linkage between the pilot policies of cross-border e-commerce and China's import structure optimization, expanding the domestic demand, and the "Belt and Road" strategy.

The marginal contribution of this paper mainly reflects in two aspects: First, this paper uses the data from 2007 to 2018 of China customs to accurately assess the trade promotion effect of the cross-border e-commerce pilot policy. Although the literature has examined the effects of China's import trade, it has not examined the positive impact of cross-border e-commerce policies on the development of China's import trade. The data from 2007 to 2018 of China Customs used in this paper provides a good data basis for evaluating the pilot policy of cross-border e-commerce, so that the trade promotion effect of the pilot policy of cross-border e-commerce can be studied.

Second, this paper further analyzes from three aspects of import structure, expanding the domestic demand and the "Belt and Road" strategy. It first examines the linkage between the pilot polices of cross-border e-commerce and China's development strategy, thus evaluates the contribution of pilot policies of cross-border e-commerce to China's economic development more comprehensively. The pilot policies of cross-border e-commerce promote China's imports, and the import structure is continuously optimized, which is conducive to providing effective supply and satisfy effective demand. It also provides a new engine for imports from countries along the "Belt and Road". Therefore, the economic impact of the pilot policies of cross-border e-commerce is not only limited to the promotion of import trade, but also conducive to promoting the construction of China's trade power and the implementation of the "Belt and Road" strategy.

The rest of this paper is organized as follows: the second part is the policies background and literature review, the third part is the data description and feature fact analysis, the fourth part uses the Difference-in-Difference model to evaluate the trade promotion effect of the cross-border e-commerce pilot policy, and the fifth part further analyses the import structure and countries of import origin.

2 Policies Background and Literature Review

This paper sorts out the policies background of cross-border e-commerce firstly, then sorts out the relevant literature on import trade and cross-border e-commerce in China, and finally reviews the existing literature and proposes the research ideas of this paper.

2.1 Policies Background of Cross-border E-commerce

In recent years, with the rapid development of cross-border e-commerce, in order to promote the healthy development of cross-border e-commerce imports, the Chinese government has issued a series of policy measures. For example, the "Notice on Issues Concerning Online Shopping Bonded Import Model of Cross-border E-commerce Services Pilot" issued on March 24, 2014 made Clear regulations on the scope of pilot products, the amount and quantity of purchases, taxation issues, enterprises management and statistics of customs. The "General Administration of Customs Concerning Strengthening the Supervision of Bonded Imports of Cross-border E-commerce Online Shopping" issued on September 9, 2015 proposed that the areas where online bonded treasury is carried out should have e-commerce customs clearance service platforms and other related facilities, and each customs should strengthen cross-border requirements for e-commerce information system construction. In order to create a fair competition market environment and promote healthy development of cross-border e-commerce retail import, the "Ministry of Finance and Others Notice on Tax Policies for Cross-border E-commerce Retail Import" approved by the State Council on March 24, 2016 made notice on matters related to the tax policy for cross-border e-commerce retail import. On April 7, 2016, the Ministry of Finance and other eleven departments jointly announced the "Cross-border E-commerce Retail Import List". On May 24, 2016, the General Office of the General Administration of Customs issued "the Notice on Matters Relevant to the Implementation of New Regulatory Requirements for Cross-border E-commerce Retail Import" put forward new regulatory requirements on the online shopping bonded mode and direct purchase mode. On July 22, 2016, "the Notice that Customs defines the Duty-paid Prices for Imported Goods of Cross-border E-commerce" put forward the principles of duty-paid price determination, preferential sales promotion, freight, and insurance premiums. On November 24, 2017, the "State Council's Notice on Adjusting Import Tariffs on Certain Consumer Goods" proposed that, starting from December 1, 2017, the import tariffs on some consumer goods will be reduced at a provisional tax rate. On November 30, 2018, the "Notice on Improving the Cross-border E-commerce Retail Import Tax Policy" raised the single and annual transaction limits, and fully levied tariffs and import value-added tax and consumption tax on goods whose duty-paid prices meet the conditions, and the transaction amount are included in the annual total transaction amount.

In December 2012, the work of national cross-border trade e-commerce service pilot jointly launched by the National Development and Reform Commission and the General Administration of Customs started in Zhengzhou. Bin Lu, deputy director of the General Administration of Customs, said at the opening ceremony: "Zhengzhou, Shanghai, Chongqing, Hangzhou and Ningbo these five cities have good economic and foreign trade foundations and conditions to carry out the pilot of cross-border e-commerce services, and subsequently established Guangzhou, Shenzhen, Tianjin, Fuzhou, Pingtan, Dalian, Suzhou, Hefei, Qingdao, Chengdu these 10 Pilot cities of cross-border e-commerce. Pilot cities achieve business collaboration and data sharing between foreign e-commerce trade companies and relevant port management departments, solve the bottleneck problems that restricts the development of cross-border trade e-commerce, optimize the customs supervision mode and improve customs clearance management and service levels through first-in-first-out and relying on the construction mechanism and platform advantages of electronic ports. This means that the development of China's cross-border trade e-commerce has entered a new stage. Bin Lu said that promoting the pilot work of cross-border trade e-commerce services is an important measure to promote the stable growth of foreign trade, and is also an inherent need to serve the development of new economics and promote customs reform and innovation. Through the work of the pilot, we can summarize and formulate management methods and standards for customs clearance, foreign exchange settlement and tax rebate that relates to cross-border trade e-commerce to promote the development of China's cross-border trade e-commerce.①

---

① The website is: http://www.gov.cn/jrzg/2012-12/19/content_2293680.htm.

Table 1 The Name and Setup Time of Pilot Cities

Name	Setup Time
Hangzhou	December 2012
Shanghai	December 2012
Ningbo	December 2012
Zhengzhou	December 2012
Chongqing	December 2012
Guangzhou	September 2013
Shenzhen	July 2014
Tianjin	October 2015
Fuzhou	January 2016
Pingtan	January 2016
Dalian	January 2018
Suzhou	January 2018
Hefei	January 2018
Qingdao	January 2018
Chengdu	January 2018

2.2 Researches on Import Trade

1. Current Situation and Trend of China's Import Trade

Some scholars investigated China's import development from the aspects of commodity structure, technical structure, products quality, import potential and so on. Wei et al made a comprehensive calculation of the changes in the structure of China's import, the study found that in 2000—2014, the share of non-agricultural primary products, high-tech products in China's total imports increased substantially. The overall technical level of import declined first and rose later. After 2007, the overall technical level of import gradually increased. Shi and Zeng found that the quality of imported products of Chinese enterprises was on the rise based on the micro-trade data of customs. Wei and Li found that since 2001, the middle and high technology commodities have been the largest import commodities of China, the share of middle and low technology commodities has increased significantly, and the share of all kinds of products in the world's total import is on the rise. Shi and Wu found that China's import has realized a slight transition from insufficient import to moderate import, but there is a certain import potential in consumer goods, and the import potential is mainly concentrated in Asia.

2. Import Trade Effect and Influencing Factors in China

Some scholars paid attention to China's import trade effects from different perspectives. Qian et al examined the impact of import competition on the cost-plus of Chinese manufacturing companies. The study found that import competition has a significant negative impact on the cost-plus of Chinese manufacturing companies. The more intense the import competition is, the lower the cost bonus of the companies is. But in the long run, the negative effects of import competition will gradually disappear. Jiang based on the multiple perspectives of imported intermediate products, and found that there is a significant "U" relationship between the diversity of imported intermediate products and the fluctuations of enterprise output. Zhang and Zou based on a price index found that the impact of import types and product quality on trade welfare is opposite to that of traditional price indexes. The improvement of China's trade welfare by diversified import types shows a volatile upward trend. Wei and Li based on the data of Chinese micro-industrial enterprises and found that imported inputs only have a significant impact on the employment growth of importing enterprises that have export behavior, but have no significant impact on pure importing enterprises. In addition, compared with general trade import, processing trade import has a more significant effect on employment growth.

The influence factors of China's import trade are another perspective that scholars have paid attention to. The scholars have conducted research on trade facilitation, import liberalization, trade policy uncertainty, productive subsidies, institutional distance, and the intensity of intellectual property protection. The above researches mainly found that trade facilitation and import liberalization increases the technology complexity and value-added of enterprises' export. The improvement of domestic patent protection in China will increase the import of high-tech products, and the increase in institutional distance and uncertainty of trade policies will inhibit the import of enterprises.

2.3 Researches on Cross-border E-commerce

1. The Trade Distance Effect and Cost Reduction Promotion Effect of Cross-border E-commerce

The development of cross-border e-commerce has changed the reality and theory of traditional trade. Some scholars have studied the influence of cross-border e-commerce on the effect of trade distance. Ma et al based on cross-border e-commerce logistics data and traditional trade export data, and conducted a study on whether cross-border e-commerce can break through the geographical distance limit. The results show that compared with traditional trade export, cross-border e-commerce export is less negatively affected by geographic distance. And the development of the Internet of trading partner countries can weaken the negative impact of geographic distance to a certain extent, and promote the growth of cross-border e-commerce export. Chang et al studied the impact of cross-border e-commerce on trade distance effect based on China's cooperation with countries along the "Belt and Road". The study found that cross-border e-commerce channels can effectively weaken the trade distance effect and indirectly stimulate trade growth. And there is a threshold effect for cross-border e-commerce to weaken the trade distance effect.

Other scholars have studied the effect of cross-border e-commerce on "cost reduction and promotion". Ma et al based on the ECI cross-border e-commerce connection index released by Alibaba, and used cross-section data composed of China and G20 countries in 2015 and China and the countries along the "Belt and Road" in 2016 to empirically test whether cross-border e-commerce can reduce trade cost. The results show that cross-border e-commerce can significantly reduce trade cost, and compared with export cross-border e-commerce, the effect of import cross-border e-commerce trade cost reduction is more significant. Mei used sample data from 16 countries in Central and Eastern Europe along the "Belt and Road" to conduct an empirical test on the impact mechanism of "cost reduction and efficiency improvement" that cross-border e-commerce has on China's international trade. The results found that cross-border e-commerce has a significant "cost reduction and efficiency improvement" effect on China's international trade. Guo et al based on the theory of heterogeneous enterprises and found that cross-border e-commerce reduces the fixed cost and marginal transaction cost for enterprises to enter the foreign trade industry, also improves the allocation of resources. Thus, by increasing trade opportunities, expanding trade entities, enriching trade content and other means have effectively promoted the growth, transformation and upgrading of China's foreign import and export trade.

2. The Impact of Cross-border E-commerce on China's Import and Export Trade

The impact of cross-border e-commerce on China's import and export trade is another research perspective that scholars have paid attention to. Xiao and Liu built a cointegration model based on China's cross-border e-commerce and manufacturing export data from 2000 to

2016 to quantitatively analyze the impact of cross-border e-commerce on China's manufacturing export scale. Research shows that there is a cointegration relationship between cross-border e-commerce and the export scale of China's manufacturing industry, and there is a long-term equilibrium relationship between the two. The expansion of cross-border e-commerce can effectively promote the expansion of China's manufacturing export scale. Zhong and Li conducted an empirical analysis of the impact of cross-border e-commerce on China's import and export trade based on cross-border e-commerce and import and export trade data from 2008 to 2016. The results show that the development of cross-border e-commerce is beneficial to China's foreign trade activities, but the degree of impact is not large, mainly because China's cross-border e-commerce is still in the early stage of development. He studied the relationship between cross-border e-commerce and import and export trade based on the import and export data of China's cross-border e-commerce companies from 2000 to 2017. The study shows that the development of cross-border e-commerce can promote the increase of China's scale of total trade. Li and Yi selected sample data of the EU and EU member states from 2008 to 2017, and used time series model and panel data model to conduct empirical research on the impact of China's cross-border e-commerce development on the EU's export trade effect. It shows that the development of China's cross-border e-commerce has a significant promotion effect on EU export trade, and it has become an important means of smooth trade between China and the EU under the background of the "Belt and Road" initiative. Wang and Yu selected two indicators of cross-border e-commerce transaction scale and total import and export trade, and collected relevant data and conducted a VAR test on the relationship between the two. The result shows that there is a two-way causality between the development of cross-border e-commerce and the growth of traditional foreign trade. Luo and Luo selected the data of 46 major trading partners of China from 2008 to 2016 as research samples, and conducted panel data analysis based on the gravity model. They found that the development of cross-border e-commerce not only promotes the development of domestic import and export trade, but also has a certain role in promoting other countries.

2.4 Literature Analysis

In China's import trade related researches, scholars mostly examined the impact on import trade from the perspective of institutional distance and trade facilitation; in cross-border e-commerce related research, scholars mostly based on national-level cross-border e-commerce development index to examine the impact of cross-border e-commerce on China's import and export trade.

In summary, although the existing literature has conducted extensive research on China's import trade and cross-border e-commerce trade, it has not investigated the impact of cross-border e-commerce policies on China's import trade. In view of this, this paper uses the data of China customs from 2007 to 2018, and uses the Difference-in-Difference model to estimate the trade promotion effect of pilot policies of cross-border e-commerce, and discusses the main mechanism sources of trade growth. On this basis, it further investigates the impact of the pilot policies of cross-border e-commerce on China's import structure, and analyzes the country of origin of the import, and then studies its relationship with the construction of a trading power, expanding domestic demand, meeting effective demand and the "Belt and Road" strategy. The linkage between them will comprehensively evaluate the positive impact of the pilot policies of cross-border e-commerce.

3 Data Description and Characteristic Facts

3.1 Data Description

The data used in this paper mainly comes from the China Customs Database and the Chinese City Statistical Yearbook from 2007 to 2018. The China customs data covers information on the HS-8 code product level, including the information on the value and quantity of import and export, modes of trade, and countries of shipment or destination. The Chinese City Statistical Yearbook covers information on urban population, comprehensive economy, trade and so on. In the base regression, this paper adds the import data of the HS-8 code product level to the city-time-HS-8 code level, so as to obtain the research individuals of this paper, and logarithmically transforms the data and shrinks it. And finally matches it with the city level data, and then analyze the impact of the cross-border e-commerce pilot policy on the import of China. The modes of trade include general trade, processing trade and others. The data of cross-border e-commerce import pilot cities comes from the Chinese government website. This data provides the time for each pilot city to be approved as a cross-border e-commerce pilot city, including the specific year and month.

In the analysis of the heterogeneity of imported product types, this paper divides the products into consumer goods and other goods according to the practice of Jiang et al and then carries out sub-sample regression. In the analysis of the source heterogeneity of import countries, this paper bases on China's "Belt and Road" initiative, which includes the east Asia Mongolia, 18 countries in west Asia, 8 countries in south Asia, 5 countries in central Asia, 7 countries of independent states, 16 countries in central and eastern Europe, and 10 ASEAN countries. There are altogether 65 countries along the route, are identified as "Belt and Road" countries, and performs sub-sample regression.

3.2 Characteristic Facts

According to the establishment of the first batch of cross-border e-commerce pilot cities in December 2012, this paper divides the sample period into two time periods, that is 2007-2012 and 2013-2018[①]. Then, the average annual import value, average annual import volume and average annual import price of pilot cities and non-pilot cities were calculated respectively in two time periods, so as to compare the growth of cities' import trade before and after the pilot policy for cross-border e-commerce was proposed. Table 2 shows the corresponding statistical results that compared with the period of 2007—2012, the import value of the pilot cities increased by 2303.333 billion US dollars in 2013—2018, and the growth rate is 41.94%; the import value of non-pilot cities increased by 2358.334 billion US dollars, and the growth rate is 36.08%. To sum up, although the import value of the pilot cities is lower, the growth rate is faster.

Table 2 Changes of City's Import Before and After Pilot Policy

City	Pilot City		Non – pilot City	
year	2007 – 2012	2013 – 2018	2007 – 2012	2013 – 2018
import	549166.7	779500	638333.3	874166.7
quantity	727333.3	1220333.3	1222166.7	2011666.7
price	0.7551	0.6387	0.5223	0.4344

Note: The data comes from the China customs database. The unit of import value is USD million, and the unit of import quantity is million.

In addition, this paper makes a statistical comparison of China's import trade modes, categories of imported goods, and importing countries before and after the cross-border e-

---

① When doing descriptive statistical analysis, the impact time cannot be unified due to the different establishment time of different cross-border e-commerce pilot cities. Since the first batch of pilot cities accounted for 1/3 of all pilot cities, this paper uses the establishment time of the first batch of pilot cities to divide the sample period into two time periods to see the import difference before and after the cross-border e-commerce pilot policy.

commerce pilot policy is proposed. The results are shown in tables 3 to 5. They show that compared with the period of 2007—2012, the import value of China's general trade increased by 1116.667 billion US dollars during 2013—2018, and the import value of processing trade decreased by 1626.666 billion US dollars; The import value of other goods increased by 222500 billion US dollars, and the growth rate is 24.82%. The import value of consumer goods increased by 437 billion US dollars, and the growth rate is 123.82%; The import value from the countries along the "Belt and Road" increased by 378.333 billion US dollars, and the growth rate is 13.18%. The import value from other countries increased by 1038.333 billion US dollars, and the growth rate is 11.53%. In summary, after the proposal of the cross-border e-commerce pilot policy, from the perspective of trade modes, China's general trade import increases, and processing trade import decreases; From the perspective of commodity categories, compared with other products, although the import value of consumer products is smaller, the growth is faster; From the source of import countries, compared with other countries, although the import value of the countries along the "Belt and Road" is smaller, the growth is relatively fast.

Table 3 Changes of China's Trade Modes Before and After Pilot Policy

Trade Mode	General Trade		Processing Trade	
year	2007 – 2012	2013 – 2018	2007 – 2012	2013 – 2018
import	653000	764666.7	423833.3	261166.7
quantity	1241500	1778333.3	573666.7	408000
price	0.5259	0.4302	0.7386	0.6400

Note: Same as table 2.

Table 4 Changes of China's Imports Category Before and After Pilot Policy

Product Category	Consumer Goods		OtherGoods	
year	2007 – 2012	2013 – 2018	2007 – 2012	2013 – 2018
import	35266.7	78966.7	896500	1119000
quantity	19033.3	26683.3	1721250	2733666.6
price	1.8539	2.9587	0.5201	0.4093

Note: Same as table 2.

Table5 Changes of China's Import Countries Before and After Pilot Policy

Country	"the Belt and Road" Countries		Other Countries	
year	2007 – 2012	2013 – 2018	2007 – 2012	2013 – 2018
import	287000	324833.3	900500	1004333.3
quantity	615166.7	717666.7	1334166.7	1895000
price	0.4665	0.4525	0.6750	0.5301

Note: Same as table 2.

4 The Trade Promotion Effect of Pilot Policies of Cross-border E-commerce

4.1 Model Specification

The sample period of the China customs data used in this paper is from 2007 to 2018, and the specific year and month of establishing the cross-border e-commerce pilot cities are taken as the time of policy impact to evaluate the trade promotion effect of the cross-border e-commerce pilot policy. Based on this, this paper uses a multi-period Difference-in-Difference model to assess the impact of cross-border e-commerce pilot on urban import trade. The estimated model specification is as follows:

$$lny_{ijt} = \alpha_0 + \beta_0 \, treat_i \cdot post_{it} + X_{it} \cdot \gamma + \lambda_i + \lambda_j + \lambda_t + \varepsilon_{ijt} \qquad (1)$$

where i is the target city, j is the HS-8 code product, t is the year, λ_i, λ_j and λ_t are the fixed effect, HS-8 code product fixed effect and time fixed effect of target city, and ε_{ijt} is the random error term. The interpreted variable lny contains the logarithm of import value—$lnimport$, the logarithm of import quantity—$lnquantity$ and the logarithm of import average price (import value/import quantity) —$lnprice$. The $treat$ variable in model (1) is a dummy variable at target city level. When the target city is approved as a pilot city for cross-border e-commerce, the value of the treat variable is 1, that is, the target city belongs to the experimental group; If the target city is not a pilot city for cross-border e-commerce, the value of the treat variable is 0, which means that the target city belongs to the control group. $post$ is a dummy variable of time, and the specific year and month issued by the policy as the impact time point in this paper. When the target city is approved as a cross-border e-commerce pilot city, the current value is (12-policy_month)/12, after the policy impact time the value is 1, and before the policy impact time the value is 0. The regression coefficient β_0 of the $treat_i \cdot post_{it}$ in model (1) can accurately reflect the impact of the cross-border e-commerce pilot policy on China's import trade.

In order to accurately estimate the regression coefficient β_0 of $treat_i \cdot post_{it}$, it is necessary to ensure the exogenousness of the target city dummy variable $treat$ and the randomness of the time dummy variable $post$. That is, whether it is a cross-border e-commerce pilot city is determined by exogenous. And whether it is a cross-border e-commerce pilot city is mainly determined by the economic status and the basis of foreign trade of the city. Therefore, this paper controls the fixed effect of the target city, the fixed effect of time and the control variable at the target city level. Among them, the control variable of target city— X_{it}, specifically includes logarithm of per capita GDP—ln$perGDP$, logarithm of actual foreign investment value—lnFDI, logarithm of year-end total population—lnpop, logarithm of total retail value of social consumer goods—ln$sale$, logarithm of the average wage of employee—ln$wage$, and unemployment rate of target city—$unemp\_rate$. For better evaluation, this paper further controls the fixed effect of HS-8 code products.

4.2 Standard Regression Results

This paper aims to explore how the pilot policies of cross-border e-commerce affect China's import trade. Table 6 shows the standard regression results. Among them, column (1)-column (3) are the estimated results of import value, import quantity and average import price. The estimated coefficient of $treat_i \cdot post_{it}$ in column (1) is significantly positive, and the pilot policies of cross-border e-commerce significantly promote the value of China's import trade by 11.73%. The increase may come from two reasons, namely the increase in quantity of import or the increase in the average price of import. The former is quantity-driven and the latter is price-driven. From the estimation results of columns (2) and (3), it can be seen that after the cross-border e-commerce pilot policy is proposed, China's import quantity increases significantly by 11.65%, and the regression coefficient of average import price is not significant, that is the pilot policies of cross-border e-commerce don't reduce China's import price. This means that the trade promotion effect of the pilot policy of cross-border e-commerce is mainly driven by the increase in quantity, that is, the increase in the value of import trade is mainly due to the substantial increase in import quantity.

Table 6 Standard Regression Results

	(1)	(2)	(3)
	ln*import*	ln*quantity*	ln*price*
treat · *post*	0.1173***	0.1165**	0.0024
	(0.0432)	(0.0541)	(0.0234)
Controls	Fixed	Fixed	Fixed
City FE	Fixed	Fixed	Fixed
HS-8 FE	Fixed	Fixed	Fixed
Year FE	Fixed	Fixed	Fixed
N	2488360	2488369	2488360
adj. R^2	0.4330	0.5889	0.7940

Notes: controls specifically include logarithm of per capita *GDP*—ln*perGDP*, logarithm of actual foreign investment value—ln*FDI*, logarithm of year-end total population—ln*pop*, logarithm of total retail value of social consumer goods—ln*sale*, logarithm of the average wage of employee—ln*wage*, and unemployment rate of target city—*unemp_rate*. The standard errors of the regression coefficients in parentheses are adjusted according to the clustering standard of the target city. The superscripts ***, **, and * represent the statistical significance of 1%, 5%, and 10% respectively.

4.3 Identification Condition Test

This paper uses the Difference-in-Difference model to estimate the trade promotion effect of the pilot policies of cross-border e-commerce. The accuracy of the estimation result depends on whether the relevant identification conditions of the model are met. This paper will test the recognition conditions of the model from two aspects: parallel trend test and expected effect test.

1. Parallel Trend Test

An important condition for the estimation using the Difference-in-Difference model is that after controlling other variables λ_i, λ_j, λ_t and X_{it}, the core explanatory variable— $treat_i \cdot post_{it}$ is not related to the random error term, that is, it satisfies:

$$E[\varepsilon_{ijt} \mid treat_i \cdot post_{it}, \lambda_i, \lambda_j, \lambda_t] = E[\varepsilon_{ijt} \mid \lambda_i, \lambda_j, \lambda_t] \quad (2)$$

In other words, after controlling other variables, the time trend of the experimental group and the control group before the impact should be consistent. This paper refers to Fajgelbaum et al. (2019), and uses the coefficient regression method to test whether the experimental group and the control group meet the parallel trend before the impact. The estimation model is as follow:

$$\ln y_{ijt} = \alpha_0 + \sum_{r=-5}^{r=4} \beta_j treat \cdot I(event_{time_i} = r) + X_{it} \cdot \gamma + \lambda_i, \lambda_j, \lambda_t + \varepsilon_{ijt} \qquad (3)$$

where i is the target city, j is the HS-8 code product, t is the year, r is the relative time, λ_i, λ_j, and λ_t are the city fixed effect, HS-8 code product fixed effect and time fixed effect respectively. Because the import value, import quantity and average import price in the standard regression need to meet the parallel trend condition, the interpreted variable ln$y$ still contains three variables: the logarithm of import value, the logarithm of import quantity, and the logarithm of average import price. I ($event\_time_i = r$) is a relative time indicator variable. And $r = (-5, -4, -3, -2, -1, 0, +1, +2, +3, +4)$ is the relative number of time period, $r = 0$ means the current period of impact, $r = -1$ means the first period before the impact, and $r = +1$ means the first period after the impact. When the number of relative time period is less than -5, it is recognized as -5; when the number of relative time period is greater than +4, it is recognized as +4. The settings of variable $treat$ and control variable—X_{it} are the same as model (1).

Figure 1 shows the parallel trend of the import value of the target cities of the experimental group and the control group after controlling other variables. It can be seen that before the introduction of pilot policies of cross-border e-commerce, the import value of the target cities in experimental group and the control group meets the condition of parallel trend. After the introduction of cross-border e-commerce pilot policy, the import value of the cities in experi-

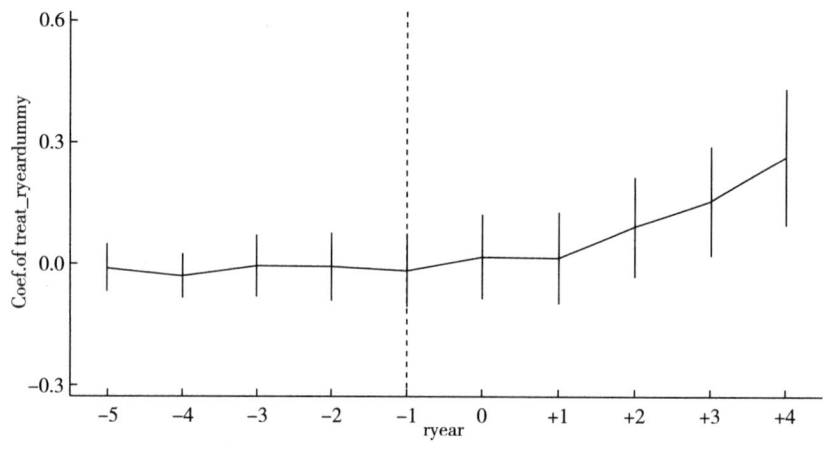

Figure 1 Parallel Trend Test of Import Value

Notes: The horizontal axis is relative time, and the vertical axis is the regression coefficient of the product term corresponding to each relative time. The vertical line represents the 90% confidence interval of the product term coefficient. Same as below.

mental group and control group begins to differ significantly, that is, the import value of the pilot cities increases significantly compared with the non-pilot cities. It should be noted that the pilot policyies of cross-border e-commerce have an obvious hysteresis effect on import value, that is, with the elapse of time, the trade promotion effect shows a trend of gradually increasing. Therefore, when evaluating the impact of cross-border e-commerce pilot policy on China's import trade, the sample period after the impact is too short to seriously underestimate the impact.

Figure 2 and Figure 3 are parallel trend charts of import quantity and average import price of target cities of experimental group and control group respectively. According to Figure 2, before the introduction of pilot policies of cross-border e-commerce, the import quantity of the target cities of experimental group and the control group meets the condition of parallel trend. After the introduction of pilot policies of cross-border e-commerce pilot policy the import quantity of the target city of the experimental group is significantly higher than that of the control group. As can be seen from Figure 3, the average import price of the target cities of the experimental group and control group also meets the parallel trend condition before the pilot policies of cross-border e-commerce are proposed, and the average import price do not change significantly after the cross-border e-commerce pilot policy is proposed.

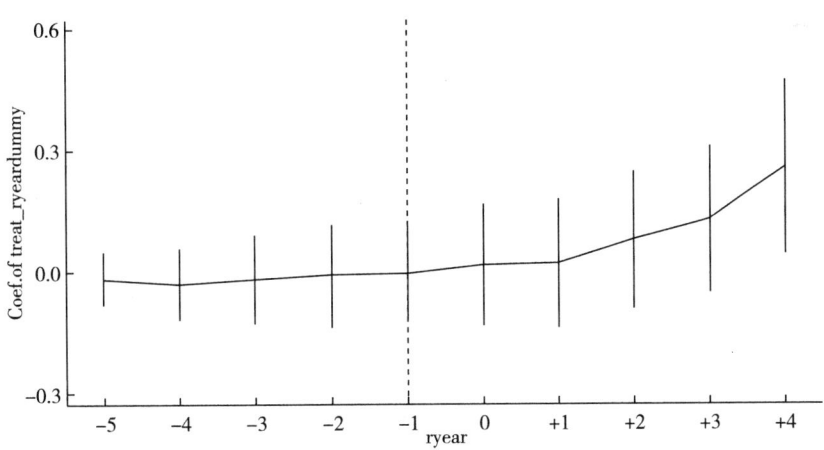

Figure 2　Parallel Trend Test of Import Quantity

2. Expected Effect Test

To accurately evaluate the impact of policy shock using the Difference-in-Difference model, another identification condition needs to be met: Before the shock occurs, the Chinese

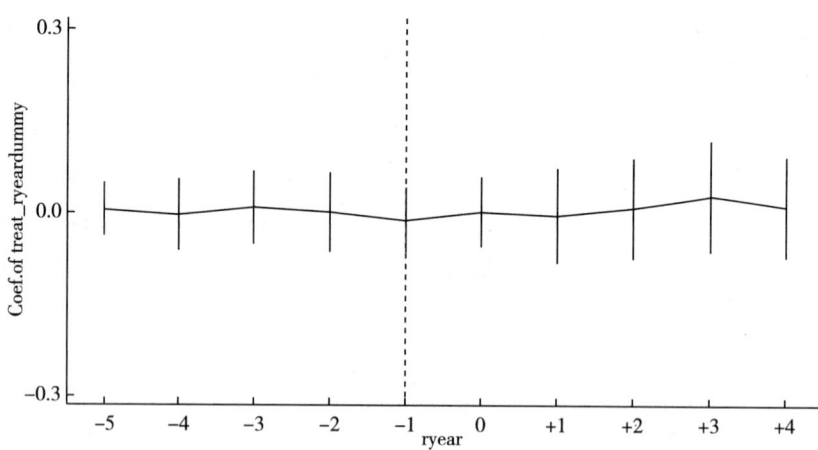

Figure 3 Parallel Trend Test of Average Import Price

government's import behavior to the target cities of the experimental group do not have the expected behavior, that is, after controlling other factors, the difference in import trade of target cities of the experimental group and the control group do not changes significantly before the shock. From the parallel trends of import value, import quantity and average import price in Figures 1 to 3, it can be found that the import behavior of the target cities of the experimental group has no obvious expected effect. In order to further test whether the expected effect is significant, this paper adds the product of the *treat* variable and the dummy variable *post*_1 of the previous period of the pilot policy of the cross-border e-commerce in the estimation of model (1), namely *treat* · *post*_1. The estimated results are shown in table 7. Observing the estimation results in columns (1) to (3), we can see that the estimated coefficients of the product term— *treat* · *post*_1 in the regression of import value, import quantity and average import price are not significant, while the regression coefficients of *treat* · *post* is basically the same as table 7.

Table 7 Expected Effect Test

	(1)	(2)	(3)
	ln*import*	ln*quantity*	ln*price*
treat · *post*	0.1138**	0.1163**	−0.0007
	(0.0471)	(0.0590)	(0.0254)
treat · *post*_1	−0.0173	−0.0009	−0.0155
	(0.0283)	(0.0343)	(0.0153)
Controls FE	Fixed	Fixed	Fixed
City FE	Fixed	Fixed	Fixed

continued

	(1)	(2)	(3)
	ln*import*	ln*quantity*	ln*price*
HS-8 FE	Fixed	Fixed	Fixed
Year FE	Fixed	Fixed	Fixed
N	2488360	2488369	2488360
adj. R^2	0.4330	0.5889	0.7940

Note: Same as table 6.

4.4 Robustness Test

This paper mainly makes two aspects of robustness test. First, we remove the non-cross-border e-commerce pilot cities from the integrated test zone in the control group for robust analysis. Second, we analyze whether the characteristic variable at the time-product level affects the estimation results in this paper.

1. Adjusting the Control Group

In the standard regression results, this paper uses 284 cities in the China customs database as samples, takes the setup of pilot cities for cross-border e-commerce as the basis, defines the city variables of the experimental group and the time of policy impact, and then uses the multi-period Difference-in-Difference model to analyze. However, the sample of 284 cities includes cities in the cross-border e-commerce integrated test zone, and it also promotes the import trade of cities. However, some cities are both cross-border e-commerce pilot city and integrated test zone. Obviously, the regression includes the cross-border e-commerce integrated test zone may underestimate the trade promotion effect of the cross-border e-commerce pilot policy. Therefore, this paper excludes the non-pilot cities in the integrated test zone, adjusts the control group, and regresses the import value, import quantity, and average import price. Column (1) to column (3) of table 8 are regression results of the adjusted control group.

Observing the regression results of the import value in column (1), we can find that the estimated coefficient of the product term—*treat · post* is significantly positive, and the coefficient value of 0.1479 is significantly higher than the regression coefficient of the product term of column (1) in table 6—0.1173. The coefficient of the product item in the regression of the import quantity in table 8 – (2) is significantly positive, and the coefficient value of 0.1246 is significantly higher than the coefficient of the product item in the regression of the import quantity in table 6 – (2)—0.1165. It can be seen that after adjusting the control group, the impact of the cross-border e-commerce pilot policy on China's import trade increases.

2. Controlling Time-product Characteristic Variable

In model (1), the product term—*treat* · *post* is a variable at the target city-year level. Theoretically, omitting the variables of target city, year, and target city-year may affect the estimated coefficient of the product term. The omission of HS-8 code product-year-level variables does not affect the estimation results. However, the standard regression results are an analysis of the HS-8 code product-target city-year level. Omitting the variables at HS-8 code product-year level may affect the standard error of the estimation results, which in turn affects the statistical significance of the estimation results.

Table 8 Robustness Test of Adjustment of Control Group

	(1)	(2)	(3)
	ln*import*	ln*quantity*	ln*price*
treat · *post*	0.1479***	0.1246**	0.0245
	(0.0418)	(0.0493)	(0.0206)
Controls FE	Fixed	Fixed	Fixed
City FE	Fixed	Fixed	Fixed
HS-8 FE	Fixed	Fixed	Fixed
Year FE	Fixed	Fixed	Fixed
N	1926923	1926928	1926923
adj. R^2	0.4280	0.5937	0.7902

Note: Same as table 6.

In view of the above analysis, based on the standard model (1), this paper further controls the fixed effect at the HS-8 code product-year level. The estimated results are shown in table 9. Observing the estimation results, we can find that the estimated results of the product term—*treat* · *post* are basically consistent with table 6. That is, the cross-border e-commerce pilot policy has significantly increased China's import trade value, in which the quantity of import has increased significantly, and the average import price has not changed significantly.

Table 9　Robustness Test of HS-8 Product-Year

	(1)	(2)	(3)
	ln*import*	ln*quantity*	ln*price*
treat · post	0.1039**	0.1264**	−0.0204
	(0.0437)	(0.0540)	(0.0230)
Controls FE	Fixed	Fixed	Fixed
City FE	Fixed	Fixed	Fixed
HS-8 * Year FE	Fixed	Fixed	Fixed
N	2483752	2483761	2483752
adj. R^2	0.4376	0.5979	0.8056

Note: Same as table 6.

5　Further Analysis

This paper mainly examines the linkage between the pilot policies of cross-border e-commerce and China's development strategy in terms of heterogeneity in import structure and the country of origin. First, it analyzes whether the pilot policies of cross-border e-commerce promote the optimization of China's import trade structure from three perspectives of trade modes and types of imported goods to promote the construction of a trading power. Second, it analyzes the country of origin of imported goods and explores whether the cross-border e-commerce pilot policy provides a new engine for the "Belt and Road" economic and trade cooperation.

5.1　The Pilot Policies of Cross-border E-commerce and China's Import Structure

The report of the Nineteenth National Congress of the Communist Party of China put forward "Expanding foreign trade, cultivating new forms and models of business, and promoting the construction of a strong trading power". Against the backdrop of the rise of trade protectionism, it is even more important to understand the current development trend of international trade and strengthen the building of a trading power. The optimization of trade structure is an important condition for building a strong trading power. To this end, this paper discusses whether the pilot policies of cross-border e-commerce is conducive to the optimization of China's import trade structure and the promotion of a strong trading power in terms of trade modes and type of imported goods.

1. Change of Trade Modes

For a long time, China's processing trade has accounted for a relatively large part of the total trade, and it has been higher than the general trade. However, processing trade is at the low end of the global value chain, and participating in the international division of labor in this way undoubtedly lacks competitiveness in the international market. To this end, the "Twelfth Five-Year Plan" of China's foreign trade development emphasizes "optimizing the structure of trade modes, strengthening general trade and gradually expanding the proportion of general trade". So, have the pilot policies of cross-border e-commerce increased China's general trade imports and its share, thereby optimizing China's import trade structure?

Table 10 shows the regression results of China's general trade import and processing trade import. Looking at Column (1), Column (3) and Column (6), it can be found that the pilot policy of cross-border e-commerce has promoted a significant increase of 10.85% in China's import value of general trade, and a significant increase in the proportion of import value of general trade import by 3.19%. The proportion of import quantity of general trade has increased significantly by 3.07%. The estimated results of processing trade in table 11 show that the pilot policy of cross-border e-commerce has led to a significant decline in import value of processing trade by 33.15%, and has no significant impact on the import quantity of processing trade. Therefore, from the perspective of import value and import quantity, the cross-border e-commerce pilot policy has significantly increased China's general trade import value and its proportion, increased the import quantity of general trade, and reduced the import value of processing trade, thereby has optimized China's import trade modes.

Table 10 Change of Trade Modes

	(1) General Trade	(2) Processing Trade	(3) Percentage of General Trade	(4) General Trade	(5) Processing Trade	(6) Percentage of General Trade
	ln$import$	ln$import$	import_share	ln$quantity$	ln$quantity$	quantity_share
$treat \cdot post$	0.1085**	−0.331*	3.1886*	0.0656	−0.2826	3.0771*
	(0.0368)	(0.182)	(1.6817)	(0.0421)	(0.201)	(1.6952)
Controls	Fixed	Fixed	Fixed	Fixed	Fixed	Fixed
FE	Fixed	Fixed	Fixed	Fixed	Fixed	Fixed
City FE	Fixed	Fixed	Fixed	Fixed	Fixed	Fixed

	(1) General Trade	(2) Processing Trade	(3) Percentage of General Trade	(4) General Trade	(5) Processing Trade	(6) Percentage of General Trade
HS-8 FE	Fixed	Fixed	Fixed	Fixed	Fixed	Fixed
Year FE	Fixed	Fixed	Fixed	Fixed	Fixed	Fixed
N	1863874	819231	1863875	186385	819231	1863875
adj. R^2	0.4498	0.4101	0.3053	0.5997	0.5795	0.3063

Note: Same as table 6.

2. Change of Product Types

The "Twelfth Five-Year Plan" of foreign trade development clearly stated that "Further expanding the scale of import, and moderately expanding the import of consumer goods and driving the upgrading of the consumer consumption structure". The outline of the "Thirteenth Five-Year Plan" also clearly stated, "Taking supply-side structural reform as the main line to expand effective supply and meet effective demand". For consumer goods, products that are not available in importing countries can create new demand and promote the development and growth of new industries. So, can the pilot policies of cross-border e-commerce respond to the national development strategy, promote the import of consumer goods, and then realize the optimization of the trade structure and expand domestic demand?

In order to answer the above questions, this paper analyzes whether the pilot policies of cross-border e-commerce pilot policies have promoted the import of consumer goods from the perspective of the type of imported products. This paper divides the products into consumer goods and other goods on the basis of end-use according to the classification standards of BEC. Consumer goods refer to social products that directly meet the needs of people's lives and are directly used as end-use products. Then, the import value and import quantity of these two types of products are respectively regressed. The results are shown in Table 11. Observing the results, it can be seen that the cross-border e-commerce pilot policy mainly promotes the import of consumer goods.

Synthesizing the estimated results of the structural effects of trade modes and the types of trade products, we can learn that on the one hand, the pilot policies of cross-border e-commerce optimize China's import trade modes and respond to the development requirements of "Optimizing the trade mode structure, strengthening general trade and gradually expanding the

Table 11 Change of Product Types

	(1) Consumer Goods	(2) Other Goods	(3) Consumer Goods	(4) Other Goods	(5) Consumer Goods	(6) Other Goods
	ln$import$	ln$import$	ln$quantity$	ln$quantity$	ln$price$	ln$price$
$treat \cdot post$	0.3861***	0.0409	0.4293***	0.0501	−0.0365	−0.0087
	(0.1063)	(0.0342)	(0.1219)	(0.0447)	(0.0389)	(0.0230)
Controls FE	Fixed	Fixed	Fixed	Fixed	Fixed	Fixed
City FE	Fixed	Fixed	Fixed	Fixed	Fixed	Fixed
HS-8 FE	Fixed	Fixed	Fixed	Fixed	Fixed	Fixed
Year FE	Fixed	Fixed	Fixed	Fixed	Fixed	Fixed
N	376594	2111763	376594	2111763	376594	2111763
adj. R^2	0.4566	0.4179	0.5382	0.5986	0.6630	0.8022

Note: Same as table 6.

proportion of general trade" proposed in the "Twelfth Five-Year Plan" of foreign trade development. On the other hand, the pilot policies of cross-border e-commerce implement the development goals of "expanding the import of consumer goods" and "Taking the supply-side structural reform as the main line, expanding effective supply and meeting effective demand", which are proposed by "12th Five-Year Plan" and "13th Five-Year Plan" of the foreign trade development. This is conducive to promote the domestic consumption upgrading and the return of overseas consumption, and better satisfy the consumer needs of the broad masses of people, and guide the healthy development of the economy and society.

5.2 The Pilot Policies of Cross-border E-commerce and the "Belt and Road" Initiative

The "13th Five-Year Plan" of foreign trade development proposed to deepen trade cooperation with countries along the "Belt and Road", expand import from countries along the route, and promote trade balance. The report of the Nineteenth National Congress of the Communist Party of China also pointed out: Focusing on the construction of the "Belt and Road", insisting on the combination of bringing in and going out, following the principle of mutual consultation, construction and sharing, strengthening the open cooperation of innovation capabilities, and forming internal and external linkage between the land and the sea, and mutually open east-west structure. To promote the construction of a strong trading power, it is necessary to optimize the layout of the international market. While consolidating the traditional market, it should also continuously expand cooperative trade with countries along the "Belt and Road". The "Belt and Road" initiative brings new opportunities to international trade development, and also brings new growth momentum to the development of the world economy. Smooth trade is an important part of the joint construction of the "Belt and Road", and does the pilot policy of cross-border e-commerce become an important new force to promote smooth trade?

To this end, this paper distinguishes countries along the "Belt and Road" from non-Belt and Road countries and investigates whether cross-border e-commerce pilot policy has promoted China's import from countries along the Belt and Road. The results are shown in Table 12. Observation shows that the cross-border e-commerce pilot policy has a more obvious promotion effect on the import trade of countries along the "Belt and Road". China's import value from the countries along the "Belt and Road" has increased significantly by 20.1%, and its import quantity has increased significantly by 16.1%, which is higher than that from other countries. This means that China and the countries along the "Belt and Road" have huge trade potential. The cross-border e-commerce pilot policy is conducive to promoting the smooth construction of the "Belt and Road" trade and injecting new forces into the development of the world economy.

Table 12 Change of Import Counties of Origin

	(1) The "Belt and Road" Countries	(2) Other Countries	(3) The "Belt and Road" Countries	(4) Other Countries	(5) The "Belt and Road" Countries	(6) Other Countries
	ln*import*	ln*import*	ln*quantity*	ln*quantity*	ln*price*	ln*price*
treat · post	0.201*** (0.0351)	0.114** (0.0268)	0.161* (0.0253)	0.124* (0.0234)	0.0462 (0.0187)	−0.00873 (−0.0037)
	ln*import*	ln*import*	ln*quantity*	ln*quantity*	ln*price*	ln*price*
Controls FE	Fixed	Fixed	Fixed	Fixed	Fixed	Fixed
City FE	Fixed	Fixed	Fixed	Fixed	Fixed	Fixed
HS-8 FE	Fixed	Fixed	Fixed	Fixed	Fixed	Fixed
Year FE	Fixed	Fixed	Fixed	Fixed	Fixed	Fixed
N	312843	2174941	312843	2174950	312843	2174941
adj. R^2	0.5055	0.4294	0.6498	0.5787	0.8105	0.7919

Note: Same as table 6.

6 Conclusion

The new business model of cross-border e-commerce has become a highlight of current foreign trade and has made positive contributions to China's foreign trade growth. China has also actively conformed to the "new normal" of economic development, and has successively established pilot cities of cross-border e-commerce. Through first trial, explores experiences for the healthy development of cross-border e-commerce. This paper based on China customs data from 2007 to 2018, and uses the multi-period Difference-in-Difference model to assess the impact of pilot policies of cross-border e-commerce on China's import trade. This paper discusses the main mechanism sources for the growth of China's import trade by the pilot policies of cross-border e-commerce in terms of import quantity and average import price. In addition, this paper further analyzes the optimization of import structure and import countries of origin.

The study shows that: (1) The pilot policies of cross-border e-commerce have prompted a significant increase of 11.73% in China's import value, a significant increase of 11.65% in import quantity, and no significant change in import price. That is, the trade promotion effect of the pilot policies of cross-border e-commerce is driven by the import quantity. (2) The pilot policies of cross-border e-commerce has promoted the import of general trade and its proportion, so the structure of the import trade has been optimized. Besides, it has a more significant promotion effect on consumer goods. (3) The pilot policies of cross-border e-commerce have a more obvious role in promoting the import trade of countries along the "Belt and Road".

The conclusion of this paper has important policy implications. First, the pilot policies of cross-border e-commerce, while promoting China's import trade, has established a strong linkage with the construction of China's trading power, expanding the domestic demand, and the "Belt and Road" strategy, which has a positive impact on the implementation of these strategies. Therefore, China should increase its support for the pilot cities of cross-border e-commerce and expand the scope of the pilot to promote the sustainable and healthy development of cross-border e-commerce. Second, the pilot policies of cross-border e-commerce have increased China's import of consumer goods, which is conducive to stimulating domestic consumption to upgrade and promoting the return of overseas consumption. Third, the pilot policies of cross-border e-commerce have mainly increased import from countries along the "Belt and Road", and fully played the role of the multi-bilateral economic and trade cooperation mechanism, while the trade potential of importing from other countries needs to be further explored, and then actively reflects the responsibilities of major powers, and gives full play to the role of cross-border e-commerce in promoting the economic development of China and the world.

References

[1] Amiti M and Konings J. Trade liberalization, intermediate inputs, and productivity: Evidence from Indonesia[J]. American Economic Review,2007,97(5):1611-1638.

[2] Antràs P,Chor D,Fally T,et al. Measuring the upstreamness of production and trade flows[J]. Am Econo Rev,2012,102(3):412-416.

[3] Bas M and Strauss-Kahn V. "Input-trade Liberalization, Export Prices and Quality Upgrading",Journal of International Economics,2015,95(2),250-262.

[4] Borenstein S & Saloner G. Economics and electronic commerce[J]. Journal of Economic Perspectives,2001,15(1):3-12.

[5] Brandt L ,Van Biesebroeck J,Wang L H,et al. WTO accession and performance of Chinese manufacturing firms[J]. American Economic Review,2017,107(9):2784-2820.

[6] Antràs P,Chor D,Fally T,et al. Measuring the upstreamness of production and trade flows[J]. American Economic Review,2012,102(3):412-416.

[7] Cao W,Wan D,Qian S T,et al. Research on the import price transfer effect of RMB exchange rate fluctuations under the background of the "Belt and Road"[J]. Economic Research,2019,54(6):136-150.

[8] Chang X and Si C Y. The impact of cross-Border E-commerce on the effect of trade distance-based on the "Belt and Road" Empirical Area[J]. Business Economic Research, 2019,(10):123 – 126.

[9] Fajgelbaum P D, Goldberg P K, Kennedy P J. The return to protectionism[J]. The Quarterly Journal of Economics,2019,135(1):1-55.

[10] Fally T. On the fragmentation of production in the US[J]. University of Colorado-Boulder.

[11] Feng L,Li Z,Swenson D L,et al. The connection between imported intermediate inputs and exports:evidence from Chinese firms[J]. Journal of International Economics,2016, 101,86 – 101.

[12] Guo S W, Zhang M G, Wang Q. The new engine of foreign trade under the new

normal: development of China's cross-border E-commerce and the transformation and upgrading of traditional foreign trade[J]. The Economist,2018(8):42-49.

[13] He W. Research on the development mechanism of cross-border E-commerce and import and export trade[J]. Business Economic Research,2018(5):142-144.

[14] Hong J J and Shang H. The theory of "Conjugated Circulation" in China's open economy: theory and evidence[J]. China Social Science,2019(01):42-64 + 205.

[15] Jiang L D, Gu K J, Chen Y B. Export frequency of Chinese enterprises: facts and interpretations[J]. World Economy,2017,40(9):51-74.

[16] Jiang Y J. "Does international trade suppress output fluctuation at the enterprise level-based on the perspective of imported intermediate diversification[J]. Financial and Trade Research,2016,27(5):48-57.

[17] Jiang X J. Reorganization of resources and growth of service industry in a highly connected society[J]. Economic Research,2017,52(3):4-17.

[18] Kang Z Y. Impact of import of capital goods and intermediate goods on the R & D behavior of Chinese enterprises: "Promotio" or "Repression" [J]. Finance and Trade Research,2015,26(3):61-68.

[19] Liang P, Li L, Wu Y et al. Trade powers and the new pattern of world trade development—A summary of the Academic Perspectives of the Fifth Trade Powers forum and the 70th Anniversary of the Founding of New China,World Trade Development High-Level Seminar[J]. Business Economic Research,2020(1):106-108.

[20] Li F. Import trade, local association and reshaping of domestic value chain[J]. Chinese Industrial Economy,2017(9):25-43.

[21] Li F J and Yi H F. Studies on the status of China's cross-border E-commerce development, problems and their effects on export trade-taking China's export trade with the EU as an example[J]. Business Economics Research,2019(17):138-141.

[22] Luo N and Luo L J. Empirical research on the impact of cross-border E-commerce based on the "Belt and Road" on China's import and export trade[J]. Business Economic Research,2018(20):132-134.

[23] Ma S Z, Fang C, Zhang H S. Can cross-border E-commerce break the geographical distance limit[J]. Economics of Finance and Trade,2019,40(8):116-131.

[24] Ma S Z, Fang C, Liang Y F. Digital trade and its value and research prospects[J]. International Trade,2019(10):16-30.

[25] Ma S Z, Guo J W, Zhang H S. Cross-border E-commerce trade cost reduction effect: mechanism and empirical[J]. International Economic and Trade Exploration, 2019, 35(5): 69-85.

[26] Mao Q L. Does trade policy uncertainty affect Chinese enterprises' import[J]? Economic Research, 2020, 55(02): 148-164.

[27] Mei H. Research on the Development of Cross-border E-commerce and its "cost reduction and promotion effect" on China's international trade[J]. Business Economics Research, 2020(1): 116-119.

[28] Pei C H. Import trade structure and economic growth: laws and enlightenment[J]. Economic Research, 2013, 48(7): 4-19.

[29] Peng S Z, Li X P, Niu X D. Does import liberalization affect firms' output fluctuations [J]. Financial Research, 2020, 46(4): 125-139.

[30] Qian X F, Fan D M, Huang H M. Import competition and cost increase of Chinese manufacturing enterprises[J]. World Economy, 2016, 39(3): 71-94.

[31] Sheng B and Mao Q L. Is import trade liberalization affecting the complexity of China's manufacturing export technology[J]. World Economy, 2017, 40(12): 52-75.

[32] Shi B Z and Wu L F. China's import potential: trends, distribution and sources[J]. Nankai Journal (Philosophy and Social Sciences Edition), 2019(3): 160-174.

[33] Shi B Z and Zeng X F. Measurement and facts on the quality of imported products of Chinese enterprises[J]. World Economy, 2015, 38(3): 57-77.

[34] Shi B Z and Zhang Y R. Trade liberalization and upgrade of intermediate quality of Chinese enterprises' imports[J]. Quantitative Economics and Technology Economics Research, 2016, 33(9): 3-21.

[35] Wang X R and Yu W C. Empirical analysis of the interactive relationship between cross-border E-commerce Development and Traditional Foreign Trade." Economics and Management Research, 2018, 39(2): 79-86.

[36] Wei H. Intensity of intellectual property protection and China's high-tech product import[J]. Quantitative Economics Technology Economics Research, 2016, 33(12): 23-41.

[37] Wei H, Zhao C M, Li X Q. Estimation of changes in China's imported commodity structure: 2000-2014[J]. World Economy, 2016, 39(4): 70-94.

[38] Wei H and Li X Q. Study on the technical structure and influencing factors of China's import trade[J]. World Economy, 2015, 38(8): 56-79.

[39] Wei H and Li X Q. Imported inputs and employment changes of Chinese enterprises [J]. Statistical Research,2018,35(1):43-52.

[40] Xiao Z H and Liu Y L. Cross-border E-commerce's impact on China's manufacturing export scale-empirical evidence from China's experience[J]. Business Economic Research, 2019(11):151-153.

[41] Xie J G and Zhou L Z. Import trade,absorptive capacity and international R & D technology spillover:a study on panel data of Chinese provinces[J]. World Economy,2009,32 (9):68-81.

[42] Xu J Y and Mao Q L. Productive subsidies and enterprise import behavior:evidence from Chinese manufacturing companies[J]. World Economy,2019,42(07):46-70.

[43] Xu J Y,Zhou S J,Hu A G. Institutional distance,adjacent effects and bilateral trade-an empirical analysis based on the "Belt and Road" national spatial panel model[J]. Financial Research,2017,43(1):75-85.

[44] Yang B Y. Import and export trade elasticity and China's trade mode structure adjustment-Based on the comparative perspective of processing trade and general trade[J]. World Economic Research ,2013,(12):39-45,85.

[45] Yang J J,Liu Y F and Li H L. Trade facilitation,intermediate import,and enterprise export value added[J]. Economics of Finance and Trade,2020,41(04):115-128.

[46] Yang J Z, Zheng B X and Yang L F. Research on the evaluation index system of cross-border E-commerce based on factor analysis[J]. Economics of Financial and Trade,2014 (9):94-102.

[47] Zhang J. Suppression effect of import on patent activities of Chinese manufacturing enterprises[J]. Chinese Industrial Economy,2015(07):68-83.

[48] Zhang Y L and Zou Z S. Import types, product quality, and trade welfare: a study based on price indexes[J]. World Economy,2018,41(1):123-147.

[49] Zhong L L and Li H. Empirical research on the impact of cross-Border E-Commerce on China's import and export trade [J]. Commercial Economic Research, 2018 (14): 143-115445.

转移支付的均等化效果评价

陈 煜[①]

摘 要：分税制改革以来，政府间转移支付的规模不断扩大。转移支付制度作为推进基本公共服务均等化的一项重要制度安排，近年来是否起到了显著的均等化作用，是本文探究的主题。本文使用泰尔指数法构造省内基本公共服务均等化指数，基于 2011—2018 年的省级面板数据，实证发现一般性转移支付对均等化有抑制作用，而专项转移支付的均等化效果则不显著。利用 2015—2018 年的样本数据进一步回归发现均衡性转移支付对社保就业和基础教育均等化有促进作用，教育类分类拨款对基础教育均等化有抑制作用，医疗卫生类专项转移支付对均等化有促进作用。为保证基本公共服务均等化目标的实现，应该进一步提高转移支付资金的透明度，加强监督管理，公平合理分配资金，使资金流向真正有需要的地方。

关键词：基本公共服务 转移支付 均等化

一、引言

2021 年是实现"十四五"规划和 2035 年远景目标的开局之年。党的十九大报告明确指出，到 2035 年，基本公共服务均等化将基本实现。目前，我国的基本公共服务制度已经基本建成，但新时期又有新矛盾不断浮现出来，投入不足、区域发展不平衡等问题成为主要阻碍。

学界已有许多文献关注基本公共服务均等化，研究视角各异。就范围而言，基本公共服务应当包括以保障人的基本生存权、健康权、自我发展权为目的的一些服务。就均等化的标准而言，有几种基本模式。其中，基本公共服务最低公平体现的是"底线均等"，虽然能保证每个公民得到最低标准的基本公共服务，但无法控制区域之间的

[①] 陈煜，对外经济贸易大学国际经济贸易学院财政学专业 2017 级本科生。

供给差距。人均财力均等化则忽视了各地资金使用效率差异带来的产出效果差距，即使考虑了各地公共服务提供的成本差异，也难以达到基本公共服务供给水平的均衡。大量研究在构建均等化指标时采用的是：公共服务标准化，即选择具体的公共服务领域，根据投入、产出和效果等维度选取子项目，综合分析构造基本公共服务水平指标。由于公共服务各领域涵盖的子项目十分繁杂，以往研究者选取的指标体系不尽相同。安体富和任强描述了公共服务均等化水平指标构建的基本方法，即选取评价指标—无量纲化—赋予权重系数—合成—构造均等化指标的基本步骤，这也是本文沿用的方法。在最近的相关研究当中，如缪小林等也提出我国基本公共服务均等化的目标应当转向"提高人民群众的获得感"。从新的角度定义了均等化标准。在指标选取方面，本文根据已有研究涉及的重点领域选取了基础教育、社会保障和就业、医疗卫生3个方面指标。

1994年分税制改革以来，全国财力向中央集中，地方政府财政支出占比不断提高，为缓解地方政府的财政压力，以税收分配制度为基础的政府间转移支付制度应运而生。Oates提出无条件的政府间拨款是实现财政平衡的适当手段。目前，我国中央对地方的转移支付资金主要分为两类。其中的专项转移支付的资金用途指向明确，往往通过项目的方式进行分配，体现专款专用的基本特征，能够更好地体现中央政府的政策意图。一般性转移支付大多通过因素法进行资金分配，其中的均衡性转移支付完全不指定用途，由地方政府统筹安排使用，目的在于平衡地区财力。而近年来种类不断增加的其他一般性转移支付则具有分类拨款的性质。分类拨款资金用途较为宽泛，且按因素法进行分配，农村综合改革转移支付、城乡义务教育补助经费、基本养老金转移支付、城乡居民医疗保险转移支付等都具有分类拨款的特征。近年来，我国中央财政对地方的转移支付规模不断扩大，由2015年的50078.63亿元增长到2019年的74415.1亿元，其中一般性转移支付占比不断提高，由2015年的56.8%提高到2019年的89%。在这一背景下，省级政府是否通过合理配置转移支付资金促进了省内基本公共服务均等化，不同类型的转移支付对基本公共服务均等化的影响有何差异，正是本文研究的重点。

国内外文献在转移支付领域的研究更多集中于转移支付对政府支出行为和地区经济增长的影响。吕冰洋等通过理论和实证两个维度探究发现，分税制改革初期专项转移支付比重不断提高的原因在于，在税收分成率下降时，为提高地区间民生发展均等化水平，上级政府更倾向于提高专项转移支付比重以直接提高地方政府的民生支出，即采取"积极均衡策略"。毛捷等通过对2000—2007年我国县级数据的实证分析证明了转移支付使得地方公共服务提供价格下降，从而导致地方政府支出扩张的"粘蝇纸效应"。吴敏等深入研究发现在年度预算平衡机制下，转移支付资金的下拨时滞在一定程度上导致了地方政府支出规模膨胀。马光荣等基于1997—2009年的县级数据，利用中央划定国贫县的自然实验，采用断点回归方法估计了一般性转移支付和专项转移支付对地方经济增长的影响。

大部分研究在涉及基本公共服务均等化时，大多只探究了转移支付制度对地区财力均等化、公共品供给水平的影响，并未直接构建均等化指数进行实证分析。分税制改革初期，国内学者对于转移支付的均等化效果研究集中于财力均等化。曾军平利用1994—1997年的省级层面数据实证分析发现经济发展水平较高的省份反而得到了更多的人均转移支付。Tsui基于县级数据发现1994—2000年间的政府间转移支付并没有缩小县域间财政差距，甚至使问题恶化了。曾红颖在考虑了各地公共服务提供的成本差异因素后，以全国基本公共服务供给的平均收支为标准，测算了理想化的均等化转移支付，发现按此分配，可以使全国的均等化水平提高9%~15%。王瑞民和陶然利用1994—2009年的县级一般预算收入数据加上上级政府的税收返还和转移支付构造了县级总财力指标，发现按财政供养人口平均财力时，两类转移支付的均等化作用明显；而按辖区人口平均财力时，两类转移支付在改革初期的均等化效果均不显著，直到2005年以后才起到一定效果。马海涛和任致伟则运用2009—2013年的县级数据研究发现，转移支付对财力均等化有积极作用。经过梳理后发现，转移支付制度在改革初期对地区间财力均等化的效果并不明显，但随着制度的不断完善，其均等化效果开始逐渐显现出来。就不同公共服务领域的均等化效果而言，研究结果也存在差异。田侃和亓寿伟构造的公共服务发展指标包括基础设施、医疗卫生和基础教育3个方面，他们采用分位数回归方法对省级数据进行实证分析，发现在不同地区、不同公共服务领域，转移支付的效果均存在差异，如转移支付对中部地区的基础设施发展和西部地区的医疗卫生、基础教育发展都起到积极作用，而对中部地区的医疗卫生发展却起到抑制作用。贾晓俊等基于河北省2002—2006年的县级数据，通过逻辑论证和实证分析发现专项转移支付更能刺激教育支出，而两类转移支付对社保支出均无显著效果。胡斌和毛艳华在使用居民对基本公共服务均等化的感知来衡量均等化水平时，发现转移支付对教育、医疗卫生、住房保障的均等化程度都起到积极作用。乔俊峰和陈荣汾则沿用马光荣等的断点回归方法，基于2000—2007的县级数据实证发现一般性转移支付对基本公共服务指数增长的边际效应为0.552个单位，专项转移支付的效果更强，为1.673个单位。

通过对上述文献进行梳理发现，以往研究者在同时关注转移支付和基本公共服务均等化时，不仅关注转移支付的总体规模，还关注其结构对基本公共服务均等化的影响。因此，本文也对不同转移支付类型分别进行探究，尤其考虑了一般性转移支付项下指定了资金用途大类的分类拨款,如城乡义务教育补助经费。对于基本公共服务均等化的衡量,大部分学者采用了综合分析方法,即通过构造基本公共服务指标体系合成均等化指数,也有部分学者从人民获得感的角度通过问卷调查获取基本公共服务均等化感知指数。考虑到数据可得性,本文采用的是选取方面指标、合成均等化指数的研究方法。从上述文献来看,转移支付对不同基本公共服务领域均等化水平的影响各异,本文也从基础教育、医疗卫生和社保就业3个领域分别研究了转移支付的均等化效果。对于均等化的维度而言,部分文献基于县级数据同时关注省内和省际均等化,但大多数文献只关注了一个维度的均等化程度,本文运用地级市数据构造省内基本公共服务均等化指数,关注省对下转移支付对省内均等化水平的影响。

首先,本文利用2011—2018年292个地级市的数据构造了27个省的基本公共服务均等化指数,通过构造泰尔指数的方法衡量省内均等化水平;其次,在实证分析阶段,利用固定效应回归模型衡量省对下不同类型转移支付对省内基本公共服务均等化水平的影响,并分领域探究了转移支付的均等化作用;最后,再进一步利用2015—2018年的样本数据探究均衡性转移支付、分类拨款和专项转移支付在等口径条件下的均等化效果。

二、实证设计

(一) 计量模型

本文采用OLS回归方法,探究不同转移支付类型对省内基本公共服务均等化的影响。计量模型的回归表达式为:

$$BPS_{it} = \alpha + \beta Tr_{it} + \gamma X_{it} + \delta_i + \pi_t + \varepsilon_{it}$$

其中,下标 i 表示省份,t 表示年份。BPS_{it} 表示基本公共服务均等化指数,在后文的回归中用 Edu_{it}、Med_{it}、Sec_{it} 替换,分别表示基础教育、医疗卫生、社保就业均等化指数。Tr_{it} 表示省对下人均一般性转移支付或人均专项转移支付,在后文的回归中用 GTr_{it}、STr_{it} 分别表示[①]。X_{it} 为控制变量矩阵。外生控制变量从社会因素和经济因素两个方面选取。根据已有文献,社会因素方面选取城市人口密度和城镇化水平作为控制变量,分别用 Pop_{it} 和 Urb_{it} 表示。经济因素方面的控制变量选取人均一般预算收入、人均一般预算支出、人均税收收入和人均GDP,分别用 FR_{it}、FE_{it}、TR_{it}、GDP_{it} 表示。本文根

---

① 此处及下文涉及的经济变量的"人均"均按照倪红日和张亮的处理,用各地年底常住人口数平均,以与一个地区实际所需的基本公共服务相适应。

据曾明等的做法选取地方财政自给率作为控制变量，用一般预算收入和一般预算支出的比值度量，用 $Self_{it}$ 表示。根据曾明等的研究，地方财政自给能力低下会抑制转移支付的均等化效果。控制变量矩阵的最终选择根据回归分析而定。δ_i、π_t 分别表示地区固定效应和年份固定效应。ε_{it} 表示误差项，α 表示常量。

（二）数据说明

1. 基本公共服务均等化指标构建

本文在构建均等化指数时更加注重基本公共服务的产出方面，根据数据可得性选取了表1所示评价指标。

表1 基本公共服务均等化指标体系

一级指标	二级指标	单项指标
基本公共服务	基础教育	每万人小学生专任教师数（人）
		每万人小学生学校数（所）
		每万人中学生专任教师数（人）
		每万人中学生学校数（所）
	医疗卫生	每万人医院、卫生院数（个）
		每万人医院、卫生院床位数（张）
		每万人执业（助理）医师数（人）
	社保就业	每万人城镇职工养老保险参保人数（人）
		每万人城镇医疗保险参保人数（人）
		每万人失业保险参保人数（人）

根据安体富和任强的做法，本文采取极值标准化方法对各单项指标进行无量纲化。由于所选指标均为越大越好的正指标，无量纲化公式如下：

$$z_j = \frac{x_j - min(x_j)}{max(x_j) - min(x_j)}$$

其中 j 代表单项指标，$max(x_j)$ 和 $min(x_j)$ 分别代表该项指标在样本区间内的最大值和最小值。

在无量纲化完成后，本文采用算数加权平均方法对单项指标进行合成，形成二级指标和一级指标，并用泰尔指数法测度省内基本公共服务均等化指数。根据田学斌和陈艺丹的做法，选用泰尔L指数衡量均等化程度，计算方法如下：

$$T = \sum_{j=1}^{n} \left\{ S_j \ln\left(\frac{S_j}{P_j}\right) \right\}, \quad n = 1, 2, 3$$

其中，n 为某省地级市样本总数，S_j 为地级市 j 基本公共服务水平指标与其所属省份总体基本公共服务水平指标的比值，P_j 为地级市 j 人口占该市所属省份总人口的比重。基础教育、医疗卫生、社保就业的均等化指数采用相同的方法构造，即用各领域水平指标代入 S_j 得到。

2. 数据和样本

在衡量两类转移支付对省内基本公共服务均等化的影响时，本文选取的样本为 2011—2018 年 292 个地级市的基本公共服务数据。相关指标数据来源于 EPS 数据库收录整理的《中国城市数据库》和《中国区域经济数据库》，部分缺失数据来自各市统计年鉴与国民经济和社会发展统计公报，省对下转移支付数据来自各省财政决算报告。在进一步回归中，为保证统计口径的一致性，本文将专项转移支付和分类拨款按照基础教育、社保就业、医疗卫生进行分类，而一般性转移支付则用均衡性转移支付代替。其中，基础教育类分类拨款用城乡义务教育转移支付衡量，社保就业类分类拨款用基本养老金转移支付和城乡居民医疗保险转移支付总量衡量，因一般性转移支付项下没有明确具有分类拨款性质的医疗卫生类转移支付，在之后的回归分析中没有涉及医疗卫生类分类拨款的均等化作用。由于数据限制，这部分实证分析只选取了 2015—2018 年的样本数据。由于转移支付数据存在缺失，在使用 stata 14.0 进行回归分析时做缺失值处理①。控制变量数据来自 EPS 数据库中的《中国宏观经济数据库》《中国财政税收数据库》《中国区域经济数据库》。为消除价格因素的影响，本文根据吴敏等的做法，以 2011 年为基期，将人均 GDP 按照地区生产总值指数调整，其余经济变量按照各省的居民消费价格指数调整。表 2 为基准回归阶段变量的描述性统计。

表 2 描述性统计

变量	单位	观测值	均值	标准差	最小值	最大值
基本公共服务均等化指数	—	216	0.171	0.091	-0.007	0.388
基础教育均等化指数	—	216	0.202	0.122	-0.064	0.655
医疗卫生均等化指数	—	216	0.173	0.096	0.006	0.404
社保就业均等化指数	—	208	0.281	0.191	0.047	1.163
人均一般性转移支付	万元/人	166	0.285	0.264	0.039	1.899

---

① 西藏自治区和新疆维吾尔自治区的转移支付数据严重缺失，故在回归中舍弃了这两个地区的数据。

续表

变量	单位	观测值	均值	标准差	最小值	最大值
人均专项转移支付	万元/人	166	0.227	0.227	0.002	1.586
城镇化水平	—	216	52.68	9.482	22.7	70.7
人均一般预算收入	万元/人	216	0.498	0.203	0.176	1.193
人均一般预算支出	万元/人	216	1.23	0.748	0.452	5.974
人均GDP	万元/人	216	4.777	1.826	1.641	11.98

三、实证结果及分析

（一）基本回归结果

表3报告的是使用2011—2018年的省级年度数据估计出的两类转移支付对总体的基本公共服务均等化水平的影响大小。第（1）、（4）列报告的是不加入其他控制变量的结果。第（2）、（3）、（5）、（6）列是在模型中加入社会因素和经济因素的控制变量后得到的回归结果。考虑到存在只随年份或只随省份变化的遗漏变量，回归中均加入了时间固定效应和个体固定效应。本文主要关注两类转移支付系数的大小和方向，从第（1）、（2）、（3）列的结果可以看出，在加入控制变量前后，人均一般性转移支付的系数始终显著为正，从第（3）列的结果来看，人均一般性转移支付每增加1万元，基本公共服务均等化指数会提高0.0784个单位，泰尔指数变大意味着均等化水平下降。第（4）、（5）、（6）列的结果显示，专项转移支付对省内基本公共服务均等化指数的影响不显著。由于城市人口密度、人均税收收入对均等化水平和核心解释变量的系数影响均不显著，本文未将其加入控制变量矩阵。由于财政自给率与一般预算收入和一般预算支出数据高度相关，本文在实证过程中选择控制一般预算收入和一般预算支出。

根据尹振东和汤玉刚的论述，完全不指定资金用途的转移支付能够更好地均衡地区间财政能力，但地方政府在官员晋升锦标赛激励下存在"重投资、轻民生"的支出偏好，而指定用途的转移支付虽然存在资金管理困难等问题，却能更好地引导和规范地方政府的行为。一般性转移支付的均等化效果可能因为地方政府支出行为偏离民生领域而大打折扣。虽然专项转移支付能更好地体现中央政府的政策意图，引导地方政府行为，但其项目繁杂、资金分散，申请和审批程序复杂、历时长，在预算平衡制度下的突击花钱现象导致资金使用效率低下，且项目申请过程中容易出现"跑部钱进"

现象，导致资金分配不公，均等化效果不显著。表3中的一般性转移支付涵盖了完全不指定用途的均衡性转移支付和指定用途大类的分类拨款，本文在进一步实证分析中将严格区分这两类转移支付。

表3 转移支付对基本公共服务均等化指数的影响

被解释变量	基本公共服务均等化指数					
	（1）	（2）	（3）	（4）	（5）	（6）
人均一般性转移支付	0.0977*** (0.0276)	0.0957*** (0.0275)	0.0784*** (0.0285)			
人均专项转移支付				0.0302 (0.0328)	0.0273 (0.0336)	-0.0293 (0.0303)
城镇化水平		-0.00225* (0.00130)	-0.00216* (0.00130)		-0.00252* (0.00136)	-0.00223 (0.00134)
人均一般预算收入			-0.0551** (0.0260)			-0.0716*** (0.0267)
人均一般预算支出			0.0279* (0.0146)			0.0586*** (0.0158)
人均GDP			0.00557** (0.00279)			0.00393 (0.00278)
常量	0.148*** (0.00734)	0.253*** (0.0626)	0.234*** (0.0618)	0.151*** (0.00766)	0.269*** (0.0654)	0.241*** (0.0640)
个体固定效应	控制	控制	控制	控制	控制	控制
时间固定效应	控制	控制	控制	控制	控制	控制
观测值	166	166	166	166	166	166
R^2	0.971	0.971	0.972	0.968	0.968	0.971

注：括号内报告的是回归标准误差，***、**、*分别表示1%、5%和10%的显著性水平。

（二）不同公共服务领域转移支付的均等化效果

表4报告的是两类转移支付对基础教育、社保就业和医疗卫生领域省内均等化水平的影响。回归将被解释变量替换为基础教育均等化指数、社保就业均等化指数和医疗卫生均等化指数，控制城镇化水平、人均一般预算收支和人均GDP。回归结果显示，专项转移支付在3个领域的均等化作用均不显著。一般性转移支付的基础教育和社保

就业均等化效果在统计上不显著，而在医疗卫生领域则发挥了抑制作用。第（5）列结果显示，人均一般性转移支付每增加1万元，社会保障和就业领域均等化指数平均增加0.0749个单位，均等化水平有所下降。

表4 转移支付对基础教育、社保就业和医疗卫生均等化指数的影响

被解释变量	基础教育均等化指数		社保就业均等化指数		医疗卫生均等化指数	
	（1）	（2）	（3）	（4）	（5）	（6）
人均一般性转移支付	0.0453 (0.0501)		0.0706 (0.0655)		0.0749** (0.0322)	
人均专项转移支付		0.0649 (0.0513)		-0.129 (0.123)		-0.0460 (0.0372)
城镇化水平	-0.00376 (0.00283)	-0.00374 (0.00282)	-0.00266 (0.00403)	-0.00287 (0.00400)	-0.00146 (0.00160)	-0.00154 (0.00158)
人均一般预算收入	-0.0566 (0.0478)	-0.0513 (0.0471)	-0.0491 (0.0846)	-0.0730 (0.0894)	-0.0272 (0.0328)	-0.0463 (0.0337)
人均一般预算支出	-0.00116 (0.0205)	-0.00277 (0.0248)	0.148** (0.0661)	0.187*** (0.0698)	-0.00825 (0.0159)	0.0254 (0.0186)
人均GDP	0.00323 (0.00399)	0.00257 (0.00367)	0.00822 (0.00789)	0.00640 (0.00768)	0.00197 (0.00387)	0.000344 (0.00391)
常量	0.332** (0.130)	0.330** (0.129)	0.270 (0.188)	0.290 (0.187)	0.220*** (0.0773)	0.228*** (0.0762)
个体固定效应	控制	控制	控制	控制	控制	控制
时间固定效应	控制	控制	控制	控制	控制	控制
观测值	166	166	162	162	166	166
R^2	0.947	0.947	0.947	0.947	0.960	0.959

注：括号内报告的是回归标准误差，***、**、*分别表示1%、5%和10%的显著性水平。

（三）进一步回归

在研究不同公共服务领域转移支付的均等化效果时，考虑到基础教育、医疗卫生和社保就业只是省对下转移支付支出的一部分，可能因统计口径不对称而导致回归结果产生偏误，因此本文将一般性转移支付划分为均衡性转移支付、分类拨款和其他一

般性转移支付，其中分类拨款按基础教育和社保就业分类，专项转移支付按基础教育、医疗卫生和社保就业分类。由于数据获取限制，进一步回归中以2015—2018年的省级数据为样本进行回归分析。表5为进一步回归描述性统计。

表5 进一步回归描述性统计

变量	单位	观测值	均值	标准差	最小值	最大值
基本公共服务均等化指数	—	108	0.165	0.0880	0.00100	0.387
基础教育均等化指数	—	108	0.205	0.124	−0.0640	0.647
医疗卫生均等化指数	—	108	0.163	0.0890	0.0110	0.348
社保就业均等化指数	—	104	0.271	0.195	0.0470	1.163
人均教育类分类拨款	千元/人	90	0.310	0.684	0.0390	3.923
人均社保类分类拨款	千元/人	91	0.7289	0795	0.1828	7.009
人均教育类专项转移支付	千元/人	85	0.174	0.241	0.0150	1.466
人均社保类专项转移支付	千元/人	86	0.237	0.167	0.0150	0.804
人均医疗类专项转移支付	千元/人	86	0.137	0.140	0	0.831
人均均衡性转移支付	千元/人	94	1.092	1.366	0.0170	8.150
城镇化水平	—	108	55.14	8.672	27.74	70.70
人均一般预算收入	万元/人	108	0.570	0.210	0.299	1.193
人均一般预算支出	万元/人	108	1.459	0.842	0.750	5.974
人均GDP	万元/人	108	5.461	1.880	2.723	11.98

表6为均衡性转移支付、分类拨款和专项转移支付在同口径下对基础教育、医疗卫生和社保就业领域均等化水平影响的回归结果。

第（1）列显示，一般性转移支付项下的均衡性转移支付对基础教育领域的均等化程度有促进作用，人均均衡性转移支付每增加1000元，基础教育均等化泰尔指数平均下降0.021。第（2）列显示，基础教育类分类拨款对均等化有抑制作用。专项转移支付的均等化作用仍不显著。

在医疗卫生领域，第（7）和（8）列显示，均衡性转移支付的均等化效果不显著，人均专项转移支付的系数显著为负，对医疗卫生的省内均等化有促进作用。在社会保障和就业领域，第（4）、（5）和（6）列显示，均衡性转移支付的均等化作用为促进作用，分类拨款和专项转移支付的均等化效果均不显著。

表6 不同类型转移支付对基础教育均等化指数的影响

被解释变量	基础教育均等化指数			社保就业均等化指数			医疗卫生均等化指数	
	(1)	(2)	(3)	(4)	(5)	(6)	(7)	(8)
人均均衡性转移支付	-0.0210*			-0.0552*			0.00635	
	(0.0113)			(0.0319)			(0.00878)	
人均分类拨款		0.0104***			0.0152			
		(0.00325)			(0.0113)			
人均专项转移支付			-0.00550			-0.0575		-0.0997***
			(0.0225)			(0.0605)		(0.0264)
城镇化水平	-0.00259	-0.00272	-0.00196	-0.00988	-0.00890	-0.00915	0.000486	0.000184
	(0.00370)	(0.00420)	(0.00378)	(0.00818)	(0.00748)	(0.00870)	(0.00223)	(0.00227)
人均一般预算收入	0.101	0.0658	0.0111	0.172	0.0651	-0.00135	0.0382	0.0629
	(0.0665)	(0.0718)	(0.0483)	(0.125)	(0.111)	(0.122)	(0.0577)	(0.0394)
人均一般预算支出	-0.0262	-0.00471	-0.0233	-0.204	0.0795	-0.140	-0.00779	0.0137
	(0.0211)	(0.0194)	(0.0180)	(0.188)	(0.180)	(0.186)	(0.0159)	(0.0116)
人均GDP	0.00301	0.00443	0.00316	-7.12e-05	0.00513	0.00121	0.00293	0.00330
	(0.00359)	(0.00283)	(0.00294)	(0.00659)	(0.00562)	(0.00601)	(0.00362)	(0.00273)
常量	0.269	0.258	0.259	0.854**	0.564	0.811*	0.0732	0.0730
	(0.198)	(0.221)	(0.199)	(0.409)	(0.344)	(0.426)	(0.118)	(0.118)
个体固定效应	控制	控制	控制	控制	控制	控制	控制	控制
时间固定效应	控制	控制	控制	控制	控制	控制	控制	控制
观测值	94	90	85	90	90	83	94	86
R^2	0.980	0.979	0.986	0.985	0.990	0.980	0.986	0.991

注：括号内报告的是回归标准误差，***、**、*分别表示1％、5％和10％的显著性水平。

四、结论

本文利用2011—2018年的省级面板数据实证检验了两类转移支付对省内基本公共服务均等化水平的影响。实证结果显示，在本文样本范围内，省对下一般性转移支付对省内基本公共服务总体水平的均等化有抑制作用，专项转移支付的均等化效果则不明显。在不同的基本公共服务领域，转移支付的效果存在差异。在医疗卫生领域，一般性转移支付对均等化有一定抑制作用，在社保就业领域和基础教育领域的作用不显著，而专项转移支付在三大领域均没有显著的均等化效果。在进一步回归中，本文利用2015—2018年的省级数据检验了均衡性转移支付、分类拨款和专项转移支付在等口径下对三大基本公共服务领域均等化水平的影响程度。结果显示，均衡性转移支付对社保就业和基础教育领域的均等化有促进作用，分类拨款对基础教育均等化有抑制作用，专项转移支付对医疗卫生均等化有显著促进作用，其他系数均不显著。

结合两次实证分析，结果显示专项转移支付的基本公共服务均等化效果不显著，一般性转移支付总体显示抑制作用，其项下的均衡性转移支付起到促进均等化的作用。根据已有文献的理论分析，转移支付制度的不规范，导致地方政府的支出行为偏离了基本公共服务均等化的政策目标。就一般性转移支付而言，应该提高转移支付资金的透明度，明确地方政府提供基本公共服务的责任，从而矫正地方政府的支出行为；就专项转移支付而言，应该加强监督管理，保证资金分配公平合理，使资金流向公共服务供给的短板地区，促进区域间基本公共服务的均等化。

参考文献

［1］曾红颖. 我国基本公共服务均等化标准体系及转移支付效果评价［J］. 经济研究，2012，47（06）：20-32+45.

［2］马国贤，基本公共服务均等化的公共财政政策研究［J］. 财政研究，2007（10）：74-77.

［3］安体富，任强. 中国公共服务均等化水平指标体系的构建：基于地区差别视角的量化分析［J］. 财贸经济，2008（06）：79-82.

［4］缪小林，张蓉，于洋航. 基本公共服务均等化治理：从"缩小地区间财力差距"到"提升人民群众获得感"［J］. 中国行政管理，2020（02）：67-71.

［5］Oates W E. An essay on fiscal federalism［J］. Journal of Economic Literature，1999，37（3）：1120-1149.

［6］吕冰洋，毛捷，马光荣. 分税与转移支付结构：专项转移支付为什么越来越多？［J］. 管理世界，2018，34（04）：25-39+187.

［7］毛捷，吕冰洋，马光荣. 转移支付与政府扩张：基于"价格效应"的研究［J］. 管理世界，2015（7）：29-24.

［8］吴敏，刘畅，范子英. 转移支付与地方政府支出规模膨胀：基于中国预算制度的一个实证解释［J］. 金融研究，2019（03）：74-91.

［9］马光荣，郭庆旺，刘畅. 财政转移支付结构与地区经济增长［J］. 中国社会科学，2016（09）：105-125+207-208.

[10] 曾军平. 政府间转移支付制度的财政平衡效应研究 [J]. 经济研究, 2000 (06): 27-32.

[11] Tsui K Y. Local tax system, intergovernmental transfers and China's local fiscal disparities [J]. Journal of Comparative Economics, 2005, 33 (1): 173-196.

[12] 王瑞民, 陶然. 中国财政转移支付的均等化效应: 基于县级数据的评估 [J]. 世界经济, 2017, 40 (12): 119-140.

[13] 马海涛, 任致伟. 转移支付对县级财力均等化的作用 [J]. 财政研究, 2017 (05): 2-12+113.

[14] 田侃, 亓寿伟. 转移支付、财政分权对公共服务供给的影响: 基于公共服务分布和区域差异的视角 [J]. 财贸经济, 2013 (04): 29-38.

[15] 贾晓俊, 岳希明, 王怡璞. 分类拨款、地方政府支出与基本公共服务均等化: 兼谈我国转移支付制度改革 [J]. 财贸经济, 2015 (04): 5-16+133.

[16] 胡斌, 毛艳华. 转移支付改革对基本公共服务均等化的影响 [J]. 经济学家, 2018 (03): 63-72.

[17] 乔俊峰, 陈荣汾. 转移支付结构对基本公共服务均等化的影响: 基于国家级贫困县划分的断点分析 [J]. 经济学家, 2019 (10): 84-92.

[18] 曾明, 华磊, 刘耀彬. 地方财政自给与转移支付的公共服务均等化效应: 基于中国31个省级行政区的面板门槛分析 [J]. 财贸研究, 2014, 25 (03): 82-91.

[19] 田学斌, 陈艺丹. 京津冀基本公共服务均等化的特征分异和趋势 [J]. 经济与管理, 2019, 33 (06): 7-15.

[20] 倪红日, 张亮. 基本公共服务均等化与财政管理体制改革研究 [J]. 管理世界, 2012 (09): 7-18+60.

[21] 尹振东, 汤玉刚. 专项转移支付与地方财政支出行为: 以农村义务教育补助为例 [J]. 经济研究, 2016, 51 (04): 47-59.